Thomas Harris and
William Blake

Thomas Harris and William Blake

Allusions in the Hannibal Lecter Novels

MICHELLE LEIGH GOMPF

McFarland & Company, Inc., Publishers
Jefferson, North Carolina, and London

LIBRARY OF CONGRESS CATALOGUING-IN-PUBLICATION DATA

Gompf, Michelle Leigh, 1970–
    Thomas Harris and William Blake : Allusions in the
Hannibal Lecter Novels / Michelle Leigh Gompf.
    p.   cm.
    Includes bibliographical references and index.

    ISBN 978-0-7864-7101-0
    softcover : acid free paper ∞

    1. Harris, Thomas, 1940– —Criticism and interpretation.
2. Blake, William, 1757–1827—Influence. 3. Good and evil
in literature. 4. Allusions in literature. I. Title.

PS3558.A6558Z66 2014
813'.54—dc23   2013039050

BRITISH LIBRARY CATALOGUING DATA ARE AVAILABLE

© 2014 Michelle Leigh Gompf. All rights reserved

*No part of this book may be reproduced or transmitted in any form
or by any means, electronic or mechanical, including photocopying
or recording, or by any information storage and retrieval system,
without permission in writing from the publisher.*

Front cover image iStockphoto/Thinkstock

Manufactured in the United States of America

McFarland & Company, Inc., Publishers
  Box 611, Jefferson, North Carolina 28640
    www.mcfarlandpub.com

To Dan Cole, my Eternal Contrary, and
Sofia, the embodiment of our balance.

Table of Contents

Acknowledgments   9

Preface   11

Introduction   13

1. "Under every *Good* is a hell": William Blake's View of Good and Evil   23
2. "The wickedness herein I took from my own stock": Thomas Harris's Creation of Evil   50
3. The Dragon and the Tyger: *Red Dragon*   68
4. Typhoid and Swans: *Silence of the Lambs*   97
5. Harris's Marriage of Heaven and Hell: *Hannibal*   117
6. Printing in the Infernal Method: *Hannibal Rising*   144

Conclusion: "Without contraries there is no progression"— Lecter's Blakean Progression to Balance   163

Bibliography   179

Index   183

Acknowledgments

I would like to thank the participants of the Blake and the Popular conference in 2002 for helping to spark this work, as well as Jason Whittaker, who helped guide and edit that early overview, which was published in *Blake, Modernity and Popular Culture.* I would also like to thank the Blake Society for inviting me to speak on an early version of this work, as well as Concord University for providing me with a sabbatical in which to complete this work and encouraging me in its completion.

Preface

This book grew out of a long-term interest in both William Blake and Thomas Harris that I first explored in a paper presented at the Blake and the Popular conference in 2002. Having studied Blake for many years and having enjoyed reading the Harris novels for pleasure several times, I had noticed connections between the two authors that went beyond Harris's referencing of Blake's Great Red Dragon and wished to explore them. This initial exploration touched on the Blakean themes in the first three published Lecter novels: *Red Dragon*, *Silence of the Lambs*, and *Hannibal*. As *Hannibal Rising* was not yet written, it was obviously not discussed then. This conference paper briefly touched on the allusions and began to set out an argument for Harris's use of Blake. The positive response to that paper led to "The Silence of the Lamb and the Tyger: Harris Using Blake to Discuss Good and Evil," published in *Blake, Modernity and Popular Culture* by Palgrave in 2007, which explored, in general, the allusions to Blake within Harris's work and the thematic connection between Blake's poetry and Harris's Hannibal Lecter novels. Not content with a general overview of the topic, and seeing a gap in the scholarly study of both Blake and Harris, I began to dive further into the allusions Harris makes to Blake, presenting a paper focusing exclusively on *Red Dragon* at a Blake Society meeting in 2003. I then began to look in depth at the thematic connections between Blake and Harris in the other Hannibal Lecter novels, eventually also exploring Blakean allusions in the film versions and considering how *Hannibal Rising* fits into the Blakean context Harris created.

This book is the result of many years of research and contemplation, including many re-readings of both Harris's novels and Blake's works, as well as viewings of the films, undertaken to understand why Harris alludes to Blake. While scholars, particularly Philip Simpson, have begun to study Harris seriously, no one has undertaken a detailed study of these allusions, particularly the implied allusions, and thematic connections. And although

Preface

Blake scholars, especially Nicholas Williams, have discussed Harris's use of Blake in *Red Dragon*, none have explored the connections in depth, especially in the later novels. Essentially, while Blake scholars have explored pop culture connections to Blake, and scholars of horror and the gothic have placed Harris in that context, no one has undertaken to read Harris—all four of the Lecter novels—in a Blakean context.

Reading Harris in a Blakean context reveals subtle connections to Blake, ones that emphasize particular thematic concerns, particularly the relationship between good and evil. Conversely, understanding how Harris uses Blake has also forced a re-examination of how I and others read Blake, causing me to consider how good and evil are connected in his work and how that is connected to other Blakean concerns like perspective and vision. For this reason, and because a groundwork of Blake must be laid before proceeding to Harris, the first chapter focuses exclusively on Blake's conception of good and evil, his insistence on the importance of contraries and his beliefs regarding vision and perspective. These concepts are examined in Blake's marginalia, poetry, comments recorded by others, and some of his visual works, mainly those found in his illuminated/engraved poetry. The close readings of the Harris novels and their film versions in the following chapters reveal how Harris establishes and makes use of the Blakean allusions and philosophies throughout the novels in order to emphasize that good and evil are interconnected. The conclusion establishes a reading of the novels as Lecter's Blakean progression and addresses reasons why the explicit Blake allusions are connected to Dolarhyde and Verger instead of Lecter.

While Harris is not working on any further Lecter novels or films, a television series entitled *Hannibal*, based upon his work but created by Bryan Fuller and produced by DeLaurentiis, began airing on NBC in April 2013. As the show has already referenced details regarding Lecter from the novels and has a compelling visual design which hints at Lecter's background and interests, it will be interesting to see if the Blakean allusions and themes appear.

I hope this book sparks further interest in both Blake and Harris and opens the door to conversation regarding not only the Blakean allusions in Harris and the necessity of reading the Lecter novels as a single narrative but also the Blakean conception of good and evil, particularly as related to perspective and forgiveness.

Introduction

William Blake has a long history of appearing in or being referenced in pop culture — everything from graphic novels (Moore's *From Hell*) to young adult novels (Pullman's *The Golden Compass*), from music (explicit settings of poetry such as Parry's "Jerusalem" and Bolcom's *Songs of Innocence and Experience*, as well as implicit inspiration and allusion, as in The Doors' "End of Night" and Patti Smith's "My Blakean Year") to films (Jarmusch's *Dead Man*). References to Blake are cataloged and shared informally and formally by scholars on websites like the William Blake Wikipedia page and *Zoamorphosis: The Blake 2.0 Blog*. Scholars have even given this cataloging of Blake allusions and connections a name: Blakespotting.

One of the reasons Blake's works may be so often referenced is their capacity for multiple interpretations. For example, when Billy Bragg sings "Jerusalem" it is as a critique of England and a call to arms for correction; however, when sung by a children's choir at the opening of the 2012 Summer Olympic Games in London it is as a patriotic anthem. Blake's works may be easily decontextualized, allowing not only multiple but even contradictory interpretations. When "Jerusalem" is read as part of the preface at the beginning of Blake's longer work *Milton*, following a call to arms of poets and painters to leave behind Greek and Roman models and to create a revolution in art and literature, it too is read as a call to arms, a rising up against tradition. In this context it is also read as a prophecy, as indicated by the passage from Numbers quoted below it, emphasizing the importance, and perhaps inevitability, of this uprising. However, when removed from the larger work it is easier to pay less attention to the rabble-rousing lines and more to the lines describing Jesus walking through peaceful England. It becomes not an angry anthem but instead a nostalgic pastoral reflection on a peaceful and sacred time to which the speaker wishes to return.

While it can be said that many writers have created works that may

Introduction

be read out of context (for example, reading Thomas Gray's phrase "ignorance is bliss" removed from his poem "Ode on a Distant Prospect of Eton College" eliminates the context of mortality and erases the idea that the ignorance referred to is ignorance of one's own mortality, making possible the interpretation that ignorance of facts or learning in general is bliss, causing the phrase to be a cry against education), Blake's illuminated works seem more vulnerable to decontextualized interpretations and uses, in part due to their use of both verbal and visual components. Given Blake's categorization as both poet and painter, he is often known as only one or the other, with the reader's/viewer's focus only on words or images, even when encountering his illuminated works.

This separation of text and image is due in part to sometimes only having access to one aspect. For example, often in literature anthologies, only the text of a poem is printed, and in art texts or in galleries the full-plate images are often printed or exhibited without the full poem. While it is more difficult to separate out the interlinear images and the images on a page of text, it is quite easy to remove the full-plate images from their poetic context. Take, for example, *Ancient of Days*. When viewed within the context of Blake's poem *Europe: A Prophecy*, the man in the image is clearly a tyrant, constraining those beneath him with his compasses; however, out of context, the figure easily becomes the Judeo-Christian God constructing his world. Further, he is no longer a tyrant but instead a fatherly figure creating order from chaos.

Works like the Proverbs from *The Marriage of Heaven and Hell* are open to even more varied interpretations due to their nature as proverbs to be decontextualized. It is this characteristic of proverbs and their relationship to readers that Mike Goode discusses in "Blakespotting." Goode addresses how "the ambiguous diction, punctuation and phrasing of Blake's proverbs certainly make them readily available to multiple and contradictory interpretations" (771) and how "Blake's proverblike poetry actively encourages readers to appropriate and resituate its lines" (776). As Goode suggests, these appropriations of and references to Blake reveal his enduring appeal; however, what can be even more interesting is trying to understand how and why Blake is referenced or used.

Artists and writers certainly do not choose his works simply because it is easy to decontextualize or appropriate them. When encountering these uses of or references to Blake, it is important to ask several questions. Is the quote used in a context or reading that scholars agree or disagree with?

Introduction

What does the use of that particular phrase or image reveal about the appeal of Blake, at least to a particular artist or generation? An important (and often not considered) question is this: Does Blake in a new context alter our own readings of his poetry and paintings? Some scholarly explorations of these Blakean allusions have been undertaken, including *Radical Blake: Influence and Afterlife from 1827* and *Blake, Modernity and Popular Culture*, as well as essays on Moore and Blake and a series on *Zoamorphosis* written by scholars that address and analyze a variety of these Blakespotting moments.

One writer often mentioned in a catalog or overview of appropriations of Blake is Thomas Harris, who has made extensive use of Blake in his four Hannibal Lecter novels: *Red Dragon*, *Silence of the Lambs*, *Hannibal*, and *Hannibal Rising*. Blake is explicitly referenced in both *Red Dragon* and *Hannibal*, playing a central role in the plot of *Red Dragon*, and Blakean themes exist in all four. In addition, some of the film versions of these novels also contain Blake allusions (interestingly, often ones not contained in the novels themselves).

This extended and sustained referencing of Blake by Harris calls for close attention. Why does Harris choose Blake? As Nicholas Williams, one of the few scholars to address this particular connection, has asked, which Blake is Harris choosing and why? In "Eating Blake" Williams discusses the use as a matter of "creative consumption" and incorporation (144). He considers how one text may incorporate another without sacrificing the incorporated text, as well as the relationship between high art and mass consumption. Williams suggests that one text is consumed by another as a means of elevating the consumer's status; in the process the consumed object is changed and altered as well, in order to fit the needs of the consumer. Ultimately, Williams uses Harris's use of Blake, and Blake's use of other authors like Milton, in order to ponder the greater question of reading and consumption.

While raising intriguing possibilities and highlighting the similarity between Blake and Harris in their own "consumption" of other, more respected or established writers, Williams's essay focuses exclusively on *Red Dragon* and does not address other possible questions regarding the connection of Harris and Blake. For example, how does Harris use Blake throughout the series of novels? Is it to further the characterizations, revealing insight into the characters by their connection to or knowledge of Blake? Or is it meant to indicate a particular mindset or commentary on the character or action? In other words, does it reveal more about the character or about how the readers are to respond to the character? Are the references meant to provide a cultural or philosophical background or context, categorizing the novels as Romantic or about revolution? Is Blake used as a positive or negative figure, an icon of art or of madness? How much of Blake is Harris assuming readers will know and recognize?

One would not expect Williams to have answered all of these questions, but they are the ones that remain unanswered by others as well. While many comment on the existence of the Blake references in Harris, no extended examination of why Harris alludes to Blake has been made. The lack of exploration of this connection and the lack of answers to these questions does not indicate that the questions are unanswerable, however. Readers coming to Harris from Blake, with a knowledge of Blake's works and themes, can examine the allusions, make the connections, and discover possible answers for themselves.

Given that Harris does not often grant interviews, there is no clear statement of what he "intended" by using references to or echoes of Blake. There is also no clear indication of how much of Blake's work Harris knows, and in what context (as poet or painter, or both), and, conversely, how much of Blake he expects his readers to know. In addition, Harris provides no explicit guidelines for how the readers should respond to Lecter, the character who best embodies Blakean ideas—should they be afraid, attracted, or both? There is obviously no definitive statement from Harris regarding any message he wished to convey about the nature of good and evil or of humanity. The most readers can do is consider what has been said by others and closely examine Harris's novels themselves.

Even if Harris had provided a statement regarding the "correct" way to read and respond to his novels and characters, that would not end the discussion becuase, as any literary scholar or English major knows, the text often reveals more than the author deliberately intended. Furthermore, an author's intention is not the only possible or valid way to read a work. Different perspectives and contexts, as addressed briefly above regarding Blake, lead to multiple valid interpretations and reactions. In addition, Harris's works will mean different things to different readers. Clearly Blake scholars or fans will grab hold of the Blake references and, with that background knowledge, read and interpret the books though a Blakean lens.

Those readers with a background in psychology or in profiling or in

Introduction

police work will, of course, read the books in another light. In addition, because of the popular film versions of the novels, the books will be read differently depending on whether the reader has seen the films first and then come to the novels or vice versa. Having seen the films first, particularly those starring Anthony Hopkins as Lecter, one may not be able to read the novels without imagining Hopkins and the charm he brings to the character. Even the order in which the novels are read changes one's view. If one begins with *Silence of the Lambs*, as many did after seeing the film version, and then goes back and reads *Red Dragon*, much time may be spent wondering where Lecter is and being distracted by his absence throughout most of the novel. As will be addressed later, if one reads *Hannibal Rising* first, instead of being disappointed in the prequel/origin story of Lecter, one may be more invested in his development and journey throughout the other three novels. Conversely, given the poor quality of *Hannibal Rising*, if one reads that novel first, one may have no interest at all in reading the other three novels.

Similarly, different interpretations are also created by reading the novels individually or reading them each as part of a longer, single narrative. As will become clear throughout this book, when the novels are read in a series a strong thematic thread is revealed that can be overlooked if one approaches each novel as a separate entity. Even fans of Harris who have read all of the novels may not think of them as a series and therefore easily overlook both the sustained Blakean allusions and the thematic thread that holds them together.

It is not simply this thematic thread that ties Harris and Blake together; it is not merely the interest in good and evil and the nature of humanity that the two have in common. The fan or readership bases of each also share a similarity in that Harris fans (of both the films and the novels) who are interested in the literary and cultural references in the novels often engage in an activity similar to Blakespotting in that they catalog, not references to Harris in other works, but literary and artistic references made by Harris. For example, the fan page "Leda and the Swan" lists allusions and links to literature, art, and music referenced in these works. Allusions are also discussed on the Hannibal Lecter Studiolo. These lists, however, are often nothing more than just that, a list or catalog of allusions. "Leda and the Swan" lists the passage from *Hannibal* in which *Ancient of Days* appears and then includes a link to a brief online biography of Blake, while the discussions on the Hannibal Lecter Studiolo do range

Introduction

into speculation regarding, for example, the connection between Dante and Harris.

Both sites, however, are fan driven, not scholar driven, which is not to say that there is no overlap between the two or that the insights raised in the discussions are not valid or interesting, but to suggest instead that they informally discuss topics that indicate a need for a more sustained and scholarly exploration of the possible connections. Scholarly exploration of Harris's allusions, however, is limited. Simpson does catalog allusions, although he does not analyze them, in *Making Murder*, a book that works well as an introduction to the literary and artistic allusions and the complexities of Harris's work, but does not delve much deeper. The rare detailed analysis is, as mentioned, Nicholas Williams's exploration of the use of Blake in *Red Dragon*.

This book will tie together the interest in Harris and Blake and work to analyze, not just catalog, Harris's use of Blake throughout the four Lecter novels. Using Blake to read Harris, particularly in regard to their portrayal of and opinion on the relationship of good and evil, as well as the nature and origin of both, reveals a consistent thematic thread: The allusions to Blake, both explicit (the paintings *The Great Red Dragon and the Woman Clothed in the Sun* and *Ancient of Days*) and implicit (portrayals of the church and the law), underline and emphasize a particular philosophy regarding good and evil — namely, that the two are intertwined and coexist, and that it is foolish to try to see them simply as opposing binaries. Not only is viewing them as binaries foolish, but it is also dangerous, leading to mental, and at times physical, harm (for example, as experienced by Graham).

The allusions to Blake, as well as the relationships between the hero and the villain, the complex nature of the characters in each of the works, and the complexity of human nature and the natural world, also emphasize this theme of the interconnectedness of good and evil. In addition, details regarding perspective and vision connect Harris to Blake and to Blake's particular theodicy because in order to accept the blurred line between good and evil, in order to *see* how the two are connected and dependent upon each other, one must first have the ability to see from others' perspectives. Seeing from multiple perspectives makes categorization and labeling difficult, if not impossible, and indicates that attempting to separate good from evil, a separation that relies on categorization, is also impossible.

Details from the novels that may seem to indicate an elitism on the part of Harris that elevate Lecter through his class status and tastes may

Introduction

in fact be markers of heightened senses that distinguish between qualities and make one more aware of quality and taste. Further connections to Blake include the difficulty of categorizing or labeling actions or people, the hypocrisy of the law and religion, the importance of imagination, and the necessity of forgiveness over vengeance.

While these specific connections tie Blake and Harris together, other, more broad connections exist between Blake and the genre in which Harris writes. It should not be surprising to discover allusions to Blake in horror fiction given that Blake's works expound on his philosophy of the complex nature of life and humanity and that "horror fiction reveals the complexities of what it means to be human" (Magistrale and Morrison 3). Intriguingly, Magistrale and Morrison also claim that "[a]t its best, horror art is visionary.... It strips us of all that we know by challenging us to invent new categories and modes of comprehension" (7).

Blake's works are also visionary, in multiple senses of the word. The poems are filled with references to visions, with one even being called *Visions of the Daughters of Albion*, and are said to have grown out of visions, at least in how Blake claimed that he learned his engraving process from a vision of his deceased brother. In addition, the engraved works are literally full of visions in that they contain a visual component as well as a verbal one. Most importantly, though, Blake's works are visionary in the sense that they confront the status quo and work to reveal a more complex truth or future path.

Since Blake's works could also be said to challenge readers to understand and invent new categories (the unique genre of the illuminated book, for example), thereby fulfilling Magistrale and Morrison's conception of the visionary as insisting upon new categories and ways of comprehending, it is not surprising to see a writer such as Harris make use of Blake in the horror genre to emphasize the visionary challenging quality of his own novels. Additionally, horror works to visualize the struggle of good and evil, order and chaos. As much of Blake's work deals with contraries and conflicts, allusions to him seem natural. It is this conflict, the struggle between and within humans, and the revelation of the dark aspect of society, the malevolent underpinnings of societal institutions, that lead to the questioning of received morality that Harris reveals in part by drawing on Blakean imagery and ideas.

In addition to the underlying exploration of human nature and conflict, another aspect of horror that relates to both Harris and Blake is the doppelganger, "one of the dominant motifs of the horror text" (Wells 8). The doppelganger may represent two sides of an individual (primal v. civilized, for example) as embodied in one person, like Jekyll and Hyde, or as two similar figures who operate according to different moralities. Harris's texts use both forms of this motif. Lecter himself can move from peaceful man at the opera to savage animal, while at the same time both Graham and Starling operate as versions of Lecter's doppelganger. The use of Starling as a doppelganger figure is particularly interesting given that, as Wells claims, the doppelgangers, the duality, can represent differing gender identities (9). Furthermore, the doppelganger motif connects to Blake's concept of Emanations, the female aspect of the male Self, as well as his idea that the Emanation and the Self are ultimately one androgynous being. The relationship between Starling and Lecter fully embodies these Blakean concepts as the two sides are fully merged into one entity, instead of, as is usual in horror films, one side taking precedence. This will be one of the main aspects focused on in the following chapters.

It must be understood that the exploration of Lecter's character and the mixed nature of good and evil in the novels is not meant to condone these actions, but merely to bring to light a particular philosophy and connection to Blake. Neither Blake's works nor Harris's novels are proscriptive, but instead are descriptive of the world and human nature. In *The Songs of Innocence and Experience* Blake describes the world as seen by both innocent and experienced people, providing, for example, in the *Innocence* "Holy Thursday" a vision of orphans and charity that leads to a positive view of the merciful nature of humanity, while in the *Experience* "Holy Thursday" a viewing of the same event leads to a negative view of the cruel nature of humanity causing the necessity for charity. Neither view is entirely correct and both together reveal a fuller description of humanity.

A view of the world from only the innocent or experienced perspective is an incomplete one, both too simplistic and narrow. Blake provides a more complex view when he includes passages of violence in order to describe the causes and effects, both negative and positive, of such moments. In *Visions of the Daughters of Albion*, for example, Blake describes a rape and its aftermath without condoning it. Similarly, in *Red Dragon*, Harris describes possible causes of Dolarhyde's violence without justifying his actions, and describing how Graham is damaged by his experiences without claiming that his being damaged is a necessarily or completely positive experience. Later, in *Hannibal*, Harris reveals humans'

Introduction

interest in cruelty by describing the popularity of the Atrocious Torture Exhibit, without suggesting that this is a positive or negative aspect of humanity, or even if it is a necessary one. Importantly, Lecter is not a role model of either how to behave or how not to behave (except perhaps in the necessity of observation and perception, which lead to acknowledgment of contraries and complexities), but is a vivid reminder that evil exists along with good qualities—that, as Blake says in his Annotations to Lavater, "that which is capable of evil is also capable of good" (594).

This dual capability of humanity and nature is at the heart of this investigation of the Harris/Blake connection. This book explores these ideas of humanity, nature, perception and duality, offering insight for two distinct audiences: scholars and fans of both Harris and Blake. For Blake scholars coming to this work, it helps, but is not necessary, to have a knowledge of Harris's works. Since numerous Blake scholars are interested in his appearances in pop culture, many will most likely already be familiar with at least a few of the novels, particularly *Red Dragon* and *Hannibal*. For them this book will not just be an exploration of how Harris has used Blake and how Blakean ideas appear in the novels, but also can act as a springboard for further consideration of Blake's own ideas, particularly his conception of good and evil, and how his works have been interpreted. For example, this discussion of Harris and Blake may lead others to re-examine how Blake portrays violence and vengeance in his own works.

After considering their own interpretations of Blake and his conception of good and evil, scholars can ultimately turn to, or return to, the Harris novels to explore their own interpretations of the connection between Blake and Harris. After all, this book seeks not to proclaim the one stable and true interpretation or explanation of how and why Harris uses Blake (to do so in a study of the necessity of complex and contrary perspectives would be hypocritical), but instead suggests one compelling interpretation that others may use as a springboard or grounding for their own interpretations. For fans of Harris, little previous knowledge of Blake is necessary, but with the information provided here they will be prepared, and perhaps inspired, to explore Blake's works on their own to further explore the Harris/Blake connection. Both audiences can use this book as a platform on which to build their own analyses of both authors, perhaps bringing in the many Blake works (particularly his paintings) not mentioned here, or finding connections not yet explored.

To provide a framework for this exploration, the first chapter gives

Introduction

an overview of Blake's philosophy of good and evil, gathered from both his poetic works and his more personal writings, such as marginalia, as well as drawing on what other scholars have said of Blake. The second chapter then examines existing Harris scholarship and how and why he has often been distinguished from other horror or procedural writers. It goes on to provide an overview of the general opinion of Harris's view of evil and interpretations of evil and the nature of Lecter in these works. Finally, this chapter summarizes what has already been said of the Harris/Blake connection.

The next four chapters explore in detail Blake references in each of the novels, as well as their film versions. The films will be examined in addition to the novels for two reasons, even though Harris had no central hand in the creation of the films (excepting *Hannibal Rising*). First, many of Harris's readers may have come to read the novels only after seeing the films and (because of the popularity of *Silence of the Lambs* in particular), the characters, especially Lecter, are closely intertwined in many readers' minds with their portrayals on film. Because of this many will have the films in mind when thinking about the novels. Second, two of the films, *Red Dragon* and *Hannibal*, have added explicit Blake allusions that are worth addressing; therefore, the use of Blakean imagery and allusions and how the films either undercut or emphasize the connection to Blake will be considered. These chapters are not merely a catalog of the similarities but an attempt to use the surface allusions to discover deeper connections and ultimately lead to a conclusion regarding Harris's choice of Blake.

The final chapter reads the novels not as separate works, but as one work in four parts, allowing the references to create a unified commentary on the nature and relationship of good and evil. Through reordering the novels and examining Lecter's progression from a young man haunted by his past in *Hannibal Rising* to finally being in balance and at peace at the end of *Hannibal*, Harris's use of the Blakean ideas of contraries, perspective, and duality are revealed. Additionally, this chapter explores why the explicit Blake allusions are connected not with Lecter, the most Blakean of the characters, but with Dolarhyde and Verger. Reading Harris through a Blakean lens also provides insight into Blake's ideas, illuminating his complex conception of good and evil and revealing that, indeed, the same hand did make the tiger and the lamb, typhoid and swans.

CHAPTER 1

"Under every *Good* is a hell"
William Blake's View of Good and Evil

Since Harris reveals his conception of good and evil through references to Blake, an understanding of Blake's own conception of good and evil becomes necessary. A complete discussion of Blake's conception of good and evil requires an entire book; therefore, attempting to address it in only one chapter may be perceived as treating it too lightly, or assuming that a standard accepted interpretation of his conception exists. This chapter's purpose, however, is to establish a possible Blakean theory of good and evil, which his writings (both his poems and what he explicitly states in marginalia and notes) reveal. Blake's statements and ideas regarding the importance and power of perspective and vision also reveal insight into his theory of the relationship of good and evil. Blake, of course, was both a poet and a visual artist; some additionally consider him a philosopher due to his production of proverbs and creation of his own mythology. This mythology is set out largely in what are called his prophetic books, which explain the creation of the fallen world and the attempt to reach Eternity. Recurring characters, such as Los and Urizen, appear throughout these books. This original mythology accounts for the difficulty of easily and quickly understanding Blake's works and the importance of reading the works in context, against the background of Blakean mythology instead of, for example, in a traditional Christian context. The majority of his poetic works, his illuminated books, include visual aspects. Blake engraved these works and included small interlinear designs, larger illustrations/designs on the plates of poetry, and separate full-plate images inserted in between the plates of poetry. However, while also providing insight into Blake's conception of good and evil, his visual images, both those of the illuminated works and other engravings and paintings, will not be addressed at length. This does not mean that all visual aspects will be ignored; obviously, some of the visual images that explicitly connect to Harris's novels will be discussed here and in later chapters, including Blake's Red Dragon paintings, *Ancient of Days*, and some recurring imagery related to enlightenment. By necessity, however, many of the visual aspects of Blake's works will be left unaddressed, with the main focus of this exploration instead on Blake's statements, both implicit and explicit, that reveal his conception of good and evil (as well as related ideas of perception and forgiveness) and on what scholars have suggested about Blake's ideas concerning good and evil and related concepts (including, of course, religion).

Many scholars have discussed religion and Blake, particularly as his ideas relate to those of nonconformist or antinomian belief systems of the eighteenth century; others have traced his connections to Gnosticism and Kabbalism.* In exploring these ideas, many have commented on Blake's thoughts regarding evil and its relationship to good. For example, Mark Schorer examines Blake's mysticism and politics, addressing many of the contraries and dialectics throughout. While Schorer discusses good and evil only briefly, some of his insights must be mentioned, especially his explanation of Blake's method for achieving a "universal order ... not by purgation, but by affirmation, which means that order is not achieved by denying elements in human nature, but by asserting their totality" (81). In other words, humans rise above the fallen world, and correct the ills of this world, not by eliminating evil, but by accepting its existence and role in nature. Like others, Schorer connects Blake's doctrine of evil to that of the Gnostics: that the God of this world is a lesser god and it is he who created evil. For Blake, this is Urizen, the rational, binding, and dividing God. This is the God with the compass in Blake's painting *Ancient of Days*, a painting that appears in *Hannibal* in connection with Mason Verger.

While not connecting Blake to Gnosticism or exploring his religious or philosophical beliefs in depth, S. Foster Damon's *A Blake Dictionary* also furthers one's understanding of Blake's conception of good and evil. While not the definitive interpretations, Damon's explanations are a useful starting point for readers of Blake, providing examples of accepted or standard interpretations. Damon does include an entry for "Evil," of which

---

*Sheila Spector's work with Blake and Kabbalism, for example, explores many aspects of Blake's theodicy, including the kabbalistic idea that the origin of evil resides in the Godhead.

1. "Under every Good *is a hell*"

he says, "[it] is not an absolute: it is an error, a delusion, a quality springing from the mistaken division of Good and Evil" (133). Good and evil have been mistakenly divided, paradoxically leading to the creation of evil itself. The mistaken belief that evil can be separated from good and easily categorized leads to some things being labeled as evil, as well as to evil actions themselves. (This idea of the attempt to divide good from evil leading to evil will be further explored later in this chapter.) The passages Damon provides in support of this definition come from *The Marriage of Heaven and Hell* (8:18) — "Every thing possible to be believ'd is an image of truth" — and *Jerusalem* (36:51) — "What seems to Be, Is, To those to whom it seems to Be, & is productive of the most dreadful Consequences to those to whom it Torments, Despair, Eternal Death" — both of which emphasize the responsibility of the mind for the evil it sees.* The mind creates the evil through a mistaken understanding of the world, due to its limited perception. Perception and the senses are intimately connected to Blake's conception of good and evil. As the passage above from *The Marriage of Heaven and Hell* indicates, anything the mind imagines is truth. What the mind imagines is shaped by what the eye sees and the other senses perceive. If one has narrow or imperceptive senses, one's imagination is limited, and therefore so is one's understanding of what is true. Perhaps this narrowed perception leads to imagining a binary world, in which good and evil are separate. For that person, this appears to be the truth, but it isn't the universal truth, and someone with expanded senses may perceive the interconnected and complex nature of good and evil (therefore, not defining evil as something opposed to good). The passage from *Jerusalem* also indicates that what is perceived becomes the truth. If one perceives an action as good or beneficial, it is; if, conversely, they view and label that action evil or harmful, it is. Importantly, one must remember that it is beneficial or harmful only to them, and not universally. If someone can see or imagine an action as possibly both beneficial and harmful, it is neither good nor evil, but both. Their expanded perception and imagination allow them to acknowledge the complexity of the world.

Notably, this definition of evil does not address what may be considered "true" evils, like murder. Surely Blake must accept that murder exists outside the construction of the mind and that murder is not, generally, a

---

**In citing references to Blake's works, plate numbers or letters are given first, followed by line numbers.*

force for good. Indeed, according to Blake's beliefs, murder does exist; however, it is human delusion that allows it to exist. A faulty vision of the world, one of limited perception in which all people are separate from each other, leads to the ability, and perhaps even inclination, to harm others. By viewing all beings as separate individuals, as unconnected, it becomes easier to oppress others, deeming one's own desires to be more important than another's. The narrow perception leads to categorization of groups of people as "other" and their beliefs as wrong, and therefore one can act against them, even murder them, because they are already separate and different. This faulty and narrow vision that attempts to categorize and label sees a struggle and separation between good and evil. Narrow vision may not lead one to murder others but can still in other ways lead to further separation and continued violence in that it can lead to a belief that those who are "evil" are irredeemable and therefore not worthy of forgiveness. This in turn can lead to vengeance and possibly other evil acts, both against the irredeemable person and by the irredeemable person, who now can only see himself as evil, with therefore no reason to change his actions.

Melanie Bandy uses Damon's definition as the foundation for her *Mind Forg'd Manacles: Evil in the Poetry of Blake and Shelley*, the only extended exploration specifically of Blake's concept of good and evil that covers the entirety of his work. Bandy focuses on Blake's belief that evil in the world can be eradicated through the use of imagination, a belief that emphasizes the connection between perception and the labeling of good and evil. The evils that Bandy explicitly discusses include tyranny and political oppression, as well as repressed/suppressed sexuality. Unfortunately, Bandy does not discuss what may be considered more traditional manifestations of evil, like murder, at length, nor does she address the connection between good and evil, exploring their ideal or even fallen relationship, but instead explains Blake's beliefs regarding how to overcome evil. If evil is created through faulty vision, she argues, then it can be overcome by enlightened vision, by imagination. This focus on overcoming evil, however, leads to a further difficulty in that Bandy admits that evil exists in what Blake calls "Eternity." If evil is overcome, how can it still exist? That evil exists in Eternity is the most troublesome aspect of attempting to define Blake's belief system. As with most difficulties in discussing Blake, this one is also caused by definitions. On the surface Eternity seems to be Blake's equivalent of Heaven, particularly as it is the highest

1. "Under every Good is a hell"

of the realms. Under Eternity is Beulah, a paradise, and under that Ulro, the material world. If Eternity is defined as equal to Heaven, the possibility that evil exists in Heaven directly opposes most religious and philosophical teachings. However, Blake's Eternity, the highest of his realms, is not the same as the traditional Christian Heaven, but is of his own invention, having in common with the Christian Heaven the fact that it is eternal and a place of reconciliation, but differing from it in that it is not governed by God and one does not attain entrance to it through confession or faith. As with many of Blake's creations, Eternity borrows from the Christian Heaven but is not equivalent, leaving out what Blake saw as flawed in traditional Christianity.

The difficulty of definition accounts in part for the lack of an extended discussion of evil in Blake's works. Particularly given Blake's use of multiple realms and his use of traditional or accepted definitions, as well as personalized definitions, determining what he means by evil (as well as other related concepts) becomes fraught with confusion and frustration. For example, when Blake discusses evil, does he set it in the Generative (fallen) world or Eternity? When he describes the Generative world, is he merely describing or is he proscribing? In addition, Blake's use of words in both their traditional meanings and his own Blakean meaning leads to further questions. The most obvious example appears in *The Marriage of Heaven and Hell*, in which devils are angels and vice versa. Particularly in this work, the question then becomes, if devils are angels, is evil good? Other words used in a contrary or ironic way include *pure, virgin, holy*, and even *God*. As Bandy indicates, God in Blake is both "God the evil tyrant, and God the Divine Humanity" (185, footnote 8). Bandy goes on to state, "In all instances ... the context makes the meaning clear" (185, footnote 8); however, while it may be clear for most readers in some instances (particularly in the explicit discussion in *The Marriage of Heaven and Hell*), in other instances and in other works, Blake's meaning is not immediately clear to readers unless they come to the work already armed with a knowledge of Blake's mythos and complex use of language. For example, in *Jerusalem* (10:38–39), as Los argues with his Spectre, the Spectre proclaims that "the law of God commands/That they [Los's children] be offered upon his Altar."* A reader coming to this passage with

---

**All Blake works are from* The Complete Poetry and Prose of William Blake, *edited by David V. Erdman (revised edition published in 1988).*

knowledge of the Bible, but not a strong background in Blake's other writings, will read this perhaps as being an echo of Old Testament stories of sacrifice to God and will interpret the call for sacrifice as a test of Los's devotion to and trust in this God. These readers may also assume that, as in the story of Abraham and Isaac, the sacrifice will never take place, so no harm will be done. They may read this as a passage referring to God the divine father and king, and assume that this God ultimately has only the best interests of humanity in mind and therefore would never require sacrifice, and if he did allow the sacrifice, then it would be for the best, even if not understood by humanity itself. If, however, the reader already knows Blake's negative connotation of "the law of God," the negative nature of the Spectre, and Blake's negative view of religious sacrifice, the reader will recognize God here as an evil tyrant, thinking only of imposing his will and, while perhaps mistakenly operating in what he thinks are the best interests of humanity, not understanding the dangers of imposing will or law indiscriminately upon them. Given this context, the reader recognizes Los's Spectre as his rational aspect (a negative concept in Blake) that wishes to create and enforce laws in the name of God. Because the Spectre is a rational aspect, these laws are unyielding, created from logical rules, and contain no emotional or individual understanding, ignoring context or complexity of actions, and instead judging and punishing based on the letter of the law alone. Furthermore, this informed reader recognizes that one-sided sacrifice, particularly that demanded of another, is merely cruelty, while mutual sacrifice and forgiveness in which two or more entities consensually agree to sacrifice themselves for the other thereby recognizing the interrelationship of all creatures, comprises the center of Blake's concept of Christianity. The two interpretations, one based on a passage taken out of context and one based on the passage within its context, differ completely. Interestingly, the importance of context and the necessity of placing Blake's work in its larger context is a central concern of Harris's novels and will be discussed at length later when considering how both Dolarhyde and Verger misread Blake because they do so out of context and without knowledge or understanding of Blake's personalized definitions and mythology.

While not terms referenced by Harris, Blake's personalized meanings of *contrary* and *negation* can lead to difficulty in understanding the relationship between dichotomies like good and evil and are therefore central to understanding Blake's conception of good and evil. Both a contrary

1. "Under every Good *is a hell*"

and a negation are what most would call "opposites"; however, in Blake's work contraries need to coexist, while negations have to be overcome and defeated. Good and evil are contraries in Blake's thought, as will become clear, but his concept of the Spectre, a negation who is a willful and rational "evil" aspect of the self, must be discarded in order for one to leave Generation for Eternity. The Spectre is a rational construction, a construction of reason divorced from all other human characteristics or aspects. Because of Urizen and the Tree of the Knowledge of Good and Evil, those in Generation have divided evil and good; it is the Spectre who encourages this categorization, so it is not evil in a traditional spiritual or Christian sense that must be defeated, but rather the rational part of human consciousness that wishes to categorize and label evil, particularly as something separate from human nature. The Spectre as a rational construction wishes to separate all irrational aspects from humanity instead of embracing the complexity of human nature. All strong emotions, particularly those usually considered negative, are viewed by the Spectre as things to be expunged. Reason wants to separate out and exterminate violence, anger, depression, and so forth. At first glance this seems like a good thing; however, as a rational construction, the Spectre would also encourage the disposal of irrational emotions like love and desire, since they make humans act irrationally. The Spectre encourages viewing evil (that is, all of the things labeled by the rational self as evil) as a negation, and not a contrary, of good, when in fact it is the Spectre itself that is a negation. Since, according to Blake, one must embrace contraries but overcome and defeat negations, evil must be embraced and the Spectre defeated. Embracing evil does not mean acting upon evil, but instead accepting it as a part of human nature, acknowledging its coexistence with good. Similarly, one can accept the rational part of human nature, but should not bow down to it and let it dominate. If the rational aspect, the Spectre, attempts to dominate, it must be overcome. Schorer addresses Blake's concept of evil as a contrary instead of a negation when he states that Blake does not discuss "radical dualism" but rather "contrary conditions of energy" and that "evil is not the opposite of good, but misdirected energy" (82), once again emphasizing that, for Blake, evil is a mistake, an error, that all can make. Like good, it is energy and only becomes categorized as evil when misdirected.

The difficulty in teasing out Blake's ideas of good and evil mirrors the difficulty in determining his ideas regarding gender, male and female. Blake's concepts of the hermaphrodite and the androgyne provide another example of difficult distinctions between seemingly similar words. For Blake, the hermaphrodite is a negative figure, consisting of two separate willful aspects, male and female; however, the androgyne is a positive figure, symbolizing the coming together of the contraries of male and female (the male self and his female emanation) in Eternity when the two are joined in one. The male does not defeat the female, nor vice versa. They are distinct genders, joined as one, neither fighting for control but instead living with an acceptance of both aspects of the self. They become one without each being willful as a hermaphroditic form, or a Spectre, is. It is this willfulness, this struggle for domination and insistence on distinctions instead of acceptance and coexistence, that needs to be avoided or overcome. In the case of good and evil it is the struggle between the two and the attempt to divide and define them that lead to the categorization of good and evil as separate and opposed (and therefore to evil actions). If good and evil are accepted as two parts of one whole, able to coexist, and if their relationship is recognized as being complex and interconnected, then balance can be achieved and evil actions eliminated.

Since good and evil coexist as these contraries for Blake, the distinction made between the two is often a matter of perspective. The Spectre, for example, will be prone to label and cast out evil from rational human nature, perhaps even where evil does not truly exist. For example, one person may view sexuality as a sin while another considers it a natural expression. Viewing sexuality as sin leads one to want to cast it out or eradicate it, which in turn leads to what Blake described in *The Marriage of Heaven and Hell* as "Brothels [being made] with bricks of Religion" (8:1). The religious view of sex as sinful does not lead to its eradication but to the creation of brothels and feelings of guilt and shame. Sexuality is not the only aspect of society that can be seen in this perspectival way. Blake witnessed both child labor and slavery viewed in this way, recognizing that those who owned slaves or used child labor did not believe either was a sin, while others were horrified and attempted to change what they viewed as sinful practices. Knowing Blake's reluctance to clearly divide good and evil, Henry Crabb Robinson asked him, "Is there nothing absolutely evil in what men do[?]," to which Blake responded, "I am no judge of that—perhaps not in God's eyes" (Kindle location 330). So, according to Blake, God may not judge any acts as evil; humanity, with its multiple perspectives and codified belief systems, does. Blake's emphasis on perspective, though, does not indicate Blake is a pure relativist, believ-

1. "Under every Good is a hell"

ing that all acts are good at least from one perspective and should therefore be allowed to continue; one need only remember that he wrote against both child labor and slavery to be convinced that he believed some actions were wrong, if not evil. However, his poems and marginalia reveal how categorization, even into good and evil, is often a matter of perspective, and that in order to understand the world and human nature, one needs the ability to acknowledge these differing perspectives, to see from a different perspective, if only briefly. By viewing from, or at least understanding, those various perspectives, one avoids hindering or oppressing others (which Blake saw as a vice and which will be discussed further later in the chapter) and knows how to respond to actions of perceived evil correctly — with forgiveness. By understanding the other's perspective, one may be able to forgive and to find a way to stop evil actions like child labor and slavery (which are indeed the hindering of others and therefore, in Blake's view, should be eradicated). However, just arguing that the actions or the people who commit them are wrong will not make these actions or people stop. One needs to understand why these actions take place, and why some people justify them; only then can one eradicate them by diverting the energy used to hinder others into something more productive.

Often, the importance of perspective and expanded vision lies in the ability to recognize both positive and negative outcomes of an action. In Blake's works a character like Enitharmon, Los, or Urizen may act to stop chaos or suffering and yet the result is further suffering. At other times, Blake will clearly posit an act as oppressive or evil — for instance, the rape in *Visions of the Daughters of Albion*— only to reveal that evil act as sparking future action toward a good or positive outcome. This rape, along with the one in the Preludium to *America*, will be discussed in depth later in this chapter to better examine their complexities of good and evil, perspective and vision, and the appropriate response to evil. What must be kept in mind is that these moments do not justify evil or encourage it, but instead accept and recognize the complex relationship between good and evil.

Blake's poems, as well as other writings such as his letters and marginalia, reveal this emphasis on the complexity of evil and its coexistence with good. Given the number of works Blake created, counting his illuminated books, notebook works, and separate engravings and paintings, as well as the fact that many of these works appear in multiple versions with variations in either coloring or order of plates that may alter interpretation, it is beyond the scope of this book to examine how each work reveals this complexity of good and evil. However, several works central to his beliefs must be discussed in detail, although any alterations in plate order or coloring between copies will not be addressed.

Most obviously, in his early works, *Songs of Innocence and Experience* and *The Marriage of Heaven and Hell*, Blake reveals how good and evil, Innocence and Experience, and Heaven and Hell are interconnected and how it is a rational error of mankind to see them as distinct. The subtitle of *Songs* is "Shewing the Two Contrary States of the Human Soul," indicating that, for Blake, Innocence and Experience are contraries, not negations, and therefore should coexist without struggle for domination. This contrary nature of the states is often revealed in the companion poems, one from Innocence and one from Experience together working to reveal both states. To look at one example of this revelation of balance of contraries from the *Songs* that connects to an image in Harris's *Red Dragon*, consider the companion poems "The Lamb" and "The Tyger." In "The Lamb" the speaker questions the Lamb about who made him and then answers that it was Jesus ("He is called by thy name,/For he calls himself a Lamb," 11. 13–14). The Jesus/God presented here is a "meek" and "mild" one.* In "The Tyger" the speaker questions the tiger about his creation but gives no answers; instead, he only wonders, "Did he who made the Lamb make thee?" (1. 20). The questions emphasize the tiger's fierceness. Is the God of good also the God of evil? Many believe Blake's answer would be yes, God made both the Lamb and the Tyger. Dena Bain Taylor, however, suggests a slightly different reading in which the tiger "represent[s] the essence of God — not as a creation separate from the Godhead but as a sefirotic power manifesting His dark nature" (82). Taylor connects this interpretation to Boehme's beliefs, with which Blake was familiar, saying "Boehme defines evil as the dark and negative principle of wrath in God, infinitely bound with the qualities of mercy and love. The tiger is a reminder that the contraries form a sacred whole as long as each maintains its proper relationship to others — in other words, as long as the tiger kills individual lambs but doesn't try to exterminate all of them" (82). Her

---

*Interestingly, Fred Dortort indicates that "mild" when used by Blake in "Milton" "establish[es] situations of unmistakable deception" (59), whereas in "Jerusalem" it marks passages of "syntactic manipulation" (59). Even a seemingly simple word like "mild" has contrary and complex meanings in Blake.

1. "Under every Good *is a hell*"

emphasis on balance when the tiger refrains from killing all lambs is apt when applied to Harris's characters: as long as Lecter kills only individual lambs, directing his wrath at those who are "deserving" instead of striking indiscriminately, he may live in proper balance with Starling. Lecter, then, is this tiger of the contraries, as will be explored in detail in later chapters.

To further support this reading of good and evil existing in the same creature and being created by the same force, the visual image of the tiger reveals neither an angry nor a wrathful creature. On the contrary, the drawn tiger clearly does not have a fire in his eyes, but instead a blank stare, soft padded feet and a smile revealing no fangs. The tiger is no more fierce than the lamb. The same God made both good and evil, and good and evil exist in all things. As Blake says in several works, "Everything that Lives is Holy," even the tiger. Crabb Robinson commented on this belief of Blake's, claiming that Blake "spoke as if he denied altogether the existence of evil and as if we had nothing to do with right and wrong, it being sufficient to consider all things as alike the work of God" (Kindle location 332).

The most explicit statement regarding the relationship between and definition of good and evil in the poetry occurs in *The Marriage of Heaven and Hell*, in which Blake lists "Reason and Energy" among the contraries, and then states, "From these contraries spring what the religious call Good & Evil. Good is the passive that obeys Reason[.] Evil is the active springing from Energy" (plate 3). It is the religious, thinking they are performing God's work, who divide the contraries, both of which are necessary for progression. Furthermore, Blake claims that one of the Bible's errors is considering "That Energy, calld Evil, is alone from the Body," when, in fact, "Energy is the only life" and "Energy is Eternal Delight" (plate 4). So, good and evil are not separate and evil is actually a positive, an active energy that provides delight, unless, as discussed earlier, it is misdirected.

Blake does not express this coexistence of good and evil in just the poems; some of the most explicit statements of this belief come in his marginalia and notebook. Many of his commentaries regarding good and evil are found in "A Vision of the Last Judgment." This work consists of passages written in his notebook and contains the title "For the Year 1810/Additions to Blakes [*sic*] Catalogue of Pictures &." As Erdman suggests, this was Blake's preparation for an explanation to accompany a public exhibition that never took place (881). Only a few of Blake's comments will be discussed here. Blake begins "A Vision of the Last Judgment" by defining "The Last Judgment" as being "when all those are Cast away who trouble Religion with Questions concerning Good & Evil" (554). If the questions of good and evil are trivial enough to "trouble Religion," then, by default, both must be accepted without attempting to discover the origin of either. Later, Blake describes the inhabitants of Paradise, who are "no longer talking of what is Good & Evil or of what is Right or Wrong & puzzling themselves in Satans [*Maze*]* Labyrinth But are Conversing with Eternal Realities as they Exist in the Human Imagination" (562). Clearly, once humans are regenerated and reunited in Blake's version of Heaven, there is no need to discuss good and evil; however, it is also clear that the mere categorizing of good and evil, the attempt to label and moralize, is, in fact, part of Satan's maze, for it is Satan who is concerned with binaries and categorization, whereas God created all in its varied complexity. The most explicit of these statements declaring coexistence is a later addition: "<Good & Evil are Qualities in Every Man whether <a> Good or Evil Man>" (563).† It is Satan's influence, the influence of a fallen nature and narrow perception, that leads to the labeling and attempt to separate these categories. Satan's role in categorization is further revealed when Blake states, "Such is the Last Judgment a Deliverance from Satans Accusation Satan thinks that Sin is displeasing to God he ought to know that Nothing is displeasing to God but Unbelief & Eating of the Tree of Knowledge of Good & Evil" (564). Here Blake explicitly states that sin, evil, is not displeasing to God. However, "Eating of the Tree of Knowledge of Good & Evil" is displeasing, not because it leads to sin or to evil, but because it leads to a distinction between the two, the desire to categorize and separate them, the beginning of Satan's Maze. Bandy interprets Blake's reference to unbelief being displeasing to God as meaning that "Blake reserves his strongest condemnation for unbelief in the Divine Humanity, the world of imagination" (51). Given Harris's use of Blake and the character of Hannibal Lecter, Bandy's suggestion is intriguing. Lecter, after all, is a murderer, and murder is an act that Blake considers the hindering of another, and therefore the restraint of action and a vice. If, as Bandy suggests, Blake's philosophy was that those who do not believe in imagination are

---

**Erdman uses italics in square brackets to indicate deleted or replaced words or phrases.*
†*Erdman uses angled brackets to indicate text written to replace deletions or text that Blake added later.*

1. "*Under every* Good *is a hell*"

worse than those who commit sin, Lecter seems to embody this belief in that he shows no qualms over his own actions, and yet disdains those who do not understand and appreciate art, music, or any of the productions of imagination. Since the audience comes to identify with Lecter, they begin to share in Blake's belief as well. This importance of imagination is also connected to enhanced perception and senses and it will be discussed further later.

According to Blake, Satan does not accept, however, that disbelief in imagination is more displeasing than sin and continues to argue for the binary opposition of good and evil in order to label and condemn evil in others. Blake emphasizes this again in "A Vision of the Last Judgment" when he states, "The Player is a liar when he Says Angels are happier than Men because they are better Angels are happier than Men <& Devils> because they are not always Prying after Good & Evil in One Another & eating the Tree of Knowledge for Satans Gratification" (565). Satan's role in the creation of this distinction also appears in Blake's "The Keys of the Gates," in which he says, "Serpent Reasonings us entice/of Good & Evil: Virtue & Vice" (ll. 7-8). The serpent does not entice us to evil but to a distinction between good and evil.

As these passages reveal, while Blake believes in a Last Judgment, it is not one of separating good from evil, but of finding them in balance and accepting their coexistence. In fact, those condemned at this judgment are those who ate of the Tree of Knowledge of Good and Evil and who refuse to stop making distinctions between good and evil in order to continue to judge and label others. Another notebook poem, "The Everlasting Gospel," also addresses the necessary coexistence of good and evil when it states, "To be Good only is to be/A Devil or else a Pharisee" (ll. 27-28). These lines, as with most of Blake's works, may be interpreted in multiple ways. In one reading, to be good is equated with being a Devil, revealing that Blake has reversed the accepted definitions of the terms, as he does in *The Marriage of Heaven and Hell*. In another, to be *only* good, and not both good and evil, is to be a Devil in the traditional sense. The first interpretation emphasizes the relativity of perspective and definition; the second, the necessity of acknowledging and balancing both contraries.

Blake's belief in the coexistence of good and evil continues in his marginalia. In an annotation to a paragraph in Swedenborg's *Heaven and Hell* in which Swedenborg discusses the various hells that exist underneath our world, Blake writes that "under every *Good* is a hell. i.e. hell is the outward or external of heaven" (original emphasis, 602). Clearly, where good exists, so must evil — and vice versa — even if it is not immediately visible. In comments recorded by Crabb Robinson, Blake reiterates this belief, stating, "I have never known a very bad man who had not something very good about him" (Kindle location 686). Interestingly, however, in his annotations to Lavater Blake says that two contraries (good and evil) cannot spring from one essence. In reply to Lavater's aphorism 489, he writes:

> Man is a twofold being. one part capable of evil & the other capable of good that which is capable of good is not also capable of evil. but that which is capable of evil is also capable of good. this aphorism seems to consider man as simple & yet capable of evil. now both good & evil cannot exist in a simple being. for thus 2 contraries would. spring from one essence which is impossible. but if man is considered as only evil. & god only good. how then is regeneration effected which turns the evil to good. by casting out the evil. by the good [594].

Does Blake believe that good and evil can exist in one person or not? Blake refers here to the idea that each human consists of two separate parts— good and evil; he contrasts this concept with one in which each human is both good and evil existing in one part, or one in which humans are only evil and God is only good. As with his concept of the androgyne, the two contraries of good and evil, or male and female, exist in separate parts within each human, as opposed to mingling in one part, and both are necessary for regeneration/reunification of humanity. Lavater's mistake that Blake corrects in this marginal comment is one that characters in and readers of Harris's novels have committed as well — that of considering humans as simple beings with one essence, and good and evil as opposing binaries, not balanced contraries. Once again Crabb Robinson's notes on Blake reiterate this belief, as is seen in his statement that Blake believed that "men are born with a devil and an angel" (Kindle location 682).

While most of the time Blake emphasizes the coexistence of these contraries, he occasionally will remark, as he does in response to Lavater's aphorism 409, "Active Evil is better than Passive Good" (592).* Would Blake really consider an active murderer better than a passive law-abiding citizen? To help answer this, one must consider Blake's use of "Active," which is illuminated by his marginalia at the end of Lavater's aphorisms,

---

*While Blake's marginal comments reveal many of his beliefs and are the focus here, an examination of the aphorisms Blake marked, even without commentary, to indicate agreement also reveals insight into his beliefs but is beyond the scope of this work.

1. "Under every Good is a hell"

where Blake explicitly addresses the idea of murder and provides us with his definition that hindering is a vice (as mentioned briefly earlier in this chapter). Drawing on his idea of evil as an "accident," Blake writes, "Accident is the omission of act in self & the hindering of act in another. This is Vice but all Act [<from Individual propensity>] is Virtue. To hinder another ... is not an act it is the contrary it is a restraint on action both in ourselves & in the person hinderd.... Murder is Hindering Another" (601). So, murder is not better than good, since it is not active. While it is a sin, however, it is still, as Blake has stated, not as displeasing to God as unbelief and the eating of the Tree of Knowledge of Good and Evil. According to Blake, the correct reaction to murder, to the hindering of another, is not categorization of the murderer as an evil man or condemnation. Instead, as Bandy claims, "Even if a man commits what in Blake's opinion is a real sin — hindering another, murder, theft — he should be forgiven" (161). After all, he is both a good and an evil man who has briefly given in to his selfhood and acted out of balance. The importance of forgiveness is connected to the importance of imagination as well, in that in order to forgive another, one must be able to imagine why the other acted as he did. It is not enough to use one's senses and imagination to feel empathy for victims; this could lead to a simplistic focus on vengeance. However, using imagination to understand both perspectives, that of victim and of victimizer, can lead to the realization of the complexity of natures and the ability to see the world as more than black and white, evil and good. Recognizing complexity leads to forgiveness and moving forward. The importance of forgiveness over condemnation appears in Harris's novels as well, most clearly in Starling being forgiving toward Lecter instead of wishing to capture and kill him.

Blake's focus on forgiveness (in part because of the inability to be perfectly good without flaw) can be seen in "To the Public" in *Jerusalem*: "The Spirit of Jesus is continual forgiveness of Sin: he who waits/to be righteous before he enters into the Saviours kingdom, the Divine/Body, will never enter there" (3:15–17). No one can ever cast out all evil and be righteous and perfect; instead, one must accept one's flaws and rely on forgiveness. It is not just Jesus who needs to provide the forgiveness, though; it is all who must act in the Spirit of Jesus, accepting the dual nature of humanity and forgiving instead of condemning. After all, throughout his works Blake refers to Jesus as the Divine Humanity; therefore, if the Divine Humanity forgives, humanity in general must at least attempt to forgive and move beyond an oppositional view of the world focused on retribution to a more nuanced view that emphasizes complexity and understanding.

Blake's disbelief in the oppositional, dual nature of good and evil reveals itself in his designs as well as his text. Sheila Spector's examination of Blake's use, both literal and symbolic, of Hebrew leads her to a similar conclusion regarding Blake's questioning of dichotomies. Discussing the use of Hebrew in Blake's inscriptions on the *Laocoön*, she notes the grammatically correct name "Lilith" placed in an empty space between Laocoön's left thigh and his son, as well as a reversed *alef* in the large Hebrew lettering at the top center. The *alef* is the first letter of the Hebrew alphabet and "[t]he most important letter" (65). It "is considered the most spiritual of the letters, having been emanated directly from the Godhead Himself" (65). While the *alef* is reversed, no errors occur in the name "Lilith." Laocoön's arm, grasping the serpent's neck, forms the top part of the triangular space "Lilith" occupies. On the other side of the arm, in a space enclosed by the arm, Laocoön's side, and another portion of the snake, there is the word "good." Reading how the reversed *alef* operates along with the correct name "Lilith" in an interpretation of the work as a whole, Spector says, "While it is always possible that Blake simply erred in executing the *alef*, we should not discount the likelihood that as a careful artist, Blake deliberately reversed the letter, perhaps in order to shift the interpretation to the readers/viewers who must for themselves reverse the perspective on the Divinity, and thereby recognize the fallacy of the 'good versus Lilith' duality" (78). In other words, Blake indicates a need to recognize that Lilith — Adam's first wife, who insisted on sexual equality and was "transformed into a she-demon [becoming] [i]n kabbalistic myth ... queen of the 'other side'" (76) — is not a figure of evil to be opposed to good. Spector's interpretation is supported by some of Blake's added inscriptions around the statue, including "All is not Sin that Satan calls so." The recognition of the fallacy of duality or opposition comes through a change in perspective that allows one to see good and evil as Blake did: coexisting, separated only by a fine line that is often crossed or blurred.

Blake emphasizes the necessity of this perspectival shift, or at least the recognition that individual vision varies, in his poetic works as well, further emphasizing that the distinction between good and evil is often a matter of vision or perception. The most obvious of these are the companion poems of *Songs of Innocence and Experience*, in which a scene

1. "Under every Good *is a hell*"

described from an innocent perspective is more positive than the same scene described from an experienced perspective. These companion poems include the "Infant Joy"/"Infant Sorrow," "The Lamb"/"The Tyger," "Nurse's Song"/"Nurses Song," "The Divine Image"/"A Divine Image," and the two "Chimney Sweeper" and "Holy Thursday" poems. It will suffice to examine just one of these pairs in order to understand how, for Blake, perspective alters categorization. In the *Innocence* "Holy Thursday" poem the speaker describes the children of the charity schools going to St. Paul's for the service. The speaker describes the children as "flowers of London town" (1. 5) and "lambs" (1. 7). Once inside the church he describes their singing and how the "aged men wise guardians of the poor" sit beneath, listening to them (1. 11). The speaker ends by emphasizing how important it is to "cherish pity" (1. 12). However, in the *Experience* poem the speaker questions the beauty and holiness of the sight of the orphaned children, who, instead of being flowers, are "Babes reduced to misery" (1. 3). He hears their singing as a "trembling cry" (1. 5), and instead of being impressed by the charity and pity shown the children, this speaker's perspective leads him to focus on the horror of poverty that made the charity necessary. The "Divine Image" companion poems reveal a similar shift in perspective regarding the interplay of poverty and charity and mercy and cruelty, and will be addressed in a later chapter since Harris uses them as epigraphs for *Red Dragon*.

Another work that reveals the importance of perspective is *The Book of Thel*. The first two lines of "THEL'S Motto" set up perspective as a main concern of the work: "Does the Eagle know what is in the pit?/Or wilt thou go ask the Mole[?]" While the Eagle can see much from his vantage point, he cannot describe the pit in the same way that the Mole can. Throughout the entire poem Thel listens to various "insignificant" beings describe their importance. These small creatures (the cloud, the worm, the clay) could easily be dismissed, but, seen from their own perspective, they are important. At the end of the poem Thel, confronted by her own grave and hearing of negative aspects of the senses (false words, false smiles, curbed desire), flees. The most common interpretation of this passage is that Thel does not flee from death back to life, but from both death and life, not realizing that death is an integral part of life. Thel wishes for only the positive aspects of life but does not realize that she cannot access that. In order to have true smiles, one must accept false smiles; in order to have desire, one must accept that it cannot always be fulfilled. Thel looks in a grave and sees only death and negativity where others may see the complexity of life.

Blake continues the discussion of the importance of perspective in *The Marriage of Heaven and Hell*. The most explicit statement regarding perspective is the Proverb of Hell: "A fool sees not the same tree that a wise man sees" (1.8). Blake also emphasizes the difference between perspectives in "A Memorable Fancy" on plates 17–20, in which an angel offers to show the speaker his eternal lot and reveals to him his place between the black and white spiders in the fiery infinite abyss as Leviathan approaches. However, when the angel leaves the speaker finds himself "sitting on a pleasant bank beside a river by moon light, hearing a harper who sung to the harp" (plate 19). The angel is surprised at seeing him and is told "All that we saw was owing to your metaphysics" before being shown his own eternal lot by the speaker, among monkeys continually coupling and devouring each other. Each imposes his vision on the other, and reverts to his own vision when not imposed upon. At the end of this fancy Blake writes, "Opposition is True Friendship" (plate 20). Opposition forces us to see from another's perspective and to understand better our own perspective; it breaks down the barriers and distinctions, including those between good and evil, leading to greater vision.

One other work that emphasizes the importance of perspective, "Auguries of Innocence," is referred to in the film *Red Dragon*. In the film, Lecter quotes the lines "A Robin Red Breast in a Cage/Puts all Heaven in a Rage" (ll. 5–6); however, the first four lines of the poem stress multiplicity of perspectives: "To see a World in a Grain of Sand/And a Heaven in a Wild Flower/Hold Infinity in the palm of your hand/And Eternity in an hour." It is possible to see both the Sand and the World; one need only vary one's perspective. Similar statements occur elsewhere as well; for example, in "A Vision of the Last Judgment" Blake writes, "When the Sun rises do you not see a round Disk of fire somewhat like a Guinea O no no I see an Innumerable company of the Heavenly host crying Holy Holy Holy is the Lord God Almighty" (565–66). He is able to see these various things because he "look[s] through" his eye "& not with it" (566). Blake reveals this way of seeing to Thomas Butts in a poem enclosed in a letter of 22 November 1802: "For double the vision my Eyes do see/And a double vision is always with me/With my inward Eye 'tis an old Man grey/With my outward a Thistle across my way" (ll. 27–30) and "in my double sight/Twas outward a Sun: inward Los in his might" (ll. 57–58).

1. "*Under every* Good *is a hell*"

This doubling or changing of vision recurs in the notebook poem "The Everlasting Gospel," in which he states, "The Vision of Christ that thou dost see/Is my Visions Greatest Enemy" (e:1–2), because "Thine loves the same world that mine hates/Thy Heaven doors are my Hell Gates" (e:7–8). Blake ends this plate with the following explicit statement: "Both read the Bible day & night/But thou readst black where I read white" (13–14). The object is the same, but the interpretation or perspective varies, with each thinking he is correct, seeing only black or white, good or evil. Blake further reveals his ideas regarding perspectives, particularly as related to his concept of good and evil, in "A Vision of the Last Judgment," where he writes, "The Last judgment is one of these Stupendous Visions[.] I have represented it as I saw it[.] to different People it appears differently as every thing else does" (555). Since everyone sees things differently, one person's evil can be another's good.

Some of Blake's works reveal the importance of perspective not in explicit statements, but in characters' actions, particularly those actions intended to be good but that lead to evil or have negative repercussions. The most explicit example of this difference between intention and result due to variation of perspective comes in *The [First] Book of Urizen* and *The Book of Los,* which both tell the story of Urizen's binding of the world and Los's binding of Urizen. In Chapter II of *The [First] Book of Urizen* Urizen searches "for a joy without pain,/For a solid without fluctuation" (4:10–11) and asks, "Why will you die Eternals?" (4:12). Urizen sees the formlessness of Eternity as chaos and the coexistence of contraries as unwelcome; he questions why the Eternals have to sacrifice themselves for each other. In order to correct what he interprets as problems and torments, Urizen writes his books of metals, in which he sets down "Laws of peace, of love, of unity:/Of pity, compassion, forgiveness" (4:34–35). While these sound like positive laws and attributes, and Urizen sees them as such, he forgets that there is no need for forgiveness without harm, and no pity without pain. He forgets that individuals are not all the same when he pronounces, "One command, one joy, one desire,/One curse, one weight, one measure/One King, one God, one Law" (4:38–40). In his attempt to give form to formlessness and ease what he sees as the Eternals' pain, he creates laws and regulations that lead to further harm, by creating punishments and the categorization of good and evil, by becoming a tyrant. This measuring and dividing Urizen is the figure in Blake's *Ancient of Days,* owned by Verger in *Hannibal.* When Urizen divides and categorizes, he separates from the other Eternals, and Los becomes "affrighted/At the formless unmeasurable death" he witnesses in this separation (7:8–9). Los then operates similarly and attempts to correct or heal what he sees. He does this by forming "nets & gins" (8:7), and as Urizen changes, Los "bound every change/With rivets of iron & brass" (8:10–11). In the next chapter Blake provides the details of these changes, describing the embodiment of Urizen. In order to stop what Los thinks is Urizen's suffering, caused by his separation from the other Eternals, Los binds Urizen in a form. However, instead of leading to good and stopping pain, this action leads to Urizen's further separation from the Eternals. This same story is retold in *The Book of Los*. It is important that it is not just Urizen who mistakenly creates evil when thinking he is acting for good. By having Los enact the same mistake, Blake emphasizes complexity of nature in that it is not just the tyrant who binds and punishes, but the hero or artist as well; all are capable of this mistake. Blake also retells this myth of Urizen and Los in *Milton*, in which, as Los witnesses the embodiment of Urizen, "he became what he beheld" (3:29). He has bound and embodied Urizen, and becomes individualized as well, causing his Emanation and his Spectre to separate from himself. This further detail of separation emphasizes the error of his actions in that it adds yet another step to the process of reunification. Los now must be reunited with his Emanation before he can reunite with the other Eternals. This scene likewise emphasizes the importance of perspective in that Los does not become what he created, but what he sees. He witnesses separation and therefore separates.

Los and Urizen, however, are not the only ones whose "good" actions create negative outcomes. In *Milton*, Enitharmon acts in a similar way. Upon witnessing the struggles of Satan and Palamabron, which involve many other characters as well, Enitharmon feels pity for all of them and forms "a Space for Satan & Michael & for the poor infected" (8:43). This creation of space, however, does not lead to an end of strife, for it only entails further separation and categorization. So, once again a character who acts in hopes of creating a positive space only leads all the characters further away from unification and, in fact, helps to create further conflict.

Blake's comments on and views of the penal system reveal this concept of evil springing from good actions as well. For example, in *The Marriage of Heaven and Hell*, "The Proverbs of Hell," he writes, "Prisons are built with stones of Law, Brothels with bricks of Religion" (l. 21), and in annotations to Watson's *An Apology for the Bible* he writes, "All Penal Laws

1. "Under every Good is a hell"

court Transgression & therefore are cruelty & Murder" (618). Essentially, humans, in the guise of law and religion, reenact Urizen's error of trying to control by creating laws and categorizing; however, drawing a line only leads to its being crossed. In addition, creation of laws leads to punishment instead of forgiveness, which is the true Gospel and the correct response to the "Accident" of evil.

Just as an action done in the name of good can lead to evil, so too may an evil act bring about a good result, as Blake claims in the first stanza of "The Human Abstract": "Pity would be no more,/If we did not make somebody Poor:/And Mercy no more could be,/If all were as happy as we" (ll. 1–4). If not for this evil, humans would have no experience of their own capability for compassion. Sometimes both the evil act and the resulting good operate on a grander scale than pity and poverty. Take, for example, the rapes in *Visions of the Daughters of Albion* and in *America*.

After Bromion, having "rent her with his thunders" (1:16), has raped Oothoon in *Visions of the Daughters of Albion*, and "her woes [have] appalld his thunders hoarse" (1:17), Oothoon calls for the Eagles to "Rend away this defiled bosom" (2:15). Oothoon believes that the rape has defiled her, has tainted her purity; she has internalized society's view and believes she should be punished. The Eagles descend and, after "rending" her, she has an increase in vision, both metaphorical and literal. She proclaims, "Arise my Theotormon I am pure./Because the night is gone that clos'd me in its deadly black./They told me that the night & day were all that I could see;/They told me that I had five senses to inclose me up" (2:28–31). Prior to the rending Oothoon's vision was narrow, and her senses only experienced what society condoned; she believed only what she had been told and saw what she was told she could see. Now she sees beyond society's constrictions. Interestingly, her literal senses seem also to be expanded, allowing her to see "the new wash'd lamb ting'd with the village smoke" (3:18). She sees details she did not see or pay attention to before. Oothoon's awakening vision and new perspective not only allow her to see the universe in a new light but also have the potential to lead to political changes regarding the fate of the Daughters of Albion. Oothoon's response to the rape is not to call for vengeance on Bromion, but instead to call for a change in how others see the world and act in it. While she does not come out and state her forgiveness, she moves on instead of brooding and plotting revenge. She does not accept society labeling her as impure and instead speaks out against lies society has told her regarding marriage, motherhood, and sexuality. This rape and its role in the narrative indicate a concept of good and evil intimately related to perspective, to a vision that sees beyond immediate effects to long-term ramifications, to a vision expanded by experience and now open and enhanced, able to see the complex details of life. This view does not justify evil or encourage it, but instead accepts its existence and the complex consequences of its actions.

A similar depiction of rape and its effects occurs in *America* when Orc frees himself and "Round the terrific loins he siez'd the panting struggling womb" (2:3), which belongs to the Shadowy Female. While she feels "limb rending pains" (2:15) and is being violently attacked, this experience leads her to speak for the first time and proclaim political changes, saying, "On my American plains I feel the struggling afflictions/Endur'd by roots that writhe their arms into the nether deep:/I see a serpent in Canada, who courts me to his love;/In Mexico an Eagle, and a Lion in Peru" (2:10–13). As in *Visions*, here too the violent experience has an effect upon her senses, expanding them, or at least allowing her to see what she has not before. Not only was she previously mute and now speaks, but the animals she sees are the same animals used to describe Orc's soul earlier on plate 1; she can now see his true spirit of revolution. The Preludium ends with the Female declaring, "This is eternal death; and this the torment long foretold" (2:17), and yet this torment leads to the Prophecy itself, which foretells revolution against political oppression.

A possible positive reading of a rape is disturbing. On a literal level the fact that in each of these cases a woman is somehow liberated, empowered through her rape, is difficult to grapple with; however, one must keep in mind that Blake is not saying that these two characters deserve rape, but instead is illustrating one positive outcome of a horrendous moment, finding strength and power in a negative, violent event. The violence of the moment has forced expanded vision and allowed the victims to heal and grow, seeing from a different and/or enhanced perspective, instead of brooding and stagnating, focusing on the past and/or revenge, either becoming passive or actively hindering others. Ultimately, and unfortunately, fallen perception is so narrow that at times evil is necessary, as it is the only thing that can rupture constrictive vision. Blake describes this limited vision in "London" as being "mind-forg'd manacles" (1. 9), created in part through society and in part through humans' acceptance of societal labeling and rules. As one would imagine, these manacles are difficult and painful to break. While the constraints may have been created externally,

1. "Under every Good *is a hell*"

by society at large (particularly the legal and religious systems), they have not been merely imposed upon the characters. Instead, the characters themselves have accepted these constraints and lived their lives by them, strengthening the manacles through their own decisions and experiences. Each time they have accepted the categories and judgments of the external systems and thereby restricted their own thoughts or actions, the manacles have strengthened. Oothoon's fear of plucking the flower increased the hold of the manacles upon her, as did her acceptance of Bromion's rape of herself, which led to her calling down Theotormon's eagles. When the Shadowy Daughter accepts her role only as Urthona's daughter, meant to dutifully serve her father by waiting upon Orc and never looking at him, her actions also reinforce her manacles. The violence of the rending of Theotormon's eagles upon Oothoon and the rape/rending of the Shadowy Female by Orc is enough to break the manacles loose. Blake reveals in these horrific moments experienced by Oothoon and the Shadowy Female the dialectical nature of inspiration or enlightenment, in which the gaining of knowledge is both a blessing and a curse. Both characters now recognize that what society has taught them is wrong, and that they do not and should not acquiesce to it any longer; instead, they shall argue against the manacles and rebel against the constraints of society and self. Blake reveals in these violent moments how good and evil are intertwined, with one evil moment leading to good actions.

Interestingly, in both *Visions* and *America* Blake includes an image of a naked female figure with a bird with wings outstretched above her. This is a Promethean moment in which the female is rended by the bird. While Prometheus is punished by having his liver eternally eaten by a vulture for bestowing knowledge and enlightenment upon humans, the human figures in Blake's Promethean images have not bestowed enlightenment upon anyone yet, but are, during the course of their encounters with a winged or winged-like figure, enlightened themselves. While Prometheus is a rebel who is punished, these figures are instead undergoing a suffering that will turn them into enlightened rebels. This image of a winged figure, or human figure with arms outstretched like wings, is found in several Blake works, both illuminated books and large prints, usually at moments indicating painful enlightenment. Examples include Keynes's plate 38 of *Milton*, and the paintings *Pity* and *Satan Exulting Over Eve*. As will be explored later, this image also occurs in some of Harris's works. A similar image of a figure with outstretched arms hovering over a prone figure appears on plate 14 of *The Marriage of Heaven and Hell*, a plate central to Blake's idea of painful enlightenment.

On plate 14 of *The Marriage of Heaven and Hell* Blake states, "If the doors of perception were cleansed every thing would appear to man as it is: infinite./For man has closed himself up, till he sees all things thro' narrow chinks of his cavern." This ability to see the infinite, this expansion of senses, "will come to pass by an improvement of sensual enjoyment." This is usually read as referring to increased sexual desire and joy; however, perhaps Blake used "sensual" instead of "sexual" deliberately, in order to imply an improvement of sensory experience. Before these senses can expand, though, "first the notion that a man has a body distinct from his soul, is to be expunged; this I shall do, by printing in the infernal method, by corrosives, which in Hell are salutary and medicinal, melting apparent surfaces away, and displaying the infinite which was hid." These lines have often been interpreted as Blake's commentary on his own printing method of acid and copper, and the interpretation is most likely correct. However, the "corrosives" could also refer to any negative or violent experience that would cut into one's "mind-forg'd manacles," thereby releasing one's vision and other senses. As with the rending of Oothoon and the Shadowy Female, Blake is not stating that violence is the only way to inspiration and enlightenment, but that sometimes the only way to open humanity's eyes is through violence, through corroding away their safety, their known boundaries. In this case the violence would act as chemotherapy does, at times harming the body in order to ultimately cure it. Tristanne Connolly describes Blake's engraving process as a "kill-or-cure method" (33) and Nicholas Williams, in discussing the power of ideology, comments on the necessity for a type of metaphorical chemotherapy, talking about "a population in need of a violent cure" (*Ideology*, Kindle location 489). While violence and evil are not synonymous, the two are often connected and an encounter with either would be a negative and powerful experience. Therefore, it is quite possible that at times one's encounter with evil may also lead to enlightenment and a greater understanding of human nature and the world.

On a lesser scale, Blake himself personally experienced how good (knowledge or enlightenment) can come out of a negative (though not evil) experience. One of the most telling comments Blake made regarding good and evil occurs in his letter of 16 August 1803 to Butts, in which he details his encounter with Scofield that led to his sedition trial. After

1. "Under every Good is a hell"

explaining what happened and asking Butts if he can gather information regarding Scofield, Blake comes to a conclusion: "Perhaps the simplicity of myself is the origin of all offences committed against me. If I have found this I shall have learned a most valuable thing well worth three years perseverance. I have found it! It is certain! that a too passive manner. inconsistent with my active physiognomy has done me much mischief[.] *I must now express to you my conviction that all is come from the spiritual World for Good & not for Evil*" (emphasis added, 733). This dark time of Blake's life leads him to believe that all acts, all experiences, lead to good results—at least eventually. His encounters with Scofield and with Hayley led Blake to understand more about himself, an ultimate good. He suggests that his view of the world, and perhaps human nature, was simplistic prior to this encounter, but that he now has a more nuanced or complex view of the world. Blake repeats this idea in his annotations to Swedenborg's *Divine Love and Divine Wisdom*, in which he writes, "Understanding or Thought is not natural to Man it is acquired by means of Suffering & Distress i.e. Experience" (602). Melanie Bandy suggests that for Blake God is "Understanding" (55). So, through suffering, one can ultimately achieve a better, divine, state. Evil leads to good. Interestingly, while understanding is not natural, Blake's list of what is natural in his annotations to Swedenborg's *Divine Love and Divine Wisdom* includes concepts considered both good and evil: "Will, Desire, Love, Rage, Envy" (602).

So, ultimately, evil is not distinct from good, but instead the separation of the two is a construct of Satan, of rationality. In Blake's Eternity, evil is not eradicated but accepted as an integral part of existence. In Blake's world of Generation, encountering evil or violence may lead to expansion of vision and understanding. Through altering one's vision and refusing to see the distinction between good and evil, realizing the adverse effects of laws and rules, society may "eradicate" evil in the fallen world, in part not through fighting and defeating it but instead through seeing it with expanded vision, allowing understanding and, to some extent, forgiveness. In Harris's novels it is the characters with the most expanded and perceptive vision, those who, like Starling and Lecter, recognize the complexities of the world, who survive. Their expanded and perceptive vision is revealed not just in their ability to track killers or see others' true nature but also in what may seem to be a surface trait that ultimately connects them: a desire for finer-quality things and attention to fragrances and food. Just as important, however, as achieving increased vision and imagination is remembering that the correct response to evil is forgiveness. Increased sensory experience leads to forgiveness by allowing understanding of the other's position and actions. As Bandy states, according to Blake, "Vengeance for sin or mistake, rather than forgiveness, is the religion of Satan" (54). Along with replacing vengeance with forgiveness and imagination, one must also attempt "to live without hatred" (Bandy 54). Interestingly, in Harris's novels, while Lecter hinders/murders others, compared to other characters like Gumb and Dolarhyde, he is less hateful, at least in the first three books. He observes the complexities of the world, growing to understand it and leave behind the hate he felt in *Hannibal Rising*. This lack of anger, hate or a desire for revenge may be a sign that while all three hinder/murder, Lecter is closer to the path of redemption.

In addition to not giving in to hatred, one must also not passively brood on the past and on past errors, but instead should act, as Oothoon does when proclaiming her new vision instead of merely calling for vengeance or Bromion's punishment. As Bandy explains when discussing Blake's *Jerusalem*, "In this fallen, opaque world ... evil takes on magnified proportions because of Albion's propensity to brood over his mistakes" (57). Brooding is essentially living passively in the past, as Theotormon does in response to Oothoon's rape, instead of acting in the present or forgiving past actions of oneself or another. Brooding leads to a continuation of evil. As Bandy states, "Lack of action — that is brooding — creates the condition under which Abstraction or Negation can come into existence" (59). The negative effects of brooding appear also in Harris's novels in several ways, which will be explored in detail in later chapters. These include Dolarhyde's brooding about how his grandmother treated him, which leads to his vengeance on others; Verger's brooding, which leads to his desire for revenge; and Lecter's brooding regarding Mischa, which leads to his search for peace.

Clearly, for Blake, the accident of evil and the creation of negations have their origins in human actions, particularly human thought and the desire to categorize. In addition, from the poetry and the marginalia, it is clear that Blake believed that good and evil coexist in everyone and everything. The question then becomes whether Blake thinks evil needs to exist. From works like the two "Divine Image" poems, it can be extrapolated that, without evil, humans have no need for good; therefore, evil must exist because without it there is no incentive to produce the good. In addition, in *The Marriage of Heaven and Hell* and other works Blake clearly indicates that what some label as evil is actually good and vice versa, due

1. "Under every Good *is a hell*"

to differing perspectives. Differing perspectives work together as contraries to create progression: if two people each think they are doing good, but from the other's perspective are evil, then the two must work together to understand the other's perspective and find a possible answer or compromise. Furthermore, in what are called his prophetic books, a character may think he or she is working for good but is actually performing evil, or at least what others view as evil. Urizen tries to stop chaos by binding and constricting, but this just creates the fallen world; Enitharmon wants to help Satan by creating a place for him, but this just results in nets and traps. Ultimately, good and evil both exist because each person's perspective or vision differs, and, since according to Blake there should be no one law or perspective for all to follow, evil must exist because there will always be someone who interprets an action or belief as evil.

While evil *must* exist given the fallen nature of the world and differing perspectives, the question of whether Blake believes that evil *needs* to exist will continue to be debated. Perhaps it is enough to recognize that it does exist in the fallen world at least (and not always separately from good), and that, therefore, it can serve a useful purpose. This, after all, seems to be what Harris takes from Blake.

CHAPTER 2

"The wickedness herein I took from my own stock"
Thomas Harris's Creation of Evil

Thomas Harris is the author of five novels: *Black Sunday*, *Red Dragon*, *Silence of the Lambs*, *Hannibal*, and *Hannibal Rising*. Of these, four can be categorized as Hannibal Lecter novels. *Black Sunday*, about a terrorist plot at the Super Bowl, is not a Hannibal Lecter novel. While Lecter appears only briefly in *Red Dragon*, particularly when compared to his appearances in the latter three novels, he is central to the plot and it is the novel that introduces him to readers; therefore, it is a Hannibal Lecter novel. *Red Dragon* focuses on Will Graham and his being called back in to service by the FBI in order to capture a serial killer, Francis Dolarhyde, whom the press have dubbed the Tooth Fairy. In order to track down Dolarhyde Graham visits with Hannibal Lecter, a serial killer he had previously captured. This contact is meant to both hone Graham's abilities by getting him back in the correct context and draw on Lecter's own observational and diagnostic abilities. Through using Lecter, Graham is able to capture Dolarhyde and is also physically injured. The Blake allusion here is explicit and central to the plot: Blake's painting of the Red Dragon. *Silence of the Lambs* likewise focuses on an FBI agent, this time Clarice Starling, attempting to capture a serial killer, Buffalo Bill, and needing to turn to Lecter for help. Lecter's presence in this novel is expanded and he becomes a central part of the plot. At the end of the novel Lecter has helped Starling capture Buffalo Bill and he has also escaped. This novel contains no direct allusions to Blake, but, as will be seen in a later chapter, it does contain Blakean themes. *Hannibal* focuses exclusively on Lecter and the FBI's and Mason Verger's pursuit of him. The explicit Blake allusion in this work is Verger's copy of Blake's *Ancient of Days*. The relationship between Starling and Lecter is also a focus of this novel, revealing Starling's protective atti-

2. "The wickedness herein I took from my own stock"

tude toward him. By the controversial end of the novel, to be discussed in detail in a later chapter, Starling has consumed human brains and is Lecter's lover. The final Lecter novel is actually a prequel, *Hannibal Rising*, which tells of Lecter's traumatic childhood and his desire for revenge, which led to his murderous and cannibalistic ways. While this novel does not contain any explicit Blake allusions, Blakean themes are present. The Blakean themes throughout the four novels are particularly obvious if considered not in publication order but in narrative chronological order, with *Hannibal Rising* considered first. What might Harris have intended through his use of allusions to Blake? Does a Blakean reading of the novels seem plausible?

While Thomas Harris does not often grant interviews or, like Stephen King, write essays regarding his view of writing and horror, he did write a preface to the Omnibus edition of the first three Lecter novels. Beyond this preface, Harris has said very little about his novels and characters, next to nothing about the relationship or natural state of good and evil in the novels, and nothing about his use of Blake. One must therefore, in an attempt to understand the relationship of good and evil in the novels and the references to Blake, begin with this preface and then speculate and make connections.

In this preface Harris describes Hannibal Lecter, not as his own creation, but as a character he encountered, one who came to him. In the preface's first sentence Harris says he wants to tell us "the circumstances in which [he] first encountered Hannibal Lecter, M.D." (vii), claiming "that when you are writing a novel you are not making anything up. It's all there and you just have to find it" (viii). Harris describes himself more as an ethnographer or documentarian than as a writer, explaining that he would leave the characters alone, so that he would be "invisible" to them while "they [were] deciding their fate with little or no help from" him (ix).

The actions of his characters, particularly those of Lecter, and the fate that is decided upon, seem to surprise and frighten Harris. He describes how, as he and Graham approached Lecter's cell, he, Harris, thought Lecter was asleep and "jumped when [Lecter] recognized Will Graham by scent without opening his eyes" (ix). This led to his feeling "uncomfortable" with Lecter because he thought maybe the doctor could see him (ix). Harris goes on to claim that this first encounter with Lecter was exhausting because he had to follow the conversation between Graham and Lecter, and because the doctor's questions for Graham were so intrusive (ix). Perhaps because of this exhaustion and the surprising nature of Lecter, Harris also claims that he did not know that Lecter would appear in other novels. He began *Silence of the Lambs* with a focus on Starling and "not two pages into the novel ... found she had to go visit the doctor" (x). Not only does Harris not necessarily control Lecter and is, to some extent, afraid of him, but he also admits "some feelings of jealousy at the ease with which Dr. Lecter saw into her [Starling], when it was so difficult for" him (x). Harris further discusses his, and the audience's, reactions to Lecter when he says (referring most likely to the reaction to the film version of *Silence of the Lambs*), "By the time I undertook to record the events in *Hannibal*, the doctor, to my surprise, had taken on a life of his own. You seemed to find him as oddly engaging as I did" (x). Finally, Harris comments on the events of *Hannibal*, making it clear that he doesn't feel he has betrayed Starling and that he was just recording the fate that had been decided upon by the characters: "I dreaded doing *Hannibal* ... feared for Starling. In the end I let them go, as you must let characters go, let Dr. Lecter and Clarice Starling decide events according to their natures" (x). He even hints that he would have drawn them differently, but for the fact that the actions in the novel were so in their characters.

Throughout the preface Harris emphasizes that he has not created the characters, but instead has merely recorded them. He, in fact, is surprised, frightened and made uncomfortable by them. In one of his descriptions of this relationship to his characters he states, "Like Graham, I found, and find, the scrutiny of Dr. Lecter uncomfortable, intrusive, like the humming in your thoughts when they X-ray your head" (ix). This statement, however, does not just reveal Harris's relationship to his characters but also hints at the type of evil illustrated in the novels and at Harris's own perspective, as revealed in the novels, on the nature of evil in the world and its relationship to good and humanity. Harris does not, after all, talk about the humming in his head or feeling like his head has been X-rayed, but instead speaks to the reader directly, suggesting that the readers are being X-rayed and feeling the buzzing as well. David Sexton comments on the insight this statement provides, saying, "This may be hokum but it's as close to an acknowledgement as Harris will give that Lecter is inside us, not out there, inside us as evil is" (111). Interestingly, Sexton uses the pronoun "us," emphasizing that Lecter is not simply a creation or discovery of Harris. Lecter is not just inside Harris; he is not a unique character available to or understood only by Harris. Instead, Lecter, the figure of evil, is inside all of us. He is the X-

2. "The wickedness herein I took from my own stock"

ray, buzzing and revealing what lies unseen behind the face we show the world. What makes Lecter's presence uncomfortable is also what makes him engaging: his familiarity and connection to the readers and viewers, Harris included. He exists not just within the pages of the novels but also within the readers as a familiar figure, and a reminder of the evil that resides in all humanity. The recognition of this familiar evil, of this connection to Lecter, even of the stirring of similar emotions inside the reader, makes the audience, and his creator, uncomfortable.

The idea of Lecter as an uncomfortable reminder of the evil residing, along with good, in all of humanity also appears in one of the most interesting statements on evil, or wickedness, that Harris has made. In the acknowledgments to *Hannibal* Harris writes, "The wickedness herein I took from my own stock" (485). In context Harris is literally stating that while he has been helped by actual people, no characters in the book are based on any actual person. However, one can also consider the statement as emphasizing that all of the wickedness or evil of the novel came from within Harris's own stock of not just imagination but also evil. Assuming that Harris is not insane or evil, and therefore Lecter is not just the alter ego of a suppressed serial killer/writer, this stock of wickedness is similar to the intrusion/humming discussed earlier in that while it exists in Harris, it does not exist *only* in Harris. This stock of wickedness exists in each individual, and Harris drew upon it to create Lecter and perhaps make his readers recognize their own stock of wickedness as well.

This view of Lecter as being representative of the evil that resides in everyone, as someone who has recognized his own evil and not suppressed it, as demonstrating the complexity of human nature and interconnectedness of good and evil, is also revealed in "a video made for the sales staff of [Harris's] publisher," in which Harris offers the "one direct statement on the record about his relationship to Lecter" (Sexton 98). According to Sexton, in this video Harris calls Lecter "a friend and [speaks] of him as an independent presence" (98), going on to state that Lecter is "the dark side of the world. He's probably the wickedest man I've ever heard of — at the same time he tells the truth and he says some things that I suppose we would all like to say" (qtd. in Sexton 99). Lecter embodies the dark side, the evil, in all things. The truth he speaks and enacts is a dark and disturbing one that audiences recognize, if hesitantly, in themselves. It is a truth that Starling hears and his ability to speak the truth is the reason she doesn't want him killed (*Hannibal* 242).

While these various statements may be read as indicative of Lecter representing how evil exists in all of humanity alongside good and how Harris has attempted to reveal this uncomfortable aspect of the nature of humanity, some readers have not admitted the existence of this darkness in all people, interpreting both the novels and Harris's explicit statements differently. Daniel O'Brien, for example, states that "Harris ... regards his best-loved character as an embodiment of Absolute Evil" and quotes Harris as saying in the video that Lecter "is the adversary for anything like kindness or hope ... he's the dark side of the world" (9). If Lecter embodies "Absolute Evil," the implication is that he has no goodness in him and therefore cannot be representative of the evil in all of humanity. While calling him "the dark side of the world" may imply that he is the darkness which exists in everyone, calling him an "adversary" once again implies that Lecter is fully opposed to kindness. O'Brien has set Lecter up in a binary situation in which he is evil opposed to the good of the world. O'Brien interprets Harris's few statements regarding Lecter as indicating that Harris considers Lecter to be Satan embodied, an "Absolute Evil" separate from most humans and their own desires and thoughts. In this interpretation, Lecter is not the dark side in everyone; he is not an aspect of the dark side, but is the dark side itself—Satan. O'Brien even states that "Doctor Lecter is at heart a supernatural creature on a par with Bram Stoker's Count Dracula" (8), and that "having dropped hints in *Red Dragon* and *Silence of the Lambs*, Thomas Harris openly suggests in *Hannibal* that Lecter is the Devil himself" (8). This interpretation (held by others as well) of Lecter as an embodiment of pure evil, of not Blake's Satan (which will be discussed further later in the chapter) but a traditional Christian Satan, a supernatural figure of evil instead of a representative human who acts upon his natural evil urges, is based in part on physical characteristics. Lecter does, after all, have maroon eyes, enhanced senses, a close relationship with animals and the seeming ability to control them, and an extra finger on his left ("sinister") hand. In *Hannibal Rising*, a sexton approaching Lecter in the cathedral at night sees his glowing eyes and crosses himself before calming down as he sees it is just a young man (170–71). Other characters, particularly those in *Hannibal*, state that Lecter is the devil.

The most direct statement of Lecter as Satan comes from Romula in *Hannibal*. Romula, a pickpocket, is working to get "Dr. Fell's" fingerprints so that Pazzi will have proof that Fell is Lecter. As she comes near Lecter in the chapel "she ... felt sucked to the red centers of his eyes ... and her

2. "The wickedness herein I took from my own stock"

hand flew away from his face to cover the baby's face" (155–56). She does not follow through on the plan and when Pazzi finds her she is "bathing the baby's head repeatedly with holy water, bathing its eyes in case it had looked at Dr. Fell" (156). She tells Pazzi, "That is the Devil ... Shaitan, Son of the Morning, I've seen him now" (156). Romula clearly believes that she has encountered Satan himself. Are we to take her statement literally, though? Is her statement the true statement of Lecter's nature or is it her own perspective, which is capable of miscategorization? There is no narrative declaration of Lecter being Satan, and one individual perspective and experience, even a moment as powerful and striking as that Romula has experienced, does not reveal the whole truth, as Blake's companion poems in *Songs* suggest. Reading Harris against a backdrop of Blake emphasizes the difficulty of one perspective providing the truth. In the "Proverbs of Hell" Blake states, "A fool sees not the same tree that a wise man sees" (1:8). An even more powerful statement of the nature of perspective and bias comes later in *The Marriage of Heaven and Hell* in one of the Memorable Fancies, when the speaker is shown his eternal lot by an angel. The angel shows him a terrible scene of an abyss, spiders, and the Leviathan. However, when the angel leaves the vision disappears and the speaker is left on a riverbank listening to a harp (plates 17–19). While Romula truly believes that Lecter is Satan, this is her perception of him and not necessarily his true identity. Perhaps her reaction is to the excess of Lecter's evil and how he, unlike others, does not attempt to suppress the evil portion of himself. Lecter is perhaps a metaphorical Satan. The question of literal versus metaphorical devil is a difficult one. Anthony Hopkins has said that "Lecter is a personification of the devil, and I have always perceived the devil as very charming, witty, seductive, sexual — and lethal" (qtd. in O'Brien 129). Perhaps what both Romula and Hopkins are commenting on is the extent of Lecter's evil. A human who embraces the evil side of himself to the extent that Lecter does ultimately becomes a figure of Satan.

However, even if Lecter is the devil himself, given Harris's allusions to Blake, perhaps he is a Blakean Satan, one who is not wholly evil. More importantly, for Blake Satan is not an individual but a state. As Damon states in *The Blake Dictionary*, "[e]verybody is born into the state of Satan" (336). Once a Blakean context for Harris is established, one could read Lecter as being the embodiment of Satan and yet still representing the evil that exists within all of humanity since everyone is Satan to some extent, having been born into the state of Satan.

This "state of Satan" into which all of humanity is born is part of one of the main themes of the novels—the exploration of evil and its role in humanity. As Benjamin Szumskyj suggests, all four of the novels "realistically depict the evil that a human mind is capable of" (10). While Szumskyj may here just be referring to the specific actions of Lecter and others, the novels may also be interpreted as a metaphysical exploration of the role of evil. The continual questioning of the nature of God throughout the novels (which will be examined in more detail in each novel's chapter) emphasizes this metaphysical exploration and the idea that the evil being explored is that which resides not just in Lecter, but in all people. Examining these details regarding God and the cruelty of "normal" or good people throughout the novels reveals the truth of Ali Karim's statement that "in all of Harris's work [there is] a questioning of the human condition and an investigation into the nature of our own wickedness" (156). Harris is not the only one with a stock of wickedness, since all are capable of wicked actions. This focus on the evil that humans are capable of leads some, like Philip L. Simpson, to argue that Harris provides "a bleak assessment of the human plight" (*Making Murder* 315). Humans are capable of both good and evil and the consequences of recognizing and fighting against that evil may be dire. After all, Graham at the end of *Red Dragon* has not only been physically damaged but also lost his family, and Starling at the end of *Hannibal* has not only become Lecter's lover, but also has eaten human brains. In addition, Simpson views the novels, with their speculation on the cruelty of God, as being indicative of an atheistic worldview (*Making Murder* 140). It is easy to see why a reader would conclude that Harris provides a negative or atheistic view of the world; however, examining the novels against a Blakean backdrop will reveal that Harris's is not necessarily a pessimistic view, but instead an acceptance of the negative aspects of the world and an exploration of how they may be put in balance with the positive. As will be discussed in later chapters, perhaps Graham is damaged not because evil is stronger than good but because he was unwilling to accept his own capacity for evil and the complex interconnection of good and evil in the world. And perhaps Starling has not been corrupted by Lecter but instead has balanced him; after all, while Barney is nervous upon seeing the couple at the end of *Hannibal*, it is possible that in this union both are at peace, with no need to give action to violent or evil thoughts. Starling and Lecter may have, in their sacrifices for each other, as the Blakean Eternals sacrifice for each other, created a world for themselves in balance with no brooding

2. "The wickedness herein I took from my own stock"

on the past and no hindering/murdering of others. Furthermore, the discussions regarding the nature of God may not be pointing to an atheistic view, a dismissal of God, but instead a belief in a different type of God — a God who can be cruel, a God who at least allows negative or evil things to happen. After all, Lecter does not wonder how or why God can allow such horrible things to happen but instead records them and contemplates them, wondering why, if God avails himself of a dual nature, humans cannot. However, regardless of interpretation, consensus is that throughout the novels Harris is exploring some aspect of evil and the nature of humanity. The question then becomes, what is the most rewarding approach for understanding the relationship of good and evil in Harris's work?

Two of the most common lenses through which to examine Harris's works are both genre approaches. One places Harris in the context of the police/procedural novel, the other in the gothic tradition. The formulas and conventions of these genres are used to help explicate Harris's work — particularly the role of evil, the gender relationships, and the relationship between hero and villain. Interestingly, while these genre discussions do not usually mention Blake, some of the conventions and qualities discussed as being aspects of the genres that Harris draws upon can be related to similar ideas in Blake. For example, both genres include ideas of duality, struggle, and the blurring of boundaries. While both approaches help to provide insight into Harris's work, place him in context, and explicate the complex relationships and blurring binaries of the works, adding a Blakean context helps to clarify some of the instances when Harris's works do not seem to fit the conventions of the given genre. For example, Simpson, in *Psycho Paths*, while considering Harris's work as gothic, also places Harris's work in the context of the procedural and focuses on the profilers in the novels (primarily Graham and Starling) and their close relationships to the killers themselves, saying, "[T]he psycho profiler and the profiler are two sides of the same belief system" (73). The focus is on the similarity of the profiler to the killer, as he or she has the ability to understand the killer. However, in this genre the killer's similarity to the profiler, a thread of goodness within him- or herself, is not generally emphasized. Simpson relates the profiler's mind-set and connection to the killer to the theme of the nature of evil and humanity by explaining that

> the need to enter the killer's mind-set threatens to bring the detective into conflict with society's prohibition against manifestation of murderous urges. In the serial killer story, these urges are often considered to be a part of

nature, ultimately beyond human control or knowledge. Similarly, Harris's novels clearly argue that man the beast has very little hope of bettering civilization [*PsychoPaths* 84].

This struggle and duality is seen as ultimately negative: these urges are here and humanity must fight against them in order to be civilized and not devolve to a lower form. The profiler must win and suppress the killer; in Blake's terms, the killer is the negation or the Spectre, not a contrary to the profiler/detective. The difficulty with this lens (besides the overall negative interpretation of the novels it necessarily leads to given that the profilers in Harris's books do not defeat Lecter) is Lecter himself. Given his level of sophistication, he complicates the binary of civilization versus man the beast. Perhaps the duality and struggle in these works is more one of contraries than negation. For an approach that comes closer to this Blakean idea of contraries, one must turn to discussions of Harris as writing within the gothic tradition.

This relationship of contraries in the gothic is revealed in how Lecter is often compared to "the Gothic hero-villains" who came before, like Vathek and Jekyll/Hyde (Magistrale and Morrison 4). Lecter, and other heroes of this nature found in King's and Rice's works, are defined by Magistrale and Morrison as "perverse mixtures of goodness aborted and greatness twisted. The horror monster is seldom wholly unsympathetic; the reader is always aware of the Gothic villain's tortured mind and soul, and of the potential that is thwarted in his or her loss of moral balance" (4). Lecter certainly is sympathetic — particularly, and surprisingly for many, in *Hannibal*, and to some extent in *Hannibal Rising* as well, in which his humanity is emphasized and his past "torture" is revealed. The blurring of categories of good and evil and the sympathetic nature of the villain in Harris's works easily fit the conventions of the gothic and the gothic provides a context in which the complication of good and evil is natural. The difficulty comes with the description of the villain-hero as having a tortured mind and soul. While in *Hannibal* it becomes clear that Lecter is tormented by the memory of Mischa, in general he does not seem tormented by the actions he takes. In addition, Lecter does not seem tormented at the end of *Hannibal*, while most gothic villain-heroes either continue to be tormented or are destroyed. Perhaps he is no longer tormented because his moral potential has not been completely lost and Starling's merger with him at the end of *Hannibal* has restored that balance. Reading with the additional Blakean allusions in mind emphasizes the

2. "The wickedness herein I took from my own stock"

necessity of coexisting contraries and balance that can help add to the gothic context and explain the end of the narrative and Lecter's lack of torment and continued survival.

A Blakean lens also seems appropriate because of other similarities between Harris's works and Blake's. In addition to the concern with blurring of boundaries, there is also the importance of perspective (particularly expanded and insightful perspective) and critiques of the institutions of law and religion.

Morrison comments on Harris's blurring of boundaries in the novels' content: "Harris complicates, blurs, and renders human the traditional horror polarities of good and evil in order to illustrate the difficulty of defining and recognizing either in the modern world — and the consequent danger of inadvertently compromising innocence and nurturing evil" (24). This type of blurring of boundaries and questioning of binaries is related to the insights provided by both the procedural and the gothic lenses discussed above. However, Harris also blurs boundaries in another way: in the difficulty of classifying his own novels. The novels may be horror, suspense, crime procedural, psychological drama, or various other genres. The difficulty of categorization applies to the films as well, particularly *Silence of the Lambs*. Tasker refers to the film *Silence* as a "hybrid creation" of horror, women's film, and FBI procedural (22). Morgan likewise places *Silence* in the category of "'hybrid works,' works that blend crime, film noir, horror, and gothic" (127–28). This hybrid nature of Harris's works may be a clue as to why he uses Blake instead of another artist. Blake also refuses categorization: he is artist, poet, and philosopher. His works contain both visual and verbal art, and while often placed among the Romantics, he has little in common with them stylistically.

Blake's focus on perspective and its importance may be yet another reason that Harris alludes to him. The importance of perspective in Harris's works is revealed in a literal way — through the ability of Graham and Starling to see from killers' perspectives; through Starling's ability to see from victims' perspectives as well; and through Graham's, Starling's, and Lecter's use of the senses to notice small details that lead to insight. This use of perspective adds to the complexity of the characters because they are not limited in their ability to understand and therefore can often comprehend that which is foreign or frightening to others. Jodie Foster has commented on Starling's ability and the importance of her perception in discussing why the character is such a favorite with audiences: "In Clarice's case she's not very strong but she has a powerful mind and she's perceptive. It's not going to be the big brawny Terminator guy that's going to save these women; it's going to be somebody who recognizes in these women their weaknesses. She sees and smells and notices things other people are too busy being heroic to notice" (*AFI 100 Years 100 Heroes and Villains*). This importance of perspective is intimately connected to the blurring of boundaries in that the shifting perspective makes the boundaries permeable. For example, the boundary between heroism and fear or vulnerability is not a stable one and the two sides often mix. Tasker describes this mixing, stating, "Starling is so powerful partly because she is a transitional rather than one-dimensional figure: both heroic and vulnerable. Border-crossing is a characteristic of heroic as well as monstrous figures" (87). Both Starling and Lecter (and, to a lesser extent, Graham) cross these borders of good and evil and other traditional binaries, revealing that the borders are permeable, at least for those who have the ability to embrace multiple perspectives and are aware of and can recognize the importance of small details—those who have highly honed and trained senses, and can therefore recognize the complexity of the world and its people and institutions.

One perspectival shift that both Harris and Blake seem to support is the necessity of seeing the negative aspects of institutions of law and religion alongside the positive aspects. One of Blake's most famous "Proverbs of Hell" is "Prisons are built with stones of Law, Brothels with bricks of Religion" (*MHH* 8:1). Not only do law and religion fail at times, but their very attempts to codify and modify behavior also lead to the transgressions of these laws and rules. Harris seems to present a similar view of these institutions in his works. His difficulty with established religion has been mentioned earlier and will be explored in the following chapters. In summary, several characters discuss the cruelty of God and, tellingly, Mason Verger, the child abuser and would-be torturer of Lecter, is the most outspoken proponent of traditional Christianity. As for the critique of institutions of law, this is visible in the ineffectiveness of the FBI to capture killers without having to call a retired profiler back in to work or to rely on the help of another serial killer; in the crassness and corrupt nature of some of the central figures associated with the law, such as Krendler; in the actions of the police during World War II; and in the court releasing Lecter from prison due to public protests toward the end of *Hannibal Rising*. Yet, even with these negative portrayals of religion and law, Harris does not present merely a simplistic negative view of either. Lecter admits

2. "The wickedness herein I took from my own stock"

that God has made good things (has made beauty, for example, in the swans, ortolans, and crickets), and positive figures associated with the law exist as well (for example, Starling's mentor Jack Crawford). Nothing is simple in Harris, or in Blake, not even a clear institutional critique.

Blake and Harris share this interest in complexity and perspective, and Harris has explicitly alluded to Blake in two of the four Lecter novels, so what has been said regarding the possible connection? Many readers recognize the "literariness" of Harris's prose, whether revealed in style or in allusions, be they to Dante, Baudelaire, or Blake. Sexton, in fact, claims that "Hannibal Lecter not only lives in books, he came out of books too" (80) — not surprising, since the name Lecter may be a play on "lecteur" (reader). There exist, or existed, websites that trace, catalog, and discuss these allusions — for example the (now defunct) *Dissecting Hannibal*, the discussion boards on the Hannibal Lecter Studiolo, and *Loving Lecter*'s sub-site "Leda and the Swan" — and it is nearly impossible to discuss *Red Dragon* without discussing Blake at least briefly. In *Making Murder* Simpson references Harris's use of Blake and occasionally draws on Blake's images, particularly that of the tiger, when discussing Lecter; however, he does not explore why Harris may have chosen Blake as a source nor does he explore thematic connections between the two in depth. In fact, excepting Williams's essay regarding *Red Dragon*, there has been no sustained in-depth discussion of the Blake/Harris connection by anyone who comments on the allusions. No one has closely examined the Blake allusions and connections throughout all four novels or attempted to address why Harris keeps referring to Blake instead of another poet or painter. Most of the works that discuss *Red Dragon* and Blake focus on Dolarhyde's obsession with Blake and the power he derives from the Red Dragon in his "becoming," but do not attempt to explain why Harris chose Blake instead of some other artist.

Daniel O'Brien, in the context of his discussion of *Red Dragon*, does address why Harris has chosen Blake to be central to the plot by discussing the inclusion of passages from Blake's *Songs of Innocence and Experience* as epigraphs to the novel. Harris quotes from "The Divine Image," included in the *Innocence* collection:

> For Mercy has a human heart,
> Pity, a human face,
> And Love, the human form divine,
> And Peace, the human dress.

He then follows with the poem "A Divine Image" from *Experience*:

> Cruelty has a Human Heart,
> And Jealousy a Human Face,
> Terror, the Human Form Divine,
> And Secrecy, the Human Dress.
>
> The Human Dress is forged Iron,
> The Human Form, a fiery Forge,
> The Human Face, a Furnace seal'd,
> The Human Heart, its hungry Gorge.

O'Brien claims that these lines show "the positive human qualities outlined in the former contrasted with the negative attributes of the latter. Mercy becomes Cruelty, Pity becomes Jealousy, Love becomes Terror and Peace becomes Secrecy. Harris appears to be citing Blake as a pioneering chronicler of the psychopathic personality" (14). O'Brien argues that Blake is used since he has explored the creation of the psychopathic personality and shown how it has shifted from the positive to the negative aspects of human personality and interaction. However, is it only psychopaths who are cruel or who can become cruel? The implication of O'Brien's interpretation is that those who do move from one state to the other are therefore not normal and are psychopaths. Given that the subtitle for Blake's *Songs of Innocence and Experience* is "Shewing the Two Contrary States of the Human Soul," it is more likely that these lines from Blake show how both positive and negative aspects can exist in humanity. Furthermore, given the complexity of the interaction of Innocence and Experience in the poems, as discussed in the previous chapter, these poems taken together reveal that all humans have the capacity for both good and evil and that, in fact, good actions and emotions are often sparked by our or others' evil actions and emotions. This interconnected reading of the "Divine Image" poems works to underline Harris's exploration of the complexity and non-binary nature of good and evil, and will be explored in the next chapter. Beyond these lines from the two poems, O'Brien provides no other explanation for why Harris uses Blake.

A more extended and theoretical exploration of Harris's choice of Blake is Nicholas Williams's "Eating Blake, or an Essay on Taste: The Case of Thomas Harris's *Red Dragon*," discussed briefly in the introduction, which explores why Harris chose Blake, focusing on what Harris reveals about the interplay between high and low art. Williams asks, "Why Blake, and ... which Blake, the painter only or also the poet, the religious Gnostic,

2. "The wickedness herein I took from my own stock"

the political revolutionary, or some other alternative or hybrid?" (137–39). Williams explores these questions in the context of "the consumption of a high-art text by a mass-market text" (139). One possible reason for the "ingestion" of Blake that Williams suggests is that of "a shortcut to literary respectability" (140). By referencing Blake, Harris indicates that his work is better than that of other horror or crime novelists. The allusion could be no more than a class marker. Williams points to Harris's error of indicating William Butts as Blake's friend and commissioner of the painting, instead of the correct Thomas Butts, as support for the idea that Harris is using Blake as a simple signifier. The error may reveal that Harris is not placing himself as a serious scholar of Blake's works and therefore he uses the reference to Blake to signify both status and "the most common cultural signification Blake carries where his name is known at all: madness" (141–42). Williams does not address the possibility that the error regarding Butts's name could be purposeful, in order to subtly indicate Dolarhyde's lack of familiarity with Blake and therefore misreading of him, an idea that will be explored in later chapters. Williams, however, does not simply agree that Blake is used merely as a cultural marker of madness, but goes on to suggest another, one in which Harris's use of Blake is "a transgressive act" (144). Harris uses Blake not to mark his status or to be a mouthpiece for his philosophies but instead to rewrite him — to, through Dolarhyde's actions, show how the consumer of art is not passive, but helps to interpret and create the work of art itself. In discussing the specific use of Blake, Williams also discusses various theories of consumption and Blake's own relation to and use of earlier writers, like Milton. In addition, he discusses Blake's relationship to his public, his audience. Blake, like Lecter and Dolarhyde, tried to balance a distance from others (maintaining a high art status) and a connection to others (selling his work to the public). Leaving behind the two possibilities for Harris's use of Blake mentioned above, Williams concludes that the use of Blake is a matter of "eating well" (158), in which the work thus consumed is changed and changes the consumer as well. Williams's exploration is interesting and highlights connections between Blake and the characters (the balance of self-reliance and necessity of others) that point to a possible reason Harris chose Blake instead of another artist. Williams's early exploration of this connection, however, only examines Blake and *Red Dragon*, not the other novels.

One other writer who explores, albeit briefly, why Harris uses Blake is Tony Magistrale in the essay "Transmogrified Gothic: The Novels of Thomas Harris." Magistrale's focus in this essay, as is clear from the title, is on transformation, which he sees as existing at the center of the horror genre. It is in the section on *Red Dragon* that Magistrale explicitly discusses Blake, connecting his works and ideas to Harris's. After stating that the Blake painting "is the dominant symbol for Dolarhyde's process of 'becoming,'" he provides a reason for the choice of Blake, saying, "As is often the case in Blake's watercolors, the painting highlights the emergence of the man–God (a vision made tangible and direct)" (28). The content of the painting, however, is not the only reason for the use of Blake. Like Williams, Magistrale suggests that it is Blake's personality or reputation that also makes him an appropriate choice for this novel: "Like Blake's conception of the artist, Dolarhyde views himself as a man pressing ... against the walls of obedience and restraint" (28). This Romantic idea of the artist as outside the constraints of society merges with the Blakean critique of law and social order, providing a goal for Dolarhyde to aspire to, "a Blakean concept beyond traditional moral codes, societal restraints, or even human recognition" (29). While these ideas are prevalent in the work of other Romantic poets, like Byron and Shelley, Blake's work as a visual artist adds a powerful component to the novel, as do his ideas regarding suffering, violence, and action. Magistrale's final explicit discussion of Blake focuses on these ideas of suffering, correctly asserting that "Blake's paintings and poetry frequently juxtapose suffering with a transcendent consciousness" (29); as discussed previously, the recurring, almost Promethean, image of a figure, either human or bird, with wings or arms outspread, hovering over a prone figure, appears at these moments of what Magistrale would call "transcendent consciousness," or what could be called violent enlightenment. Blake's Red Dragon (in both versions that will be discussed later) appears in this position associated with both suffering and knowledge. Magistrale suggests that it is this connection between suffering and knowledge or transcendence as embodied by the Red Dragon that draws Dolarhyde to the painting and in part directs his actions, causing him to act "[l]ike Blake's Satan in *The Marriage of Heaven and Hell* ... liv[ing] to destroy individual lives ... believ[ing] their destruction to be a source of energy" (30). Most Blake scholars would believe that this interpretation of Blake is incorrect, and Magistrale does admit that Dolarhyde's actions simplify and misread Blake's symbolism. One must remember Blake's redefinition of terms, particularly in *The Marriage*

2. "The wickedness herein I took from my own stock"

of Heaven and Hell, in which angels are devils and vice versa, and where Blake declares that "in the Book of Job Milton's Messiah is call'd Satan" (plate 5), conflating and reversing figures of good and evil. For Blake, this Satan is Milton's rebel Satan, leading a revolution against a Urizen-like God who enforces strict and unyielding laws, attempting to restrain all desire and energy, which are positive forces in Blake's philosophy. For Blake it is not that the destruction is a source of energy, but that anything active is energy and is good, as opposed to the passive, which is bad. The active Satan fights against a God who wishes to make all passive. However, instead of seeing Blake as emphasizing struggle against an oppressive (and in some cases overly masculine) society, Dolarhyde himself becomes the violent oppressive tyrant. The difficulty in Harris's deliberately including a misreading of Blake, though, is that it is never indicated in the novel that Dolarhyde misreads Blake; there is no correction of his mistake. Magistrale suggests that there is no correction because Harris wishes "to indict Blake by twisting and critiquing the naïve and destructive potential inherent in the romantic urge to recreate self" (30–31). While an intriguing point and one that connects to the gothic reading that Magistrale produces, this also seems a misreading of Blake in that Blake is not a typical Romantic whose goal was to simply re-create self. This reading also overlooks the other possible connections to Blake that are more gothic than Romantic in nature.

Interestingly, Magistrale hints at these other connections to Blake when he opens his essay with lines from Blake's *Jerusalem* that comment on both the nature of God and the necessity of coexistence: "when the Male & Female/Appropriate Individuality, they become an Eternal Death./Hermaphroditic worshippers of a God of cruelty & law!" (90:53–55). In these lines the male and female have not accepted their necessary union and instead have insisted on individuality. They have become a hermaphrodite and not an androgyne (concepts discussed in the previous chapter). This passage also reveals that the God that is then created, the God of Generation and not Eternity, is one who is cruel in his desire for all to obey the law. This is the Urizenic God portrayed in *Ancient of Days,* the painting that Verger owns. The lines warn of separation from one's contrary and the dangers of rigid laws and boundaries. Oddly, Magistrale quotes these lines but does not refer to them or make any explicit connection between them and Harris's novels. These lines do, however, resonate with his discussion of both the complexities and the contradictions of characters and of human nature itself. He calls Lecter "[a]n angel with horns" who "fascinates us with his dualities" (32) and suggests that "Lecter's attractiveness to readers" is due to how Lecter "fully embodies this dialectic within his own personality" (33). Magistrale also discusses Starling's complexity, suggesting that "[i]t is [her] simultaneous vulnerability and strength ... that establishes whatever respect Lecter is capable of summoning toward another human being" (33). The two are not the hermaphrodites of Blake's passage but instead have integrated and embraced contrary aspects of themselves. In addition, Starling is capable of embracing negative or dark aspects of herself, and yet in his discussion of how "[o]nly Starling is able to integrate harmoniously the opposing parts of herself" (37) and how it was Lecter who put her in touch with her own dark side, Magistrale does not refer to the passage from *Jerusalem* quoted at the beginning of the essay that warns against lack of integration, but instead refers to Jung's ideas of the animus, anima, and shadow self.

In addition to discussing the duality of individual characters, Magistrale discusses the complex nature of life and humanity itself, claiming that Harris, as the gothic does, comments on the capacity and necessity to balance good and evil, and how if "their impulses remain unchecked humans were more likely to perform acts of perversity than poetry" (31). In order to keep these impulses in check one must first be aware of one's capacity for both good and evil. If one is not aware of the capacity for evil, one cannot control it; however, if aware of it, one may be able to control it or place it in balance with one's good natures. Both Lecter and Starling acknowledge this necessity of balance, with Lecter acknowledging Starling's capacity for rage and Starling acknowledging Lecter's humanity. However, once again Magistrale makes no connection between these ideas and the passage from *Jerusalem*, leaving the connection unclear or available only to those who come with a prior knowledge of Blake, as perhaps Harris does himself.

The difficulty in determining why and how Harris uses Blake stems in part from not knowing how Harris understands Blake and not knowing the level of familiarity with Blake that Harris is assuming on the part of his audience. Unless Harris comes out with a definitive statement regarding knowledge and interpretation of Blake, one must speculate. However, the context of the explicit allusions, as well as the connections discussed in this chapter regarding duality, complexity, and critique of law and reli-

2. "The wickedness herein I took from my own stock"

gion, create a foundation upon which the individual novels and film adaptations may be discussed to provide the, as Blake might say, Minute Particulars. These particular connections between Blake and Harris include the aspects listed above, as well as a focus on the importance of imagination (not surprising, as it is related to vision), the role of suffering or pain in expanded vision or understanding, and the dual nature of nature itself. The following chapters will examine these connections and read Harris through this Blakean lens, revealing, whether intentional or not, Harris's use and echoing of Blake's ideas of the interconnectedness of good and evil.

Chapter 3

The Dragon and the Tyger
Red Dragon

It would be difficult for anyone reading Thomas Harris's *Red Dragon* to miss the references to William Blake. After all, the title of the novel comes from Blake's painting *The Great Red Dragon and the Woman Clothed in the Sun*, which plays a major role in the novel since Francis Dolarhyde, the serial killer, communicates with the dragon in the painting and has the dragon tattooed on his back. In *Red Dragon*, Harris explicitly and repeatedly establishes a link with Blake that then continues through the other three Lecter novels.

These explicit connections to Blake in *Red Dragon* are clear: the Blake painting is the name of the novel, a tattoo on Francis Dolarhyde's back, and a painting Dolarhyde is obsessed with. The novel also contains a scene with a sleeping tiger that alludes to "The Tyger" and Harris uses lines from Blake's "The Divine Image" and "A Divine Image" as epigraphs. These two "Divine Image" poems were discussed in the previous chapter and are central to creating the Blakean foundation on which to read not only this novel but also the entire series of Lecter novels. These poems, one from *Songs of Innocence* and one from *Songs of Experience*, reveal that humanity has the capacity for both mercy and cruelty. The human form contains both negative and positive aspects and each person is capable of acting from either alternative — is capable of being merciful or cruel. A third poem from *Songs of Innocence and Experience* that is not used in the epigraphs but is often considered alongside "The Divine Image" and "A Divine Image" is "The Human Abstract." As "The Human Abstract" reveals, not only are humans capable of both mercy and cruelty, but the two contraries are also interdependent:

> Pity would be no more,
> If we did not make somebody Poor;
> And Mercy no more could be,
> If all were as happy as we; [ll. 1–4]

3. The Dragon and the Tyger

It is only humanity's capacity for cruelty that allows us to experience mercy. Implied in these lines is the idea that if we were to eradicate cruelty completely, mercy would disappear. The two "States of the Human Soul," as Blake calls Innocence and Experience in the subtitle to the collection, must exist together, in balance. It is this necessary balance of the contraries that Harris begins to explore in *Red Dragon*.

After the epigraphs the first explicit Blake reference in the novel itself comes as Dolarhyde looks at his copy of the painting: "He felt that Blake must have peeked in his ear and seen the Red Dragon" (71–72). Dolarhyde admires the dragon's power and, as mentioned previously, has had the massive dragon from the painting tattooed on his back. He comes to the conclusion that "if he followed the true urges he had kept down for so long ... he could Become" (214). Dolarhyde's killings serve as the process of his "becoming." Through the killings he believes he will cease to be Francis Dolarhyde and will fully become the Dragon. Even though he has implied that the Dragon is a part of him by saying that it seemed like Blake was able to peek in his ear and see it, and even though he admits he has had these evil and bestial urges in him, his comments regarding his "becoming" imply that he sees the Dragon and himself as separate entities and believes that he will be subsumed into the Dragon eventually. He and the Dragon are as male and female in Blake's concept of the hermaphrodite: two willful entities living in the same space and struggling against each other. He and the Dragon are not like Blake's androgyne or contraries—two parts of one whole. However, even though Dolarhyde seems to already consider himself as separate from the Dragon, he is surprised and scared when, after his night with the blind Reba McClane (during which he has felt accepted and at peace), he feels divided from the Dragon and worries that the Dragon will take her. It is this morning that the Dragon speaks to him for the first time and "[t]his new twoness with the Dragon disoriented him" (254). He is frightened because he has been considering himself and the Dragon as being one but now feels as if they are two (265). However, looking closely at the way he has described the situation, he and the Dragon have not been one; instead, he is Francis, who has this evil inside of him, and who aspires to be the Dragon and leave behind Francis. He is not a Blakean figure who has recognized the positive and negative aspects of his life and is deciding if and how to keep them in balance. He has divided himself in two from the beginning and has decided to leave behind one half of himself to become the other. However, when Reba stays with him and he feels love, he further separates the two sides of himself, not wanting to hurt her. He now wishes to not only contain but also defeat the Dragon and eradicate it. Like Blake's Urizen, he creates boundaries in order to stop what he sees as harmful. While his intentions here are good, his mistake is in seeing the negative aspects of himself as a separate entity, as revealed in his listening "for himself coming down the stairs" (253); he is worried that this separate identity may hurt Reba instead of recognizing that it is the Francis holding Reba that could hurt her. If he were more aware that it is not a separate entity that may harm her but himself, if he acknowledged that the Dragon and Francis are the same person, he could better protect her and keep her from harm. Instead, his attempt to separate himself from his evil urges in an attempt to protect Reba only leads to that dangerous aspect becoming stronger, commanding Francis to give him Reba.

Eventually, in order to silence the Dragon, Dolarhyde travels to New York, gains access to the original painting, and eats it. He devours the painting hoping to stop the Dragon's need for destruction and violence. However, instead of the Dragon ceasing to talk to him once he has ingested the painting, it returns stronger than before, and is able to take over Dolarhyde completely. When he returns home he still plans on one more killing, to appease the Dragon. Even though he has ingested the painting and the Dragon appears to speak through him, this has not made him one with his dragon aspect but instead has further separated the two. Believing the Dragon to exist outside of himself, viewing it as an external object that can be ingested, when in fact it is already an internal aspect of himself, is Dolarhyde's error. Although Dolarhyde believes that he has the power now and has won the binary struggle, when he sees Graham at Gateway and knows they will find him soon, the Dragon speaks again, and soon has taken him over, a reversal in the struggle. The Dragon and Dolarhyde are not one. They are two separate entities existing in the same body, each fighting for dominance. Eating the painting does not lead to the defeat of the Dragon because, while Dolarhyde feels a strong connection to the Blake painting, he has misread Blake. He views the Dragon as a force outside himself even though it is not an external force. The Dragon represents an aspect of himself that already existed inside him, a force urging vengeance and violent action. The desire for vengeance comes from his abusive experiences as a child. He broods over these memories, which can lead, as Bandy suggests and was discussed earlier, to the creation of a negation.

3. The Dragon and the Tyger

His abuse and torment did not lead to his murders but his brooding over this past torment led to a desire for revenge. Therefore, his ingestion of the painting is not a defeat of an outside force but an attempt to repress and ignore an internal one. Dolarhyde suffers from the binary thinking that Blake wrote against. Because of his brooding he sees the Dragon as separate from himself (a negation) instead of an aspect to be acknowledged and balanced (a contrary). Prior to deciding to eat the painting, prior to loving Reba, Dolarhyde suffered from this binary thinking in a slightly different way, seeing Francis and not the Dragon as the negation to be overcome.

Even though at this crucial moment Dolarhyde has misread Blake, he does reveal a partial enactment of Blake's philosophy elsewhere in the novel. It is his love for Reba that leads him to want to stop committing evil acts. It is through her that he realizes that he can be good; he recognizes that he does have a positive aspect and can be accepted by others. Her love for him helps him to (momentarily) forget and move past his memories of torment at the hands of others. However, instead of using this insight to move forward with Reba, in balance, and, while recognizing them, not act on his evil urges, he instead identifies the evil as existing outside of himself as an adversary. By not accepting the Dragon as an internalized aspect of himself, he cannot defeat it; if anything, he makes it stronger.

As discussed in the previous chapter, Magistrale also comments on how Dolarhyde has simplified and misread Blake by interpreting Blake's focus on the necessity of destruction for creativity to mean that butchery of others is necessary. This misreading, though, is understandable, given that Dolarhyde's knowledge of and familiarity with Blake's other works is never indicated and that Blake, particularly in his later prophetic works, is quite complex. As discussed earlier, misreading Blake is easy and understandable given the multiple versions of his works and the ease of taking them out of context, unmooring the text of an illuminated work from its imagery or a smaller poem or proverb from a larger work, like removing "Jerusalem" from *Milton* or only examining the *Songs of Innocence* and not reading those of *Experience*. Additionally, several aspects of Blake's works are the center of scholarly debate — particularly the role of women, and the portrayal of women as victims. It is also important to remember that it is not Blake, but the Red Dragon, a bestial humanoid figure of evil, who speaks to Dolarhyde.

A possible indication of Dolarhyde's focus on the Dragon instead of on Blake, and consequently his misreading of Blake, comes in what has been read as a factual mistake on Harris's part: referring to Thomas Butts as William Butts. When Dolarhyde meets Paula Harper at the Brooklyn Museum and she asks what kind of research he is doing, he tells her he is writing about Butts. Harper asks, "On William Butts?" identifying him as Blake's patron (281). Dolarhyde does not correct the naming error, implying that he does not know that it is an error. As Nicholas Williams suggests, this may be a mistake on Harris's part; however, it could be an indication of how little Dolarhyde knows about Blake. Harper is not a Blake scholar and could easily have gotten the name wrong, but the important thing is that Dolarhyde does not correct her. Perhaps this small detail is a flag indicating Dolarhyde's ignorance of Blake's works and ideas. Unfortunately, without a narrative correction the reader is left unaware of this indication of misreading. Harris perhaps wanted to avoid a narrative intrusion, a voice interrupting to correct the error; however, he could have had another character come in and correct the mistake, or even have had Harper correct herself, the way one does when misspeaking and then realizing it. Nevertheless, Dolarhyde does not recognize or correct Harper's error because his focus is not on Blake. Dolarhyde acts, especially toward women, the way he witnesses the Dragon of the painting act.

As Magistrale suggests, "The narrative action of *Red Dragon* is completely male-generated ... while the novel's female characters appear as parallel models to Blake's feminine representation in his 'red dragon' painting: terrified, supplicant, victimized" (36). On the surface this parallel seems quite clear; however, when examining the plot, important distinctions appear. Clearly, the women that Dolarhyde has killed were terrified and victimized. Additionally, Reba's blindness at first aligns her with the woman in the painting, as it (wrongly) implies a vulnerability and perhaps a naiveté or innocence. Graham's wife Molly also at first appears to be vulnerable and victimized, terrified of what will happen to her and her son because of her husband's work. She is also a widow, which, like Reba's blindness, may wrongly indicate a vulnerability, suggesting perhaps that she needed Graham to save her from loneliness earlier, and that she needs him now to protect her. However, Reba's sexual aggressiveness and Molly's shooting of Dolarhyde at the end and thereby saving of Will's life are not the acts of victims or supplicants. Perhaps it is in this difference between the female of the painting and the two main female characters of the novel that Harris provides his authorial comment on Dolarhyde's misreading of Blake. Through the independent and strong actions of both Reba and

3. The Dragon and the Tyger

Molly, Harris counters Dolarhyde's reading: women are not helpless victims, and powerful males are not powerful because of the violence they inflict on female victims. If this characterization of Reba and Molly is a counter to Dolarhyde's misreading, though, it is very subtle, and without a direct commentary on Blake readers are left with the disturbing fact that the explicit references to Blake (in the four novels, although not the films) come from Dolarhyde and Verger and not from Starling or Graham, or even Lecter. (This disturbing direct connection between Blake and the most negative characters will be explored in more detail in the concluding chapter, after all of the Blakean allusions have been addressed.)

The painting of the Red Dragon, while the central and explicit connection to Blake, is not the only connection to Blake in the novel. In addition, there are minor details like Dolarhyde's handwriting, which is described as "a fine copperplate script — not unlike William Blake's" (88). More importantly, a telling scene involving a tiger occurs when Dolarhyde starts dating Reba McClane. Dolarhyde at first watches a report about this tiger with a toothache on the news. Through the muscular nature and the tooth problems of both (Dolarhyde has a cleft palate, wears dentures, bites his victims, and has been dubbed "the Tooth Fairy" by the tabloids) Harris connects Dolarhyde and the tiger. In fact, David Sexton calls the tiger "the public version of Dolarhyde's identity as a big predator" (75). If he who made the lamb made the tiger, he also made Dolarhyde. When Dolarhyde takes Reba to visit the tiger while it is sedated, Harris provides another detailed description of both its power and vulnerability as Reba "sees" the tiger by touching a paw and then a claw, feeling both its soft fur and its muscles and teeth. As she moves around the tiger "her fingers trailed over the furry testicles. She cupped them and moved on" (246). The tiger's sedated state makes it safe for Reba to touch inside its mouth and feel its tongue. The visit ends with her touching its chest and being "filled with the tiger heart's bright thunder" (246). The use of "bright" to modify a sound, "thunder," reveals a poetically deliberate choice. This tiger, like Blake's, burns bright. The tiger, in its vulnerable sedated state, is proof of something great and wonderful, as well as a warning of the destructive power of this force, just like Dolarhyde and Lecter.

Reba's encounter with the tiger is echoed in her encounter with Dolarhyde when, after the visit to the tiger, he takes Reba to his home. As he keeps his distance, Reba approaches him and, finding "his mouth with her fingers and kiss[ing] it, [she] lightly press[ed] his lips against his clenched teeth" (249). He is the passive, yet imposing figure. When she realizes that it is his shyness and not disinterest keeping him passive his vulnerability is revealed. She feels both his vulnerability and his power, just as she did with the tiger. The tiger lay passive while she cupped his testicles; Dolarhyde sits still while Reba unzips his pants. While some, like Sexton, have connected Dolarhyde and the tiger, only a few have made the connection to Blake's tiger, and this connection is usually made only in passing. O'Brien's comment is typical of those making the connection, saying, "Presumably Harris ... [is] drawing on the William Blake connection once more, as the scene has obvious echoes of Blake's poem 'The Tyger'" (52). The obvious echoes are ones of descriptions of the tiger's strength, which, importantly, lead to questions regarding his nature and creator. If the tiger consists of contradictions and is made by the same person who made the lamb, so is Dolarhyde.

Dolarhyde, however, is not the only character who illustrates this complexity of contradictions. Will Graham also has a complex nature that leads to questions regarding the relationship of good and evil and the nature of God. When talking about the doubling of killer and hunter/profiler in *Red Dragon*, Simpson states that Graham is able to empathize with Dolarhyde "because he realizes he will always be more hunter than prey — a dragon more than a lamb" (*Psycho Paths* 88). Clearly, Simpson uses the words "dragon" and "lamb" here to allude to or play on the titles of two of the Harris novels; the word choice is interesting because in *Silence of the Lambs* (and in *Hannibal*), Starling is also more dragon than lamb. Instead of Blake's tiger/lamb contrast, seen in the companion poems "The Lamb" and "The Tyger," Simpson creates a dragon/lamb comparison. However, since Harris equates the dragon with the tiger, and Dolarhyde with the tiger, we return to Blake's tiger and lamb.

The tiger and the lamb are made by the same being and can therefore understand each other. Graham, the agent who captured Lecter originally, also is one of the few who understands Lecter, as Clarice Starling will later. Graham recognizes that just as he has a "criminal mind" (41) that allows him to visualize the killer's movements and motivations, Lecter is, in some way, normal. As Graham talks with a detective who asks about Lecter being crazy, Graham responds, "Dr. Lecter is not crazy, in any common way we think of being crazy. He did some hideous things because he enjoyed them. But he can function perfectly when he wants to" (49). Lecter is not a strange nonhuman creature, but shares similarities with "normal"

3. The Dragon and the Tyger

people. Graham, in turn, shares similarities with Lecter. Graham admits that he captured Lecter because he just knew he was the killer. He calls it a coincidence, but knows it is more than that—it is a connection. When he goes to see Lecter he fears feeling Lecter's madness in his own head (58). This fear is not because Lecter can impose his thoughts or madness on others but because at a distance Graham can ignore his similarity to Lecter, but cannot when near him and reminded by Lecter himself. Lecter, however, recognizes and acknowledges this connection and wants Graham to admit it, the connection of good and evil (60). As Graham leaves, Lecter tells him, "'The reason you caught me is that we're *just alike*'" (original emphasis, 62). Lecter refers here perhaps not only to the existence of Graham's evil urges (and therefore his ability to understand Lecter) but also to what may seem like a superficial similarity but is actually quite telling: their shared enhanced senses, and willingness to use these senses. Part of Graham's skill in profiling lies in closely examining crime scenes and people, and noticing and paying attention to details that others overlook or dismiss. Graham's, and Lecter's, enhanced senses connect to Blake's idea of the Doors of Perception being opened through improved sensual experience (*MHH* 14). Both of them have a greater understanding of the world around them and of themselves because their senses (all of their senses and not just sight) have been honed to pick up on subtleties and small differences. Graham, however, resists admitting this, or any, similarity to Lecter. Simpson draws on Graham's resistance of this recognition in discussing the deeper meaning of Harris's novel, claiming that Graham's worries about his over-identification with killers "is not ill-founded in the philosophical terms established by Harris's text. Harris implies that the Tooth Fairy's murder of reporter Freddy Lounds is at least a sort of wish-fulfillment for Graham" (*Psycho Paths* 89). These "philosophical terms" involve the blurring of good and evil, their coexistence, and the natural capability of humans for both. Stated this way, the philosophical terms are those of Blake himself.

Allusions to Blake not only emphasize the blurring of boundaries and the capability of humans to be both good and evil but also emphasize that the best response to this realization is not to fight against it and struggle to create clear boundaries, but to accept the connection of the two. Lecter accepts the coexistence of his natures while Dolarhyde, although seeming to accept his dual nature, in fact separates Francis from the Dragon. Graham's problem, and one that may lead to his being damaged by the end of the novel, is to not accept this state but instead attempt to fight against the blurring and erect walls between the two contraries. Graham will not admit his similarities to Lecter, his desire (however small or subconscious) for Lounds's death, or his pleasure in killing Hobbs. He attempts to keep the wall up between himself and Lecter, between good and evil.

Lecter, on the other hand, not only recognizes and acknowledges the interplay of good and evil but also realizes that both come from the same source: that evil can be natural and that God also commits evil acts and causes suffering. He explains human nature to Graham, saying, "We don't invent our natures ... they're issued to us along with our lungs and pancreas and everything else. Why fight it?" (259). He goes on to tell Graham that when Graham had to shoot Hobbs and killed him, he wasn't depressed because of the shooting itself but "*because killing him felt so good*" (original emphasis, 259). Lecter then asks, "Why shouldn't it feel good? It must feel good to God — He does it all the time, and are we not made in His image?" (259). As proof that God does it all the time, he provides examples of a church roof collapse in Texas that killed 34 people and a plane crash that killed 160 (259). In the later books, Lecter expounds further on God's cruel acts and his being the source of both good and evil. These statements do not reveal that Lecter is an atheist. He has not rejected the notion of God, but instead embraces a different perspective on God, the God who created both the tiger and the lamb.

Lecter is both the tiger and the lamb himself, something that will be made clearer in the ensuing novels. However, even in his brief appearances in *Red Dragon*, he is clearly established as being both highly savage and highly civilized. The highly savage aspect is highlighted in Chilton's warning to Graham about how, after a year of cooperation, Lecter attacked a nurse and tore out her tongue, while his pulse rate never increased (56). The calmness revealed during this savage attack indicates his outward civilized demeanor, which is accentuated by the reading material we first see him with, Dumas' *Le Grand Dictionnaire de Cuisine* (58). Lecter's sophistication and taste are capable of making audiences side with him as opposed to his jailers or the more typical serial killers like Dolarhyde. This, in part, heightens the effect of his savagery and leaves audiences not sure of the "proper" reaction. There could be some elitism at work here: even though Lecter is a cannibal, he is a refined one and therefore is better than boring middle-class people like Dr. Chilton. However, there may also be a thematic reason for the contrast between the styles and personalities

3. The Dragon and the Tyger

of Chilton and Lecter. Chilton represents the law, the establishment, and psychiatry (with its categories that Lecter defies). By making the symbol of established law and categorization unappealing, Harris may be adding to his Blakean critique of the legal system. This critique, however, does operate on a visceral and simplistic level by having the readers experience how drab and boring the upholders of laws are, how often they are wrong, and how, while they try to maintain a sense of decorum, they easily cross the line into vulgarity or awkwardness.

The distinction between Lecter and Chilton also reveals a distinction between their senses. Lecter's senses are more honed, more perceptive than Chilton's. Perhaps Chilton is less refined because he does not literally see or taste the difference between his pursuits and Lecter's. Perhaps it is not that Chilton cannot afford finer things, nor that he doesn't care about them, but maybe instead he literally cannot see or taste the difference between the finer things and more average things. His senses are lacking, leading to the surface distinction between the two and also indicating a reason for Chilton's lack of success in his field or in understanding Lecter. Chilton's senses fail him; his observations are flawed and narrow. In *Red Dragon* Chilton is not so much vulgar or awkward as trying desperately to understand Lecter, to prove that he, too, is a good psychiatrist and that his observations can lead to insightful diagnoses. When Graham comes to speak with Lecter and has to first speak with Chilton, Chilton dominates the conversation, warning Graham about Lecter and prying into Graham for any insight he may have into Lecter. He tries to read Graham's face and cannot (56), and when they are finally finished and Graham does not answer Chilton's inquiries, Chilton clearly sees hostility in Graham's face (57). Graham feels hostile in part because he is delayed in seeing Lecter and in part because of Chilton's clear attempt to get a psychiatric reading of Graham. Lecter knows this has bothered Graham and says to him of Chilton, "Gruesome, isn't it? ... he fumbles at your head like a freshman pulling at a panty girdle, doesn't he? Watched you out of the corner of his eye. Picked *that* up, didn't you?" (original emphasis, 60). Not only does this scene denigrate Chilton, it also serves as a reminder of the importance of the senses. Chilton looks for clues, for signs from Graham, something to read, but finds none. His senses fail him, only being able to read the outright signs of hostility and not more subtle clues. Chilton cannot understand Lecter because he cannot read the subtleties of other humans. Chilton is also described as "seeing" the hostility with no indication that he attempts to use other senses (for example, smell) to read people, as Lecter does. Graham, however, like Lecter, can read Chilton's probing and can avoid it. Graham, like Lecter, has honed his senses—not just sight, but smell as well—and can use this to avoid labeling by others, as well as to better understand others. Chilton, with his narrowed and limited senses, with his fumbling manipulation and blatant attempts to discover insight, continues to serve as a reminder of the weaknesses of the law in *Silence of the Lambs*, while in *Hannibal* Chilton's contrasting role will be taken over by Krendler.

It is not just in representatives of a flawed system that Harris reveals the ugliness and vulgarity of human nature, though. Harris reveals brief glimpses of the, if not evil, certainly ugly and vulgar thoughts that reside in humanity as a whole. The clearest example of this comes early in the novel as Graham is returning to his hotel room in Atlanta. He shares the elevator with two men who have been attending the convention in the hotel. One points to a woman in the lobby and says, "God damn, I'd love to tear off a piece of that." The other responds, "Fuck her till her nose bleeds" (15). The men casually use violent terms, not hiding this savage aspect of themselves, aware that Graham is in the elevator and not caring. Sexton describes this encounter well when he says, "The scene is brutal; the rhythm, though, is formal, almost Flaubertian. It has the effect of making the monstrous crimes seem not so removed from common ugliness" (73).

All of the indications of the dual nature of humanity and the melding of good and evil come to a head in the last pages of the book when Graham thinks back to a visit to Shiloh, Tennessee, the site of a Civil War battle in which 23,746 men died. He remembers the trip and his reaction:

> Now, drifting between memory and narcotic sleep, he saw that Shiloh was not sinister; it was indifferent. Beautiful Shiloh could witness anything. Its unforgivable beauty simply underscored the indifference of nature, the Green Machine. The loveliness of Shiloh mocked our plight…. In the Green Machine there is no mercy; *we* make mercy, manufacture it in the parts that have overgrown our basic reptile brain.
> There is no murder. We make murder, and it matters only to us. Graham knew too well that he contained all the elements to make murder; perhaps mercy too…. He wondered if, in the great body of humankind, in the minds of men set on civilization, the vicious urges we control in ourselves and the dark instinctive knowledge of those urges function like the crippled virus the body arms against. He wondered if old, awful urges are the virus that makes vaccine [original emphasis, 339].

3. The Dragon and the Tyger

Here at the end of the novel, Harris emphasizes that humanity can be both good and evil, that in fact we need our evil urges in order to be good. Evil works as a vaccine to combat further evil. The relationship of evil and vaccine is similar to that of cruelty and mercy in Blake's poems, particularly "The Human Aspect." Without cruelty there is no knowledge of or need for mercy. Without evil, humans may not be aware of their ability to help and care for others. Knowing that there is evil in the world may strengthen these bonds and humans' ability for empathy. This knowledge of evil may be related to Blake's concept of corrosion leading to increased vision from *The Marriage of Heaven and Hell*. This evil, with its accompanying violence, may work as a corrosive to enhance one's vision and allow one to have empathy for others. Connected to the idea of vaccines and viruses in this passage, perhaps the evil and violence operate as a powerful medicine or therapy, such as chemotherapy, which can weaken and harm in the process of ultimately healing. Simpson comments on the idea of virus and vaccine, claiming that "the 'vaccine' that only partially restores Graham to psychic equilibrium is the knowledge of his capacity for murder" (*Psycho Paths* 90). Acknowledging the dark aspect of his own nature allows Graham to recover, at least partially. Unfortunately, he fought this acknowledgment throughout the novel. In addition, by acknowledging that evil, the dark urges, are an aspect inherent in nature, Graham realizes that he is not a monster and therefore can recover, can live with himself, even if his wife Molly and stepson Willy cannot. Simpson quotes Christopher Lehmann-Haupt musing on the same scene, claiming that he doesn't like the viral image because "it suggests that evil is a matter of biology, and has little to do with moral choice" (qtd. in Simpson, *Psycho Paths* 215). This, however, is Harris's point — that evil is a part of nature. However, while natural, it is not determined and therefore characters have the choice of whether to accept or deny these aspects of themselves and then whether to act upon them. Lecter accepts and acts, while Graham struggles to accept and then, most likely, not act.

Unfortunately, many readers have overlooked or ignored this ending, and instead choose to categorize this novel and the subsequent novels as ones about the struggle of good against evil, rather than an exploration of both in all of humanity and nature. Most of these readings then suggest that Harris provides a dark and pessimistic view of the world, one in which good cannot triumph. Sexton exemplifies this simplified binary reading when he claims that "in his [Harris's] world, predation is the norm, in both animals and humans" (54). This does acknowledge Harris's point that evil must exist; however, it places good and evil out of balance, positioning one as more natural than the other. Also, considering Graham's conclusion regarding Shiloh, nature, mercy, and murder, clearly all is not predatory so much as indifferent, accepting the necessity of death and killing, as well as life and creating. The killing of one animal by another is not murder, but an aspect of nature. For example, when the wild dogs that Graham, Molly, and Willy take care of dig up some turtle eggs, the act is accepted as part of nature and Willy merely covers the eggs back up (40). The dogs are not punished or restrained. The collapsing of a church is not God murdering believers. On a simplistic level, humans make murder through the literal creation of the definition of "murder" and then application of the definition. On a deeper level, we "make murder" by acting on our impulses instead of acknowledging them and dealing with them in another way.

Instead of leading to a philosophical contemplation of human nature or a clear connection to the Blake allusions, this ending regarding Shiloh has led, in some cases, to a negative review of the novel. For example, Sexton claims that this ending is "perhaps an artistic mistake" (55). He later explains,

> It's an uncharacteristically awkward, opaque and actually badly written paragraph for Harris. It is perhaps meant as a rationale for the novel, as much as for Graham's insight into murder. It's as if Harris is saying "the old awful urges" are worth thinking about as part of the price of civilization—and therefore his kind of crime novel deserves consideration as a serious form of literature [70].

Sexton's primary interpretation of the passage—that just because we are civilized that doesn't mean we can ignore those old urges—does sum up properly Harris's emphasis on the coexistence of civilized and savage, good and evil, and perhaps Harris was worried that without this final thought by Graham, readers would miss his point. Sexton also connects his claim that the ending passage is a justification of the novel as serious to Harris's use of Blake, stating, "The Blakean frontispiece ... followed by the quotations from *Songs of Innocence* and *Songs of Experience*, locate the book within the literary tradition much more effectively" (70). Unfortunately, this conclusion seems to assume that the use of Blake is merely as a literary marker. However, Harris could have chosen any canonical author to reference if his only goal was to mark his work as better than other genre fiction, so surely Blake was chosen for other reasons as well. The Shiloh episode makes the connection clear, especially when read against the epigraphs: Harris wishes to allude to Blake's ideas regarding the coexistence of good and evil and the dual nature of humanity.

Manhunter— *Film*

Harris's novel was first turned into a film in 1986: Michael Mann's *Manhunter*. Not only is *Red Dragon* no longer the title of the work, the painting itself plays a much smaller role in the film. The print is seen only twice: once when Dolarhyde (spelled "Dollarhyde" in the film) shows the slide to Freddy Lounds and once right before we see Reba in Dolarhyde's apartment during their date. Dolarhyde identifies the painting when showing it to Lounds, and when he shows a slide later of himself at one of the crime scenes he refers to himself as "the Dragon rampant." Nothing is said regarding the painting in the second scene. He does refer to himself explicitly as the Red Dragon in the message he has Lounds record. Lounds says, "I have seen the wonder and awe of the Red Dragon," and warns Graham, "You will be awake in fear of what the Red Dragon will do." While Dolarhyde refers to his "becoming" in his toilet paper note to Lecter (here spelled Lecktor), he does not explicitly say he is becoming the Dragon, although when he stops by Reba's apartment and kidnaps her he has apparently become the Dragon since when Reba asks if it is Francis there, he responds, "No, not Francis. Francis is gone forever." The Red Dragon kanji is still referred to but only briefly, and no explicit connection is made between that and the Dragon painting. There is no tattoo and no scene of Dolarhyde eating the painting itself.

Originally there was to be a tattoo of the dragon in the film. Tom Noonan, who played Dolarhyde, explained on the "making of" featurette on the DVD that they tried to create the tattoo but it never looked right and finally Mann told Noonan, "I think the tattoo trivializes your struggle." Dolarhyde's struggle, however, does not clearly come through in the film, as the focus is mainly on Graham and there are only brief hints of Dolarhyde's possible struggle against the Dragon. In addition to his belief that the tattoo would trivialize the character's struggle, "Mann also appears to have been concerned about audiences misinterpreting the tattoo as a deliberate Oriental touch, despite the explicit references to William Blake's

'Red Dragon'" (O'Brien 53). This is supposedly the same reason the title was changed.

Instead of Blake, the strongest influence on Dolarhyde in this film seems to be the moon. The timing of his killings to be in conjunction with the full moon is emphasized and his apartment is overwhelmed with astronomical décor, implying a different compelling force. The dragon is not obviously the source of desires or the object of his "becoming." Simpson, however, actually draws a connection between the painting in the novel and the décor in the film: "Dolarhyde attempts to transcend his human weaknesses by imaginatively transforming into an omnipotent, transcendent being — quite literally, a cosmic force of nature manifested in the masculine sun devouring the feminine moon. Dolarhyde is fascinated by William Blake's painting, *The Great Red Dragon and the Woman Clothed in the Rays of the Sun*. His house is full of photographs and murals of planetscapes and stars" (*Psycho Paths* 110). Interestingly, the version of Blake's painting that Mann uses is different than the one Harris describes in the novel. As with many of Blake's works, the Red Dragon exists in a few different versions, revealing different perspectives. The version Harris describes is the work that is most commonly titled *The Great Red Dragon and the Woman Clothed in the Sun*, in which the back of the dragon is dominant and the woman is at the bottom of the canvas with the dragon's tail wrapped around her. Harris does refer to it as *The Great Red Dragon and the Woman Clothed with the Sun*, as does the Brooklyn Museum's website, but most other sources use "in" instead of "with" in the title. In the print seen in Mann's film called *The Great Red Dragon and the Woman Clothed with the Sun*, the dragon is above the woman, looking down at her, and the woman is free from his tail. She has what appear to be wings and seems ready to fly away. Instead of the Dragon dominating the image, he is relegated to less than the top half while the woman dominates the lower half of the painting. Both paintings do contain Blake's recurring image of a figure with wings or arms spread, hovering or standing over another figure, and in that way they both may contain the same theme of painful or violent enlightenment. However, in the one used by Mann the female figure is not prone, but rather kneeling and looking up at the Dragon; interestingly, she, too, appears to have outstretched arms and wings. Her position and wings indicate that she is not a passive receiver of enlightenment. The moment of painful enlightenment in this painting therefore may be read as perhaps a mutual one, with both Dragon and

3. The Dragon and the Tyger

woman being enlightened and active. Conversely, in the painting referenced in the novel, the female figure is almost entirely prone and does not have outstretched arms or wings. She is more typical of the prone figures in the Blake images of painful enlightenment, the minor difference being that her head is slightly lifted to look in terror at the Dragon. While the titles of the two paintings are often confused, since Harris clearly and specifically describes the painting in the novel, it is unlikely that Mann just chose the wrong one. O'Brien suggests that "Mann may have used the later picture as a subtle hint that Dollarhyde's [sic] next scheduled victim, as personified by the Woman, would escape the coils of his tail" (50). However, since this version de-emphasizes the Dragon and makes the woman more active and independent, why would Dolarhyde be drawn to this version? The painting in the film is not a coherent or central part of the plot.

The other central symbolic connection to Blake in the novel is the tiger. Mann does retain the visit to the tiger but its connection to Dolarhyde is not established or emphasized; in addition, Reba does not respond to the tiger and Dolarhyde in similar ways, revealing the strength and vulnerability of each. The tiger's need for a cap on his tooth is mentioned, but because the tiger only appears in one scene and appears to be part of an impulsive trip, Dolarhyde's connection to him is de-emphasized, as we do not see him earlier watching the tiger and considering taking Reba to see it. While we do see Reba touching and exploring the tiger, and she does initiate the kiss with Dolarhyde afterward, the scenes are not as parallel as they are in the novel. While Dolarhyde in the novel is not an overly sympathetic character, Harris does provide the reader with details regarding his childhood and his internal struggle with the Dragon after he has met Reba. In the novel, the connections to the tiger and his interactions with Reba also reveal aspects of his humanity. While there are brief moments of insight into his humanity in the film, overall, he is more of a pure villain. His relationship with Reba is not established over several meetings but consists of one date. Noonan's facial expressions do indicate Dolarhyde's growing feelings for her both after their night together and in the car as he waits to meet her for the second time, but there is no indication that he is willing to fight the Dragon to be with her. In addition, his villainous nature is further emphasized in the film when he kidnaps Reba and attempts to kill her. While the Dragon does take over fully in the novel, Reba is not a targeted victim but instead has to be kept alive to witness Dolarhyde's faked death.

Interestingly, while the connection between Dolarhyde and the tiger is not emphasized, this version of Lecter has been connected to the tiger. According to O'Brien, "One element Cox particularly wanted to bring across in Lecktor [sic] was the incarcerated Doctor's utter sense of boredom. Lecktor is like an animal confined in a cage at a public zoo, prodded and gawped at by curious visitors" (43). O'Brien comments further on this connection later when discussing the scene with Reba and the tiger: "Reba's encounter with a symbolic sleeping tiger is especially effective, staged against a clinical white backdrop similar to Lecktor's cell" (51–52). Lecter here is the caged creature, a dangerous, yet beautiful and intriguing, creation of nature, not allowed to act on its nature. Lecter is still the character who best embodies the balance of good and evil, although he is not in complete balance, yet. His conversations with Graham remain virtually the same and he is portrayed as being both quite savage, in descriptions of his crimes (although the attack on the nurse is not mentioned), and quite civilized, in his polite and calm interactions with Graham, and as indicated by his posture and bodily movements. Some aspects of his civilized or elite nature are erased or downplayed in the film, however. For example, the books in his office are solely psychology books and journals, no cookbooks. The book code used by Lecter and Dolarhyde in the film is not from *The Joy of Cooking* but from the State of Maryland Statutes. His crimes are also more "ordinary," as Hobbs's crimes are attributed to him. We are left with a Lecter who attacked college girls.

Even with these changes, Lecter remains the embodiment of Blake's belief in contraries. His discussions of human nature, his similarity to Graham, and the nature of God are all retained almost exactly, with Lector emphasizing that Graham caught him because they are the same, that Graham felt bad after killing Hobbs because it felt good, that God kills indiscriminately (including his worshippers), and that our natures are issued to us. The noticeable changes in these discussions actually further emphasize the dual nature of humanity and God and strengthen Lecter's connection to Blake's philosophy. He emphasizes Graham's similarity to himself and to a killer's mind-set by telling him, as he leaves the hospital, not just that they are the same but that if Graham "wants the scent, [he should] smell [him]self." This not only emphasizes their connection but also emphasizes the centrality of senses to understanding, merely substituting smell for sight. Then, in his final conversation with Graham, Lecter explains that Graham's killing of Hobbs felt good because killing feels good. This is "because God has power and if one does what God does enough times, one will become what God is." While Graham applies this statement to the investigation and to Dolarhyde's desire to be wanted and accepted by others, it is more likely that Lecter meant it to be a general comment regarding both God's and humans' nature. If one kills as much as God does, one will become a killer, like God. Lecter does emphasize, in both the novel and the film, that God will always be ahead in the body count. He could, however, also be justifying his own violent murders: Since God kills and he has made us in his image, why should we not also act on these impulses and be like God, eventually reaching his capacity for destruction? This idea of becoming like God is reminiscent of the "Application" part of Blake's "There Is No Natural Religion [b]": "He who sees the Infinite in all things sees God. He who sees the Ratio only sees himself only. Therefore God becomes as we are, that we may be as he is" (3). While Blake does not say that God is violent and therefore humans should be violent as well in order to become like God, this passage emphasizes the relationship between humans and God and that humans can become like God by acting, or — once again emphasizing the importance of senses — seeing, like God.

While Lecter recognizes this dual nature and pushes Graham to recognize it as well, and while Graham does retain his ability to understand those like Lecter and Dolarhyde, he, too, has become a simplified character. Graham still can understand and see from the perspective of evil. He tells his son, "I tried to build feelings in my imagination like the killer had, so I would know why he did what he did that would help me find him.... After my body got OK, I still had his thoughts going round in my head ... they're the ugliest thoughts in the world." It was this, retaining thoughts like Lecter's, and not killing Hobbs, as in the novel, that necessitated his time in a psychiatric ward. Graham's movements through the crime scene echo those of Dolarhyde and throughout the film he tries to figure out what the killer's dream is. He knows that seeing from another's perspective will lead him to understanding. He also realizes the necessity of asking Lecter for help, recognizing that evil can serve a purpose, and that understanding that which is frightening or foreign is sometimes necessary. On a more minor note, his own capability for violence is revealed in his reaction to Lounds when he throws him against a car and breaks the windshield. However, many other aspects from the novel that add to the theme of the blurring or mixing of good and evil have been left out, leading to a more straightforward police procedural film with Graham as the hero, the Manhunter.

Graham is clearly the focus of the film. Dolarhyde only appears an hour into the film, and, as discussed previously, the audience gets little insight into his motivations, emotions, or struggle. While Graham has to be persuaded to return to the FBI and help, once involved he takes charge. It is no longer Crawford's idea to use Lounds to get to Dolarhyde, it is Graham's. He volunteers himself as bait instead of having to be convinced to be bait. At the end of the film, he goes in alone to save Reba, and he, not Molly, kills Dolarhyde. While he feels anger toward Lounds and does throw him against a car in their first scene together, the intensity of his anger is downplayed and his implication in Lounds's murder is downplayed as well. In the novel, he puts his arm around Lounds for the photo, and later blames himself for Lounds's death, thinking that in that photo he had identified Lounds as his pet, to be killed first before himself and his family. In the film, however, it is Lounds who puts his arm around Graham. Simpson also addresses how Graham's hatred for Lounds and his implication in his death are not as pronounced in the film as in the novel. According to Simpson, "Michael Mann's film softens this crucial plot development to the point that much of its disturbing ambiguity is purposefully lost, probably in the commercial interests of making Graham a more sympathetic character for a mainstream audience" (*Psycho Paths* 215). He becomes the hero who unfortunately gets called in to work on these difficult cases because he can use his imagination to better understand the killers, and who survives and triumphs, keeping his family intact the entire time. While Molly is clearly scared and shaken by these events, as is Kevin, the son, their family is only in danger of being destroyed by Dolarhyde killing them, not by Graham's actions or any already existing difficulties. Emphasizing the strong intact family is the fact that Graham is Kevin's father, not stepfather, in the film. Molly and Kevin also were both with Graham during his earlier work on the Lecter case, although Kevin was too young to really remember. Graham in the film is no longer the man from the novel who often feels as if Molly and Willy are not his. His relationship to Willy is already precarious and becomes shakier when Molly and Willy go to live with Willy's paternal grandparents, returning to their earlier family. Although this represents a minor change in relationships, making Graham part of a solid stable and traditional family simplifies the themes and emphasizes his role as hero.

3. The Dragon and the Tyger

Another change that might be easily overlooked or considered minor, and yet reveals much about the different themes in the novel and the film, is that while in the novel Graham takes care of wild dogs, as discussed earlier, in the film he tries to protect newborn turtles. Instead of taking care of ugly and possibly vicious dogs that no one else wants, and that occasionally dig up turtle eggs, here Graham protects the innocent and vulnerable. The film begins with Graham and his son building a protective fence around the turtle eggs, as Graham explains that crabs and dogs would otherwise get the eggs. He promises Kevin that "they're all going to make it." At the end of the film, when Graham returns home, Molly asks him, "How many of them made it?" and Graham replies, "Most of them made it." The hero was able to protect the vulnerable turtles, as promised.

It is the ending of the film that is most changed and that causes the major shift in tone and theme. Given the nature of film, in which voiceovers can be clumsy, it is no surprise that Mann does not include Graham's thoughts on Shiloh; however, with this section left out and with the emphasis on Graham as hero, the film ends on a more optimistic note, emphasizing the triumph of good over evil. The film ends with Graham confronting and killing Dolarhyde and saving Reba from Dolarhyde's attack, as opposed to Molly confronting and shooting Dolarhyde in order to protect Graham, who then ends up alone in a hospital, knowing that Molly and Willy will be returning to Willy's grandparents. However, not only does Graham save Reba from Dolarhyde, but he also leads her from the house out into the dawn, literally a new day. O'Brien defends this change, stating, "A lot of Thomas Harris fans are critical of Mann's rewriting of the book's ending, yet *Manhunter*'s climactic night-time shootout is both visually—and aurally—spectacular and dramatically satisfying" (56). O'Brien also justifies this ending by claiming that "Mann gives Graham back the hero role denied him by Harris. Graham recovers to blow the 'sickfuck' Dollarhyde to hell" (57). By giving him a role he was denied in the novel, Mann alters the theme, making a hero out of a man who originally represented the struggle to acknowledge the coexistence of good and evil and accept the fact that there are no uncomplicated heroes. While O'Brien states that "Mann stresses that Graham finds the killing of Dollarhyde a painful act" (57), the only thing that Graham seems pained about is the actual physical pain he is in. He is in no psychological pain because, unlike the Graham of the novel, he doesn't believe that killing someone even if they are bad is one of the ugliest things in the world, as he tells

Willy in the novel regarding his reaction to killing Hobbs (127). At the end of the film Graham is clearly Graham, good FBI agent, protector, strong hero. At the end of the novel, while he also has uncovered some of his identity, he has done so only through uncovering the natural role of evil and the recognition that there are no "happy" endings.

Red Dragon— *Film*

Due to the success of *Silence of the Lambs*, and particularly the popularity of Anthony Hopkins's portrayal of Lecter, in 2002 Brett Ratner's version of Harris's *Red Dragon* was released. Much debate surrounds which is better, *Manhunter* or *Red Dragon*. This debate usually centers on who is the better Lecter: Brian Cox or Anthony Hopkins. However, regardless of whether one prefers *Manhunter* to *Red Dragon* as a film, clearly *Red Dragon* more faithfully reproduces the Blake connections and Harris's view of good and evil. While some of the same changes or deletions that *Manhunter* made are made in *Red Dragon* as well, most likely in the interest of simplifying plot or due to the nature of film versus novel, the film emphasizes and even adds Blake connections, along with an expanded role for Lecter, who embodies the coexistence of savage and civilized, evil and good, a man almost in balance.

The film retains Dolarhyde's obsession with Blake's Red Dragon (the version Harris described in the novel), as well as his tattoo of the dragon itself. The dragon also is seen on the first page of Dolarhyde's journal, on which, over a pencil sketch of the dragon, he has written "Behold a Great Red Dragon." Ratner even includes the scene of Dolarhyde devouring the painting. Dolarhyde's fascination with Blake is emphasized even more in the film portrayal of his trip to the Brooklyn Museum. In the novel he poses as a Butts scholar; in the film he is a Blake scholar. Apparently he has been posing as one for a while and carrying on an exchange with the woman at the museum. When they meet, she says that his dissertation should be almost finished and that it is good to finally connect a face to his name. While this change does emphasize his connection to Blake, it also makes his misreading of Blake, discussed previously, even more disturbing, since the film does seem to clearly connect Dolarhyde to Blake with no indication that Dolarhyde could be misreading him.

Not only is Dolarhyde's obsession with Blake's dragon clear, but the

3. The Dragon and the Tyger

film also emphasizes his connection to the tiger. Dolarhyde's scrapbook contains a photo of a tiger's face and eyes. While it is not Blake's tiger, it does briefly establish an existing connection to tigers that will be built on in the scenes with Reba and further emphasizes the connection with Blake and the idea that he who made the lamb also made the tiger and Dolarhyde, creatures of both innocence and experience. As in the novel, the connection between Dolarhyde and the tiger is emphasized in the scene where Reba "sees" the tiger by touching it. She feels its sleeping body, touches its testicles and experiences its power as it sleeps helplessly, growling in its sleep. Upon returning from the zoo, Reba touches Dolarhyde's lips in the same hesitant way she touched the tiger and then cups him, as she did the tiger, before proceeding to perform oral sex. Here not only is Dolarhyde equated with the tiger, but Reba is also sexually aggressive and Dolarhyde, while powerful, is vulnerable and shy.

Dolarhyde's complexity, his human qualities, and his struggle with his dual nature are also highlighted more in this film than they were in *Manhunter*. This is accomplished in part by revealing some of his childhood. When we first see Dolarhyde's home, about 40 minutes into the film, there is a voiceover of himself when young and his grandmother. This voiceover is of the scene in the novel where the young Dolarhyde wets his bed at night and the grandmother tells him he is disgusting and threatens to cut off his penis (194–95). The camera takes us through the house, in which we see paintings and pictures of Grandmother, as the voiceover plays, and the sequence ends as we see Dolarhyde lifting weights in the room where he has the print of the Red Dragon and the safe where he keeps his journal. Toward the end of the film, Graham reads Dolarhyde's journal, learning about this and other incidents with the grandmother, leading him to tell Molly, "When I read his journal it was sad ... so sad. I couldn't help feeling sorry for him. He wasn't born a monster, he was made one through years and years of abuse." Graham seems to disagree with Lecter that our natures are issued to us. He is also able to use this information to anger Dolarhyde, to make Dolarhyde vulnerable by recalling his painful childhood, and thus save his own son Josh during the later confrontation. This knowledge of Dolarhyde's childhood humanizes him and is given to the reader alone in the novel. In the novel, while Graham wants to know what created the Dragon, he is unable to and never reads the diary (324, 338). Therefore, in the novel, Graham never explicitly disagrees with Lecter regarding how our natures are given to us and not made.

Thomas Harris and William Blake

In addition to the information on his childhood, Dolarhyde is humanized by expanding the relationship with Reba and making his struggle with the dragon part of himself explicit. Instead of just one date, as in *Manhunter*, a relationship is established in the film, as is the rationale for taking Reba to "see" the tiger. Dolarhyde first meets Reba when picking up the IR film for, as he tells her, filming nocturnal animals. He sees her later at the bus stop and offers to drive her home. At her home, she invites him in for coffee and pie and asks about the zoo project. This leads to her saying, "One of my earliest memories is seeing a cougar." Since she saw the cougar when she was 5 and lost her sight at 7, she wonders if her memory is true to life or if it has faded too much. This both establishes a reason why Dolarhyde thinks Reba would want to visit the tiger and reveals a human, caring aspect of Dolarhyde in that he wishes for her to have this gift, this connection to her childhood and sight. The trip to the zoo is a later meeting/date between the two, extending the time that they know each other.

The morning after their night together, Dolarhyde's struggle with his dual nature becomes clear. Earlier, when he kidnapped Freddy, he spoke of himself and the Dragon as one, telling Freddy, "I am not a man. I began as one but each being that I change makes me more than one," and then "I am the Dragon." However, now he is clearly separate from the Dragon; he has gone through the same shift he did in the novel. When he wakes and sees that Reba is no longer in bed, he runs up to his weight room and sees the print of the Red Dragon. He then talks to the Dragon, clearly having a conversation with it, of which we only hear Dolarhyde's part: "No, no, I won't give her to you.... Please, just for a little while. No, you're hurting me." His struggle and pain is so strong at this point that he gets his gun and aims it at the print, saying, "No, she's nice; she's OK." He then places the gun in his mouth, intending to shoot himself. It is only when he sees the words "Brooklyn Museum" at the bottom of the print that he removes the gun, now having another idea about how to stop the Dragon. The film does change one aspect of the scene at the museum that further emphasizes Dolarhyde's struggle against the dragon part of himself. In the novel, he does not hesitate to kill any museum workers he encounters, while in the film, he attacks but does not kill the two women. When Crawford tells Graham about the incident, he asks two questions: "If that painting meant so much to him, why destroy it?" and "Why didn't he kill the two women at the museum? They both got a good look at him." Graham's

3. The Dragon and the Tyger

response, contradicting what he said earlier in the film about the killer not stopping, is "Maybe he is trying to stop." While in the novel Graham does recognize that because of Reba Dolarhyde was attempting to stop (319), Dolarhyde still kills the museum workers. His not killing them in the film indicates an attempt to not necessarily act on all of his violent urges or instincts.

Dolarhyde's attempt to stop also includes not wanting to hurt Reba. Even though he is enraged at seeing Reba and Ralph Mandy together and he kills Ralph, when he kidnaps Reba it is not to kill her, but instead, as in the novel, it is a way to save her and fake his own death in a fire. He is angry at her, thinking that she may have found something and told the FBI about it, but he is not angry enough to kill her and let the Dragon have her. Dolarhyde confronts Reba and reveals his struggle, saying, "Sit still or he'll hear us ... he's upstairs. He wants you, Reba. I thought he was gone but now he's back. I didn't want to give you to him. I did a thing for you today so he couldn't have you. I was wrong." As he pours gasoline for the fire he says, "No, no, you can't have her." Graham does not have to save Reba from Dolarhyde in the novel or in this film version because while he has a dragon aspect of himself, the human one would never hurt her.

While Dolarhyde's dual nature is revealed in the film, he is not capable of balancing both aspects of his nature, and fails ultimately in trying to reconcile them, in part through a misreading of Blake, as discussed previously regarding the novel. As in the novel and in *Manhunter*, the character who most embodies and gives voice to the Blakean theme of Harris's work is Lecter.

While Lecter's role is expanded in this film (most likely because of the audience's interest in Hopkins's Lecter), his characterization is not changed much, and this film, as did *Manhunter*, retains much of Lecter's dialogue with Graham, while adding scenes that further develop the theme and connection to Blake. For example, the additional opening scene of *Red Dragon* reveals from the outset Lecter's opinion regarding punishment, justice, and the necessity for what others call evil acts, as well as the evil, or at least evil thoughts and desires, hidden in most people. After the mistake-prone flutist from the symphony disappears and Lecter hosts a meal for the other members of the symphony board, one of the board members says, "Shall I confess something wicked? I can't help but feel the tiniest bit relieved." While not as vulgar as the conventioneers Graham shares an elevator with in the novel (who are missing in both film versions), the board member's statement and the silent assent of the others at the table indicate the underlying wickedness of all humanity. Lecter adds to the board members' complicity in the flutist's disappearance with the amuse bouche he prepares. One member asks what it is and Lecter tells her, "If I tell you, I'm afraid you won't even try it." This, connected with the later discussion with Graham that indicates that parts of victims' bodies are being kept and eaten, and a recipe for sweetbreads marked in Lecter's *Larousse Gastronomie*, implies that the amuse bouche is part of the flutist. Of course, the board members wouldn't eat it if they knew what it was, but they happily enjoy it and do not even wonder about it beyond that first question. The implication is that there is not an instinctual negative reaction to something like cannibalism. If one doesn't know what one is eating, one may enjoy it. If no category or label is introduced, it is not recognized as a vice or evil.

This added scene not only establishes this thematic idea of the savage aspect underlying humanity's civilized veneer but also reveals Graham's early interactions with Lecter as the two are working together to solve Lecter's own crimes, since in this film Lecter is a forensic psychologist. When Graham meets with Lecter after the dinner he says that he is "starting to be able to think like this one," revealing already Graham's ability and willingness to view events from a different perspective, which allows him to understand evil. It is Graham who realizes that body parts are not kept as souvenirs but are eaten, and, upon seeing the sweetbreads recipe, he makes the intuitive leap to knowing it is Lecter and is therefore able to fight back. Lecter in this scene tells Graham that he has "an artistic imagination," which allows him to assume the emotional point of view of other people. It is this imagination, the term that Crawford uses as well for Graham's ability, that connects Graham to Lecter and in turn connects the theme to Blake's ideas, as it is imagination in Blake that is important for seeing the reality of the world and expanding vision. This ability to access the point of view of others also connects to Blake's idea of perspectives: Graham can see the hell under every heaven.

As with *Manhunter*, *Red Dragon* retains Lecter's recognizing a similarity with Graham. The first conversation between the two regarding the Red Dragon killings is very similar to their conversation in the novel. In the film he tells Graham, "You caught me because we're very much alike. Without our imaginations we'd be like all those other poor dullards." It

3. The Dragon and the Tyger

is their imaginations, their insightful use of their senses and ability to change their perspectives, that make them similar. He also recognizes that while he and Graham are alike, what Graham is missing is the ability to embrace this imagination; he is too afraid. He tells Graham, "Fear is the price for our instrument but I can help you bear it." It is fear that ultimately keeps Graham from embracing his dual nature completely.

Lecter comments again on Graham's imagination and fear in their second conversation, which is original to the film. He says to Graham, "You sensed who I was back when I was committing what you call my crimes. So you were hurt not by a perception or a fault in your instincts but because you failed to act on them until it was too late." It is the denial or lack of response to what he senses, both in the meaning of what he perceives through his senses and in regard to his instinct, that hurts Graham. If he were to embrace his instincts and not be afraid of his imagination, he could be active instead of passive or reactive, and would be less likely to be hurt or damaged.

It is also in this second conversation that the added Blake reference appears. During the conversation, Lecter is chained and walking around a track. After Graham shows him the kanji and identifies it as the Red Dragon, Lecter says, "Red Dragon, correct. This boy begins to interest me." While he does not say why the boy interests him, it is in this conversation that Lecter points Graham in the direction of Blake, and so perhaps it is Dolarhyde's interest in Blake that intrigues him. Perhaps Lecter hopes to encounter someone else who has recognized the two states of the human soul. Lecter points Graham toward Blake by saying, with no introduction or commentary, "A Robin Red Breast in a Cage puts all Heaven in a Rage." Lecter knows that Graham will trace the quote to Blake, as it is from Blake's "Augeries of Innocence." As Graham hunts for the quote in the library, he is directed to Blake's paintings as well, and scans through a book of Blake prints, seeing *Ancient of Days*, *The Body of Abel found by Adam and Eve*, and *God Blessing the 7th Day* before stopping on *The Great Red Dragon and the Woman Clothed with the Sun*. Graham stops because the title connects to the kanji the killer carved. This additional scene and allusion not only create a fluid way for Graham to piece together the clues but also reveal Blake as a key to understanding perspective and evil. This scene also illustrates Lecter's knowledge of Blake and therefore connects their beliefs on good, evil, and the nature of God. However, in addition to providing Graham with a clue, Lecter could also be using Blake to comment on himself. Given that Lecter quotes from "Augeries of Innocence" while he himself is chained, is in a cage, he could be suggesting that he, like a robin, is a creation of nature and should be allowed to be free to follow the nature given to him, instead of being chained.

Lecter does not, in any of their conversations, state that "our natures are issued to us" but does in the quote about the "Robin Red Breast" imply that one should not chain one's nature. Other points Lecter makes about the nature of God are retained, though. In their third conversation Lecter congratulates Graham on "disposing of the annoying Mr. Lounds," implicating Graham in Lounds's death and asking him if he enjoyed it, his "first murder." The discussion in the novel of how it felt to kill Hobbs is here transferred to the killing of Lounds. Lecter tells Graham that of course he had to have enjoyed it because it feels good and killing feels good to God as well. He then provides the example of the church roof collapse and states that God "wouldn't begrudge you one journalist." While Lecter does not say that killing makes one like God (as he does in *Manhunter*), early in the film at the briefing in Atlanta, Graham tells the police that Dolarhyde won't stop killing "because it makes him God." Graham may mean not just that, like God, Dolarhyde has power over the life and death of others, but also that, just as killing feels good to Dolarhyde, it feels good to God too.

Ratner retains Harris's emphasis on the complexity of God and the difficulty of teasing out good from evil. In addition, he retains Harris's characterization of Chilton, which, as discussed previously, can be read as a negative example of the law, revealing its weaknesses and hypocrisy. When Graham first goes to see Lecter, Chilton prods him, saying that he wants some insights on Lecter because he wants to publish them. It becomes clear that he does not want to publish them for the good of psychiatry but for his own ego, as his emotions are revealed when Lecter mentions Chilton's rejection letter — his "latest rejection." As in the novel, Lecter comments on Chilton's attempts to analyze people, commenting, as in the novel, on Chilton's fumbling for insight. Chilton's foolishness is also emphasized in a brief reaction from the orderlies. When Lecter eats his fine meal, part of a deal with Graham, he knows Chilton is watching and raises his glass in a toast. Chilton is visibly disturbed and walks away, while the orderlies, including Barney (who appears in the other Lecter films), chuckle, seeming to enjoy his discomfort.

Part of Chilton's foolishness stems from the idea that he should be

3. The Dragon and the Tyger

able to categorize Lecter. Graham, for all of his insights into Lecter, and even though he calls him insane, doesn't attempt to pigeonhole Lecter or explain him. He knows that Lecter cannot be easily labeled. Graham, too, while triumphing in the end and reuniting with his family, is not a simplistic hero. He has to be coaxed into working on the case and is quite willing to return home after the briefing in Atlanta, leaving the police and FBI to finish the job. It is Crawford who convinces him to stay on the case and see Lecter, and Crawford who has the idea to make use of Lounds and use Graham as bait; Graham does not heroically volunteer. Graham is also more implicated in Lounds's death in this film than the earlier one, and he is not the hero who saves the day at the end. While he does get Dolarhyde to release his son Josh, it is Molly who kills Dolarhyde, as in the novel. While there are no turtles that he has protected, there are no wild dogs he has taken in either.

Graham does admit the complexities of the world and human nature. He recognizes to some extent that Dolarhyde is not a monster and that he has some goodness and vulnerability in him. As he does in the novel, he believes in the film that Reba "didn't draw a freak" but instead "drew a man with a freak on his back" (319). Just like the Dragon is part bestial and part human, Dolarhyde is part freak and part human. Graham, unlike Lecter, however, still does not fully accept the idea of evil being a part of our nature. As commented on previously, he says of Dolarhyde, "He wasn't born a monster, he was made one through years and years of abuse." The leaving off of the Shiloh scene also adds to the idea that monsters are made, not born. The film's final scene leaves Graham recovered and not damaged. Instead of in a hospital bed knowing that his wife will take her son and return to live with her deceased husband's parents, this Graham is on a sailboat with his wife and his son, a complete stable family unit. Has he learned to live with the fear that accompanies his imagination? Will he act on instinct next time?

Importantly, in this new ending, while we see Graham and his family, we hear Lecter, who has written to Graham. He implies that perhaps Graham is damaged internally, and comments on his physical damage as well, telling him, "Scars have the power to remind us the past was real." Perhaps these scars, then, operate like the virus referenced in the Shiloh passage, protecting us from the future. The letter then continues, sounding much like Lecter's final letter in the novel to Will in the hospital (335): "We live in a primitive time ... neither savage nor wise." However, even though he claims that humanity has a dual nature, he implies that it has not yet learned how to deal with this double aspect of itself, claiming that "half measures are the curse of it." Like Graham, society has instincts but, instead of acting upon them, waits and is injured. Surprisingly, Lecter says, "Any rational society would either kill me or put me to good use." In the novel, too, he complains of half measures, but suggests, not that he be put to good use, but that he be given his books (335). It is hypocritical of society to claim he is savage, an animal, and yet not put him down. In addition, it is ridiculous that society admits his insight and intelligence and yet does not make use of it and learn from him (except in extreme cases). One thing they could learn from him, one way he could be put to good use, is in revealing the complexity of life and the intertwined nature of good and evil. While Graham doesn't yet admit or recognize the necessity of evil or pain, the power of corrosion to lead to vision, or the coexistence of the savage and civilized, Lecter does, and in the film he has the last word.

Chapter 4

Typhoid and Swans
Silence of the Lambs

Although Harris includes no explicit references to Blake in *Silence of the Lambs*, the novel continues the exploration of the nature and relationship of good and evil, emphasizing the coexistence of the two, the dual nature of God, and the dual nature of humanity. The novel likewise highlights the necessity of understanding evil, as well as recognizing and accepting that all humans are capable of evil. Heightened senses and an imagination able and willing to see from another's perspective are central to this understanding. The novel also reveals how violent or evil, corrosive, experiences can lead to insight and understanding. In *Red Dragon*, Graham and Lecter, while not exhibiting the explicit connection to Blake that Dolarhyde did, reveal Harris building upon Blake's idea of contraries, particularly the contraries of good and evil. In *Silence*, Graham is replaced by Clarice Starling. Starling differs from Graham in being more willing to accept the dual nature of humanity and her own relationship to evil.

As discussed previously, Graham fights against this recognition of dual nature, particularly his own capacity for evil or violence, and his resistance leads to his being damaged. While at the end of *Red Dragon* Graham is alone, with Molly and Willy presumably leaving him, and he is physically hurt and reflecting on lessons of Shiloh, a reader could always presume that Graham could recover. However, references to Graham in *Silence* make it clear that he has been irredeemably damaged by his experiences. Starling is warned not to let Lecter know much about her and Graham is given as an example of that danger: not only did Lecter gut Graham but he also pointed Dolarhyde to Graham so that now "Will's face looks like a damn Picasso drew him, thanks to Lecter" (6). Graham's damage goes beyond the physical, though, as he is also described as being an alcoholic (67). Graham is shown drinking in *Red Dragon* but not to the extent that he is a drunk; now, due to his experiences, he drinks to excess, perhaps to attempt to forget the revelations of the truth of not only human nature but also his own nature.

Starling will not end up like Graham, even though she does let Lecter know about herself, because she is more willing to accept the necessary coexistence and balance of contraries, like good and evil, even within herself. When Lecter asks her how she manages her rage (155), Starling does not deny that she has rage. She seems less likely than Graham or even Crawford to attempt to characterize and label in an attempt to control, in part because she recognizes the difficulty of simple categorization. Perhaps her ability to be more accepting or perceptive of this dual nature and the futility of categorization stems from her being female and of a lower class than those she has gone to school with and now works with. She therefore defies some traditional classifications herself and is and has been an outsider in several situations, compelling her to observe instead of participate. This observation has helped to hone her powers of perception (a similarity to both Graham and Lecter that will be further discussed later), and allowed her to witness the dangers of simplistic categorization, as well as the duality of human nature (particularly in men's treatment of women) where others have not or do not see it. For example, when first told about the questionnaire and the paperwork, Starling is wary of possibly being categorized in a way that will limit her future; she does not want to be labeled and thought of as only a secretary (3). Her knowledge of men's savage or denigrating treatment of women extends from the subtle, and possibly subconscious, statements of Chilton, who calls her Miss instead of Agent or Officer (as Lecter calls her when he doesn't call her Clarice) and asks her where all the "office girls" are (9), to the vulgar statement and action of Miggs, who says he can "smell [her] cunt" (12) and flings semen on her (22). While Miggs's actions are outrageous, Starling compares walking past him to walking past other men in her daily life (22), and the mentality behind his actions is not far removed from the discussion of the conventioneers that Graham overhears in the elevator in *Red Dragon*. In addition, her being female ties this novel further into Blake's ideas by now also adding the supposed binary of female and male to the already existent one of good and evil.

While there is no explicit allusion to Blake in this novel, it is possible to read Starling and Lecter together as halves of a whole, of a Blakean persona made of Self and Emanation, in which Starling is Lecter's Emanation.

4. Typhoid and Swans

The Emanation at first refuses reintegration into one being with two aspects and wishes to retain an individual will and be together with the Self while remaining separate, but eventually (in Starling's case, over the course of two novels and culminating in *Hannibal*) submits to reintegration and acceptance of the coexistence of contrary traits and natures. In *Silence*, Starling has not yet fully recognized and accepted the necessity of coexistence, as she is just beginning to understand contraries and balance; however, her growth is revealed throughout.

Part of her progress comes from witnessing the hypocrisy and vulgarity of characters symbolic of the law, which tarnishes her view of it and allows her to step out of seeing simple binaries and instead see the messiness and complexity of life. Much of this tarnished view comes through her interactions with Chilton and his contrast to Lecter, particularly in how the two treat her. While speaking more specifically of the film, Tasker's observation applies to the novel as well: Lecter's "intelligence and vision serve to underscore Chilton's fatally limited insight. Moreover, Lecter's insistence on courtesy — appealing at a distance, whatever his proclivities — contrasts with Chilton's clumsy attempts to hit on Starling" (83–84). Tasker's use of "vision" and "insight" in describing the difference between the two highlights that the difference in their styles, manners, and tastes may not be just elitism but instead surface markers of their vision and imagination. It is Lecter's expanded and perceptive vision that draws him to Starling and she to him, while it is Chilton's limited vision, his "mind-forg'd manacles," that blind or limit his vision, which pushes Starling away. Chilton's character and clashes with Lecter in this novel are the same as they were in *Red Dragon* but are now expanded. Like in the previous novel, Chilton clumsily attempts to control all information about Lecter and to publish about him, while Lecter and others see through his attempts and counter them. He not only treats Starling dismissively (calling her Miss and assuming she was asked to help just because she is an attractive female), but he also exhibits, as Tasker calls it, "limited insight" (83). Instead of focusing on helping the FBI, he focuses on helping himself. Crawford is aware of Chilton's focus on himself and warns Starling that they cannot trust him to work in their best interests (121). Crawford is proven correct when Chilton secretly tapes Starling's discussion with Lecter so that he can reveal to Lecter the FBI's lies and make a deal with Lecter himself, ensuring that he, not Lecter, will be the one who publishes on Catherine Martin being taken by Buffalo Bill. This action leads, in turn, to the investigation being hindered and to Starling realizing that in one night Chilton has completely ruined her investigation (173). Starling is angry not just that Chilton is working against the FBI's interests and her work, but also because she is concerned for Catherine Martin and blames Chilton for any harm that will come to her, thinking, addressing him, "*You've killed her, Dr. Chilton*" (original emphasis, 173). His hindering of Starling's and the FBI's investigation may well lead to a murder, an interesting connection to Blake's idea that murder is hindering another (discussed earlier). Chilton wants to be in control and have the focus on himself, regardless of any damage it may do to the hunt for a serial killer or the attempt to save a victim. He only sees what is advantageous for himself. He cannot imagine the ramifications on others of his actions. Chilton sells the tapes to the *Tatler* for his own monetary gain. He also arranges for the meeting between Senator Martin and Lecter to be filmed, so that he can get some media attention. He "remove[s] the mask [over Lecter's face] with a flourish," further damaging the search for Catherine Martin since his "showmanship frightened Senator Martin as much as anything" that may have happened to her daughter and erodes her confidence in him, leading her to "fear that he was a fool" (183). Chilton's vision is focused narrowly on his own struggle for domination over Lecter, and his own ego and wallet. He serves to reveal to Starling the dangers of limited vision (that it endangers others as well as oneself) and to be a foil to Lecter, revealing how the law and its agents are not necessarily superior to those who operate outside of the law, and how law and justice are not equivalent.

In addition to Chilton, Paul Krendler also serves as a warning to Starling about the law. Krendler will be a major figure in the next novel, *Hannibal*, but only appears briefly here. However, in this brief appearance he serves to reveal the pettiness of the law enforcement system and to convince Starling that sometimes working outside of the system is better than working within it. Krendler orders Starling to return to Quantico and leave the investigation, characterizing her as a child and warning her that she'll be nothing more than a secretary — the very thing she feared upon being given this assignment (200). After Krendler leaves, however, Starling realizes that being a part of the institution of the law, having the label of "Special Agent," is not worth ignoring her instincts and imagination and living in a limited hypocritical world (201). She also realizes that if she listens to Krendler now, he will have her forever labeled and she will always

4. Typhoid and Swans

have to listen to him. More disturbingly, she wonders if, regardless of her actions, he has already labeled her in his mind and she will have to be wary of him (267). It is her fear of the simplicity of labels, and her recognition of the difficulty of escaping others' labels and categorization, that leads her to her decision to escape those labels now. She is particularly aware of the rigidity of labels imposed by those above her, and the possible far-reaching negative consequences, not only for her but also for others, of being labeled, and therefore she decides to create her own path. Starling goes on to jeopardize her work with the FBI by working on the investigation instead of staying in her dorm and studying, seeing beyond what would best serve her own interests (unlike Chilton in this novel and Krendler in *Hannibal*) to what will help others (specifically, Catherine Martin), and realizing that working within the bounds of law is not always the best way to achieve results.

It is Lecter, clearly operating outside the bounds of law, who not only helps Starling grow into accepting the coexistence of contraries and the duality of all natures, including hers, but also best embodies this coexistence of good and evil and difficulty of categorization. Most obviously, Lecter is the killer who works to capture another killer, thereby revealing that he is willing to acknowledge a good side to himself, even if not for completely altruistic reasons. Tasker claims that "the twist in *The Silence of the Lambs* is to conflate the twin figures of reason and of unreason more completely, so that Lecter is both perverse profiler and psychopath" (76). While Tasker discusses Lecter as a conflation of reason and unreason, one can also read him as a conflation of good and evil.

Lecter also does not look for an explanation of his evil but recognizes it as a part of himself. In his first meeting with Starling she wants to know about what happened to him to make him a killer. He says, "Nothing happened to me ... *I* happened. You can't reduce me to a set of influences. You've given up good and evil for behaviorism" (original emphasis, 19). This statement is an echo of his statement to Graham that our natures are issued to us with our organs. When Lecter asks Starling if she could label him evil, she says he is destructive and those are equivalent (19). This leads Lecter, in a moment reminiscent of his telling Graham in *Red Dragon* that killing feels good to God and providing church roof collapses as an example, to discuss his own understanding of destruction, particularly "Acts of God": "I collect church collapses, recreationally. Did you see the recent one in Sicily? Marvelous! The facade fell on sixty-five grandmothers at a special Mass. Was that evil? If so, who did it? If He's up there, He just loves it.... Typhoid and swans—it all comes from the same place" (19). As Simpson says, "Lecter doesn't cite Blake here, but he nevertheless raises the same theological question Blake does" (*Making Murder* 198). Here Lecter essentially asks, "Did he who made the lamb make thee?" and responds with an emphatic "Yes!" Simpson also sees this scene as the central metaphysical scene: "Lecter here attempts to shift Starling's focus away from inherited modes of discourse ... and onto a reckoning with the cultural question of evil and its resistance to definition. Lecter ... forces her to confront the issue of teleology itself" (*Psycho Paths* 94). Simpson is one of the few who reads Lecter's role, in part, as leading other characters (Graham and Starling, in particular) to an understanding of the complex nature of evil and the difficulty of categorizing or defining it when it exists as an aspect of all things, including all humans.

Lecter, as he does with Graham, notices in Starling a person of similar capabilities and perhaps capacity for evil or violence. He notices an undercurrent in her and asks how she manages her rage (155). He notices in her not only a complexity but also the possibility that she, unlike Graham, will be able to recognize and accept her similarity to Lecter himself and admit her own shadow side. Perhaps it is this similarity and this hope of recognition that makes him want to help her by giving Jame Gumb to her (157). From their conversations it becomes clear that Starling, like Lecter, is wary of simplistic categorization. When discussing the papers published by Behavioral Science, Lecter asks Starling for her opinion regarding their attempt to categorize serial killers as either organized or disorganized. She hesitates, looking for a word, and says, "It's ... fundamental." Lecter responds by saying, "*Simplistic* is the word you want" (original emphasis, 17). While Starling does not come right out and critique the categories, her search for a word to describe her opinion implies that she, too, believes the binary categories are simplistic. She understands that human nature in particular cannot be easily labeled, given that humans are complex and contain the possibility of multiple and contradictory actions and emotions.

Lecter's recognition of this capability within her, the possibility of her understanding not only him but also the nature of humanity and of good and evil itself in all things, leads to a deepening of their relationship and his respect for her. They treat each other politely and respectfully during all of their conversations, and without realizing it, Starling begins to

4. Typhoid and Swans

learn from Lecter. In their second meeting Lecter asks her if she has "memories or tableaux ... [t]hings from your early life" (55) that help her at difficult times. Starling says she doesn't but that she will now be more attentive to see if she has anything she hasn't been aware of. She begins to draw upon and be aware of these memories during the investigation, thinking of her mother at the sink to help her at the West Virginia funeral home, for example. She doesn't brood on the past but draws upon it and her connection with other people in order to face and complete difficult tasks, and in order to focus her perception on the task at hand. She begins to trust Lecter, more than Crawford does, perhaps because she understands him more than Crawford does. While Crawford and others say that Lecter is just playing with the case and doesn't really care about catching Buffalo Bill, Starling begins to see that he does care, even if it is only to help her. One of the clearest revelations of this is after she has retrieved the file from him in Tennessee. On the map Lecter has written a note suggesting that the sites are "*desperately* random" (original emphasis, 269). In thinking about this note, the only one in the file, Starling wonders why he would have bothered looking at the map and commenting on it if he were just playfully reading the case (271). She is correct; if reading just for fun, he would not leave a clue on how to proceed with the investigation. She trusts him, even though no one else does. Since Lecter has been told by Chilton that they have lied to him, all but Starling would expect he would not wish to help now. In addition to understanding that Lecter is truly helping her, Starling comes to realize, even against Crawford's warnings to the contrary, that she is safe from Lecter even though he has escaped. They have a connection, a shared vision of the world to some extent. Starling understands how Lecter views the world and that he'd believe it would be "rude" to come after her after they have established this relationship, and that as long as she is interesting to him and complex, willing to answer his questions and sincerely engage with him, she will be safe (328). He will never harm her (as he says in his letter to her, he has "no plans to call on" her [337]) and she, recognizing his complexity, knows this to be true.

He will not harm her in part because of her desire to expand beyond the labels others have placed on her and because she wishes to increase her vision and sensory abilities and experiences. This desire for expansion of experience is exemplified in part through what may appear to be a superficial desire to grow beyond her class and previous style. Her interest in style connects her to Lecter, perhaps in an elitist way, but this connection also reveals her attention to detail, her ability to see and experience things more closely than others, just as Lecter does. While Graham's power of perception was greater than that of others, Starling's seems to be not only greater than that of other agents but also closer to that of Lecter in what types of details she pays attention to. Starling's attention to detail, as it relates to style, is revealed early in the novel when Starling connects Crawford's cleverness to the color and texture of his clothing (2). Starling's attention to and interpretation of detail, revealing her use of imagination, is also apparent when she goes to investigate Catherine Martin's home and the spelling of the complex's name, "Stonehinge Villas," bothers her; she imagines "white wicker and peach shag. Snapshots under the glass of the coffee table. The *Dinner for Two Cookbook* and *Fondue on the Menu*" (190). While seeming petty, this criticism also indicates Starling's attention to detail and belief in the importance of detail. The inclusion of the cookbooks in particular further connects her to Lecter in what she sees or imagines. Details can label and define one, so if one wants to break out of a particular label, details can help make the change. Lecter comments on Starling's attempt to break out of a class label with her "good bag and ... cheap shoes" (20), proceeding to comment on how she must have a necklace of gold add-a-beads that she now thinks is tacky. He suggests to her that she "[g]et some loose drilled tiger's eyes" to add to the necklace because "[t]he tiger's eyes will pick up the color of [her] own eyes and the highlights in [her] hair" (21). Not only is Lecter commenting on her desire to grow and change, but he also connects her to a tiger, perhaps Blake's tiger, both powerful and vulnerable.

While *Red Dragon* contains an explicit reference to a tiger who embodies both good and evil, vulnerability and power, and there is this brief reference to a tiger here, *Silence of the Lambs* obviously contains a direct reference to lambs. The lambs in this novel are used traditionally — as a symbol of innocence. Starling woke to hear "the lambs screaming" when she was young (211), and since she couldn't save them she left with her horse Hannah in order to protect at least one creature. She now wishes to save Jame Gumb's victims. Lecter asks her if she thinks that catching Buffalo Bill and saving Catherine Martin will make the lambs stop screaming (211), and while she says she doesn't know, she does begin to feel a silence when she goes on the hunt (282) and by the end of the novel "she sleeps deeply, sweetly, in the silence of the lambs" (338). Interestingly, something as innocent as lambs introduces Starling to evil, in her encounter with Lecter. Without the desire to preserve the good, she has no need to encounter evil. For her, evil does operate as the vaccine that Will Graham speculated it was; it helps to end further evil. In addition, interest in helping the lambs leads to an encounter with a tiger (Lecter) and the eventual realization that he who made the lamb also made the tiger.

While the lamb remains essentially an image of innocence, the death's-head moths raised and used by Gumb reveal a duality in much the same way that Blake's tiger does. When Starling visits the Smithsonian and sees a death's-head moth it is described as being both "wonderful and terrible" (239). Its design is exquisite and yet strikes fear in those who see it. Blake's tiger inspires a similar awe. The moth also resembles Lecter, with his elegant sophistication and frightening power. The moth is nature's reminder of the coexistence of the savage and the civilized, the beautiful and the destructive. If nature contains this duality, it should not be a surprise that humans do as well, and it is those humans who are willing to see the complexity of nature — in fact, to some extent it is those who are willing to just pay any close attention to nature — who come closest to recognizing this complexity in humanity as well. While Gumb uses the moths and seems to be intrigued by them, his is not a recognition of their dual nature, of both their beauty and their ability for destruction. Instead, for Gumb the moths are more simply a symbol of change and transformation, moving from one form to another as he would like to do. He is similar to Dolarhyde, who saw himself as either Francis or the Dragon. Gumb sees an ugly, perhaps destructive caterpillar and then a beautiful moth, not a creature who is both at once, containing the possibility of moth in its early form and remnants of caterpillar in its later form. Gumb focuses on the change from one to the other, the differences between the two, instead of their connection and similarities. While he is associated with nature, he does not recognize its complexity. Lecter and (eventually) Starling do see this complexity of nature. Interestingly, Starling tells Lecter that he is destructive and that is the same thing as evil, and she describes moths as destructive as well (96), but she is corrected by Pilcher, who points out that, like humans, they all live in different ways, some destructive, some not, and that "more than one ... lives only on tears" (96), suggesting a compassion for others that may be disguised or unnoticed at first.

It is Starling's ability to see the details, and to acknowledge how something may be both "wonderful and terrible" at the same time, that allows her to accept the coexistence of seeming contraries and understand the nature of evil. As Tasker says, "Catching the killer lies in understanding. Starling has to learn about vision to see and understand the smallest signs" (52). Not only does Starling have compassion for others (for example, the lambs and Catherine Martin) based on her ability to see or understand from their perspectives, but she also is eventually able to both have compassion for Lecter and recognize his own capability for compassion. Once again, it is vision that is important to attaining this knowledge — the same vision that Blake emphasizes throughout his works, a vision that is expanded and leads to understanding. As Starling comes to see and understand, she also becomes accepting of (acknowledging, if not embracing) her own dual nature. While not explicitly discussing the duality of good and evil, Magistrale addresses a similar idea when he claims that Starling alone is able to integrate the opposing masculine and feminine aspects of herself, and this is implicitly tied into her understanding of her "personal devil," "her shadow" (37). Lecter is the one who places her in contact with this shadow; he forces her to deal with human nature, with pain, and with himself. Furthermore, "Contact with the shadow instructs her in how to integrate the positive characteristic with the negative" (Magistrale 37–38). Without saying so, Magistrale here comments on how Starling alone has realized how to integrate the good and evil, to keep them in balance through acknowledging the shadow side. Without making a connection to Blake, Magistrale states, "Starling discovers the positive side of what the shadow proffers and integrates into her personality" (38). While in Blake's works the shadow or self-hood is annihilated, the Emanation and the Self are reintegrated. Starling, like the Emanation or Self, recognizes aspects of herself that seem opposite to who she has been and, instead of suppressing them or ignoring them, she accepts them, even if they are frightening. The acceptance of the contrary leads to a fuller understanding of Self. Starling is unlike Blake's Thel, who runs from the world of experience and never grows. When Thel looks into her grave and hears of the sorrow of the Generative world she flees, returning to her Eternal and yet stagnant world. One must embrace what at first looks like death in order to enter the world of experience and grow into a fully integrated person. Starling's perspective and attention to detail allow her to see that "the grave" is a part of, not an end to, life. Her contact with the world of experience has corroded her "mind-forg'd manacles," providing her with expanded vision. She therefore enters into this dark and frightening world,

4. Typhoid and Swans

and experience and knowledge allow her to grow and remain undamaged, unlike Graham, who entered but resisted.

Starling is not the only one, though, who can grow and remain undamaged while encountering evil. Barney also not only survives his encounter with Lecter but also grows, as will be seen in the next novel, *Hannibal*. Barney is able to do this through being willing to understand Lecter and treat him as a human being instead of a case study or a monster. While treating him as a human being, Barney also never underestimates Lecter, as he understands and acknowledges the violent and evil aspect of him. Both Barney and Starling understand Lecter better than the trained psychiatrists do and recognize his capability for kindness. When Lecter wishes to see Starling's credentials, Barney doesn't just say no or angrily threaten, but agrees while reminding Lecter that if her FBI identification is not returned when he asks for it, he will be upset and there will need to be punishment. Because he places the direction and threat in the context of the relationship they have, Lecter agrees (15). The two speak politely to each other and respect each other. When Chilton tells Lecter that the Tennessee state police will be taking custody of him, Lecter thinks, "*Police are not as wise as Barney*" (original emphasis, 163). When saying goodbye, Lecter thanks Barney for being "decent to [him] for a long time" (171). Barney warns Chilton that the police need to "treat [Lecter] all right" (171) and lets Starling know he is concerned as well, knowing that if Lecter is not treated well, is not respected, he will act out in violence. Chilton dismisses his concerns and the Tennessee state police are not careful with Lecter, allowing him to escape.

Lecter's escape adds to the complexity of the ending of the novel. While Buffalo Bill has been killed and Catherine Martin is freed, and while Starling is sleeping peacefully, Lecter is at large. One of the last scenes in the novel is of Lecter sending a thank-you note and tip to Barney and then a letter to Starling. While Barney was working for Lecter's captors and worked to keep Lecter contained and under control, Lecter respects Barney for the respect shown to him; Barney made an attempt to understand Lecter and view him as a complex human being instead of as a label, an example of a mental illness, or Satan. Lecter recognizes in Barney the ability to see the complexity in the world and admires his desire to move beyond his current station in life, as we will see in *Hannibal* when Barney speaks of how Lecter encouraged him in his studies. He therefore thanks Barney for seeing more than just a prisoner in him, and provides a tip, perhaps knowing how poorly Barney is understood and compensated by others. Lecter does not indicate any further correspondence with Barney; however, he wishes to maintain a correspondence with Starling, having recognized her ability to move beyond labels and rules, her recognition of the complexity and duality of both his nature and the world's, and perhaps her willingness to fully accept her own dual nature, with his encouragement. Lecter ends the note by talking about how he can see Orion outside his windows. He then adds, "But I expect you can see it too. Some of our stars are the same" (337). This connection between them reveals that, even if they appear to be opposites, they share a commonality. They are Blakean contraries. This moment underscores their relationship, which will be emphasized, to the chagrin of some readers, in *Hannibal*.

Silence of the Lambs— *Film*

In 1991 Jonathan Demme's film version of *Silence of the Lambs* was released. The film was both a critical and commercial success, sweeping the major Oscar awards and sparking interest in Harris's novels. The film has also been the focus of most of the critical discussions of Harris's work. Many of these works attempt to categorize the film or to explain how a work of horror became so popular and acclaimed. Skal, for example, while emphasizing Lecter's similarity to earlier film monsters, also points out the clear and frightening distinction here, which is that "the monster, this time, looked very much like us" (382). Wells explores a similar reading, categorizing *Silence* as an "adult drama" or "erotic thriller," containing "variations of the sociopath as monster, existing within established parameters of human interaction" (100). Wells explains that these types of films "imply that any man or woman, dependent upon the lives they lead, the needs they have, and the stress they experience, can become capable of anti-social and brutal acts" (100). It is important to note that Wells does not say that experience makes a monster, but instead that it makes one "capable" of being a monster; it is this choice that is stressed in Harris's novels and will be discussed at greater length in later chapters. Both Skal and Wells identify an aspect of what Harris takes from Blake (without explicitly referencing Blake): that good and evil are not binaries and cannot be easily classified as "other."

4. Typhoid and Swans

However, the film, while at times blurring the lines between the binaries, does not emphasize this blurring or the dual nature of God as much as the novel does. As Tasker points out, "the film aims to be a faithful adaptation.... There are plenty of minor differences between novel and film. But the key difference is one of tone" (19). Explaining further, she says, "Harris's vision is bleak, at times undercutting Starling's heroism. By contrast, Demme's film enacts a heroic quest narrative in which the heroine's motivation is clear and direct" (21). Because the film more clearly draws a line between good and evil, the tone of the work shifts. This shift, this emphasis on the opposition of and struggle between good and evil, comes in part from the structure of the medium itself. Films have a more difficult time revealing characters' inner thoughts than novels do and, in addition, because of time constraints conversations must often be shortened. In the novels, Harris can reveal to readers more of the characters' thoughts, which may reveal further their complexity, their "stepping over the lines" of good and evil. For example, in *Silence* Harris can emphasize how Lecter is not just amusing himself by helping with the investigation, but does actually want to help by including the comment, quoted earlier, regarding why, if he was just reading for entertainment, Lecter bothered to comment on the "random" locations on the map. In addition, in the novel, Harris includes scenes of Lecter contemplating how he would like to help Starling, while in the film, we only get what Lecter articulates to other characters. As Tasker explains, "The film ... explicitly offers Starling's point of view, aligning the audience with her *heroic quest*" (emphasis added, 21). The necessary cutting down of conversations also leads to not only a strengthening of the heroic identification with Starling but also a dampening of the burgeoning relationship between Lecter and Starling and of discussions of evil and nature/God.

The biggest change, though subtle, that aligns Starling securely in the heroic law enforcement camp in the film is that she is never removed from the case or threatened with failing to complete her studies and graduate. In the novel, as discussed earlier, Starling wonders if being an agent is worth all of the difficulties; she particularly wonders if she will have to deal with or watch out for people like Krendler for the rest of her career. When told to go home, she retains her ID and goes unauthorized to speak to Lecter in his cell in Tennessee before being kicked out by Chilton. She eventually decides that being an agent is not worth it and leaves school to continue the investigation on her own, willing to deal with whatever consequences befall her, even if that means she cannot re-enter the Academy. She decides that if she needs to work outside of the law to make the lambs stop screaming, she will. However, in the film, while Chilton does remove her from the Tennessee cell, that is not because she is no longer working for the FBI on the Buffalo Bill case. There is never a scene that indicates her wondering about her future or reveals a superior removing her or warning her. Starling never steps outside of the law on purpose, except when lying about Senator Martin's deal. While she does want the lambs to stop screaming, her other goal in the film is personal job advancement, aligning her with, instead of distinguishing her from, Chilton and Krendler, who also desire career advancement. This is a subtle change but in the truncated first discussion with Lecter, he does not say he will give her a valentine when he provides the information that leads to the finding of Raspail's head. Instead, Lecter says that he will give her what she wants most: "advancement." Starling is much more concerned with staying inside the boundaries here and seems to have a more narrow vision. While her vision/insight is good, good enough to catch Buffalo Bill, it is also narrowly focused. While she does want to save Catherine Martin, it is in part because she wants personal advancement. Her vision is narrow in another way as well — in the lack of discussion of her taste. Not only does this indicate a more limited vision, it also lessens her connection to Lecter. While Lecter comments on her good bag and bad shoes, he doesn't mention how she now finds the add-a-beads tacky. There are also no indications that she is afraid that Senator Martin sees a tackiness in her and is right. There are also no judgments of taste regarding Catherine Martin's home. The omission of the add-a-bead discussion additionally negates any connection between Starling and tigers, as established in their discussion of the beads in the novel.

In general, the shortened conversations between Lecter and Starling, coupled with the lack of insight into characters' thoughts, and the playful way Anthony Hopkins plays the conversation scenes, make the relationship between Lecter and Starling not as solid or deep as in the novel. This lack of depth is also revealed in the fact that Starling's leaning on memories from her childhood to anchor her in difficult situations does not seem to come from a suggestion by Lecter. Instead, the memories of her father come unbidden and, instead of anchoring her, seem to come at vulnerable times and mirror previous vulnerable times. Lecter's comments to her are limited to his playing with her and his comments on her past and her class

4. Typhoid and Swans

status. She and Lecter do not discuss how the Behavioral Science categories are simplistic, nor do they discuss simplistic diagnoses of mental illness. Lecter also does not ask her how she handles her rage.

Starling's outsider status as both female and lower class are referenced but not to the same extent in the film as in the novel. While the scene with Starling telling Crawford that it does matter how he treats her because the police look to him for guidance is retained, other scenes, like her concern that she will get pegged as a secretary and Chilton wondering about "office girls," are cut. In addition, her thought about how walking past Miggs is no different than walking past other groups of men is cut. With these details gone, the emphasis on Starling's ability to see past and fight against labels and categories is lost, as is the important connection between Miggs's vulgar and violent actions and those of average men Starling encounters every day, thereby erasing the idea that evil thoughts reside in all humans.

Not only are Starling's character and relationship with Lecter simplified, so are Barney's. In the novel, the fact that Barney also understands Lecter and can have a respectful relationship with him indicates that anyone is capable of understanding evil, and that if one does understand it and accept it, one will not be damaged. In the film Barney seems like a nice man and he does appear to treat Lecter well, but there are no extended discussions between him and Lecter. He does not walk Starling down to the cell, so the first conversation between the two, revealing how they interact, is cut. The discussions with Chilton and Starling, revealing Barney's concern over how Lecter will be treated and how he will then respond, are also cut, as is Lecter's verbal thank you to Barney and his subsequent letter and tip.

While Lecter's relationships with Starling and Barney have been altered, the nature of the relationship between Chilton and Lecter has been retained. Interestingly, the film emphasizes Chilton's vulgarity and lack of vision in some ways while downplaying it in others. The central way that the film reveals Chilton's incompetence is not present in the novel. In the novel, Lecter has had his "handcuff key" for a while and was able to fashion it from a pen left by a researcher and a paperclip left by an orderly, both on days Barney was off. In the film, it is Chilton who leaves the pen behind in the cell with Lecter. Chilton, who is so meticulous about Starling and everyone else following the rules, leaves the forbidden pen behind because he is gloating. His ego has blinded his vision to the extent that he doesn't realize what he has done or the dangerous consequences of this action. He has discovered the FBI's lies to Lecter and in his fit of feeling superior to both the FBI and to Lecter, he leaves the pen behind. This is the most egregious of Chilton's flaws. His other flaws include flirting with Starling, taping her without telling her, and, after Lecter has been moved to Tennessee, holding a press conference, making sure that the media know his name and that it was "through [his] own unique insight that this breakthrough [was] possible." As Tasker suggests, "Ultimately, audiences can enthusiastically endorse Lecter's contempt for Chilton" (85). Of Chilton, O'Brien claims he "is an extreme example of the casual chauvinism Starling must face every day of her life.... Even 'normal' men, Harris seems to be hinting, are capable of treating women as mere objects" (74) and "Doctor Chilton is in many ways as distasteful as the psychopaths he claims to study" (94). While this is true, the film also softens Chilton in certain ways. For example, while he does flirt with Starling and imply that she is being used because she is attractive, he does not patronize her to the same extent he does in the novel, nor is he as crude in his speculations regarding her attractiveness to Crawford and Lecter. In addition, while Lecter clearly does not like Chilton, he makes fewer comments regarding him that focus on intellectual inferiority. Chilton is the focus of Lecter's insults more in the novel, to the extent that the false lead, the fake name, Lecter provides to Senator Martin in the novel is Billy Rubin, not Louis Friend (the name given in the film), and refers to bilirubin, which Lecter says is the color of Chilton's hair and the chemical that gives shit its color. He also incorporates Chilton's name into the chemical notation for the substance. Lecter's reminder to Starling that Chilton does not have a medical degree is his way of further insulting Chilton by claiming that he is too ignorant to put together the details of the false lead. This extended insult of Chilton is missing from the film. Finally, while in the film Chilton does hold a press conference and take credit for getting information from Lecter, he does not make a filmed spectacle of the meeting between Senator Martin and Lecter, nor does he sell the tapes of Lecter and Starling's conversations to the *Tatler*. While these omissions do not make Chilton a likable character, they do soften his crassness.

Some of the most thematically important omissions involve nature and God. One omission regarding nature, in a way, has already been mentioned: the lack of an identification of Starling with a tiger through the color of the tiger's eye beads. This removal, along with the removal of the

4. Typhoid and Swans

horse from the childhood memory, leaving Starling instead carrying a lamb, fully identifies Starling with innocence. The moth, too, is now a simplified object. Instead of being something that is both terrible and wonderful to look at, it is simply a moth that represents change and can lead to the discovery of the killer. Also missing is Starling's reference to the moth as destructive and her then being told that some moths live on tears. The complexity of the symbol has been erased, as has its connection with Lecter.

Just as the moth is not described in the film as being destructive, neither is Lecter. He does not ask if Starling can stand to say he is evil and so she does not tell him he is destructive, which is the same as evil. Because this lead-in to the discussion is missing, there is no chance for Lecter to discuss his church roof collapses and the idea that God made both typhoid and swans. The discussions central to the idea that nature is complex and that God created both good and evil are missing from the film. The resolution of the film, though, does indicate some of the complexity of not only the relationship between Lecter and Starling but also the nature of each individual, being a mixture of good and evil. If Lecter were completely evil or destructive, if he were the evil set against Starling's good, he would surely use his freedom to hunt Starling. However, Starling tells Mapp, "He won't come after me. He won't. I can't explain it. He would consider that rude," and on the phone call with Starling, after Lecter asks her if the lambs have stopped screaming he says, "I have no plans to call on you.... The world's a more interesting place with you in it." He does not mention that their stars are the same, but he asks her to extend him the same courtesy of not calling on him. Starling's reply that she cannot make that promise emphasizes that she still puts her faith and time into the law. The last scene of the film, when Lecter says he has to go because he is having an old friend for dinner and then leaves to follow Chilton, both simplifies Lecter into someone who merely looks for revenge and complicates the ending of the film. It is a happy ending in which the law has triumphed by rescuing Catherine Martin and stopping Buffalo Bill, but it is also a system from which Lecter has escaped and is now free to roam and hunt.

While the Blakean themes remain, they are muted because of all of these changes. And, in the absence of any explicit Blakean allusion in the novel or the film, these themes of the importance of vision and understanding, the relationship of good and evil, and the nature of God and humanity are easily overlooked or ignored. However, while the film does not add any explicit Blake references, one particular scene looks startlingly like a Blake painting—the Red Dragon painting, in fact. When Lecter escapes from his Tennessee cell and the police come in and discover the cell empty, they are struck by the sight of one of the guard's bodies hanging on the cell itself. The guard has been hoisted onto the side of Lecter's cage. His arms are outspread and the fabric used to hold him up is behind his arms, looking like wings. It looks somewhat like an image of crucifixion as well as the Brooklyn Museum's version of the painting of the Red Dragon. Others, too, have noticed this similarity. Tasker suggests that "*Silence* exploits a tradition of dark, religious iconography that extends from Hieronymous Bosch through William Blake (a key figure for Harris) to Francis Bacon, Kristi Zea's [production designer for the film] immediate inspiration for the grotesque crime scene" (32). While Tasker mentions Blake here, and includes a print of the Red Dragon painting in the book (on page 31—one page after a still photo of this scene) in order to implicitly suggest the connection between Harris and Blake in this film, she does not state explicitly how Blake is a key figure for Harris, nor does she attempt to suggest why this may be. In addition, while visually stirring and stunning, and definitely evocative of Blake's Red Dragon as well as the recurring images of figures with their arms or wings spread (assuming the viewer is familiar with Blake's work), if the viewer is not familiar with Blake, the connection is nonexistent. In addition, while one may notice a visual similarity to Blake in this scene, a clear thematic rationale for its use is lacking. Given how these figures with outstretched wings or arms in Blake are associated with moments of painful enlightenment, perhaps this image is meant to convey that the Tennessee police and the FBI have received a painful enlightenment regarding Lecter. The Tennessee police were cocky about their ability to contain Lecter while Barney knew just how careful they would need to be. Both Barney and Lecter knew that the police were too certain of themselves and therefore not careful enough. The FBI believed that they could trust the Tennessee police to do the job correctly and were more concerned about Starling interfering than Lecter actively attacking and escaping. This moment painfully and violently reveals their mistakes and Lecter's own capabilities. Perhaps the image, however, is not meant to indicate this enlightenment but instead works as an indication of Lecter's familiarity with Blake, and therefore his knowledge of the Blakean ideas of good and evil.

4. Typhoid and Swans

As in the novel, Lecter is the character who best embodies these Blakean ideas. He is the mixture of high and low, human and monster. He eschews categories and labels and has the vision and insight that allow him to see how any dividing line is blurred or crossed. Because he can see how the lines are crossed, he does not attempt to confine himself to any one category and, in fact, ridicules those who do attempt to categorize him.

Even though in the film Lecter is characterized by Crawford and Chilton as a "monster" and a "pure psychopath," and even though in the scene when Chilton leads Starling down to the cell the screen is suffused with a red light that indicates a descent into hell, one of the most discussed and engaging aspects of the film is the trace bits of humanity that Hopkins brings to the role of Lecter. It is Lecter's humanity, after all, that makes him so frightening. However, this trace, at least, of humanity in Lecter leads to difficulties of response in the viewers who either desire a simplistic response to characters or are disturbed by their own mixed reactions. What is the correct response to Lecter? Are Lecter's actions condoned or condemned? Tasker is not the only one who questions whether "Lecter [is] too appealing for our own good" (33). She states that "the question in relation to *Silence* became one of tone — what kind of message was the film sending?" (35), particularly because there existed "a sense that the film celebrated Lecter despite his violence, a celebration regarded as both morally troubling and rather snobbish (since Lecter is so explicitly coded as 'cultured' against Buffalo Bill's inarticulate white trash)" (36). Essentially, when Tasker states that "while *Silence* was widely read as symptomatic, critics disagreed as to precisely *what* it was symptomatic of" (original emphasis, 36), she implicitly makes a connection with Blake in the possibility of a multiplicity of interpretations, including those that on the surface appear to be contradictory. In addition, Tasker discusses the reaction of critics to Lecter's charisma and culture: "The contradictions of Lecter's persona — 'charming psychopath' we might dub him — helped make him a cause celebre on the film's initial release. For some reviewers, Lecter's cultured tastes suggested an endorsement of his violence. He is just *too* charming. Peculiar that we do not seem to think that the reverse might equally apply — that Lecter's savagery might question the culture to which he lays claim (and which Starling desires so badly)" (original emphasis, 84). No one has followed up on Tasker's suggestion that Lecter's connection with culture may reveal the underlying evil of that culture itself. Not only is the culture evil, but so is the humanity that created it. Sexton attempts to explain the appeal of Lecter by stating that he "is the face that looks back at us out of our own boredom. He is our monster. The evil we embrace for our diversion" (97). To restate his point slightly, Lecter is the face that looks back at us out of our own mirrors, if we are willing to look and truly see with expanded vision and open imagination.

CHAPTER 5

Harris's Marriage of Heaven and Hell
Hannibal

After waiting ten years for a sequel to *Silence of the Lambs*, readers had mixed reactions to *Hannibal*. Sexton states that the novel "rapidly disappointed and affronted many of its readers" and that "it has the distinction of having, among its more than 2,500 reader-reviews on Amazon.com, nearly 700 which give it the lowest possible rating" (131). Many of the negative reviews, from those written by readers on Amazon to those of published reviewers like Martin Amis, objected to the gore, the focus on Lecter more than on Starling, the "explanation" of the origin of Lecter's evil, and the move to a more gothic genre than a procedural. These changes in tone, focus, and genre may account for many of the objections. If one expects Grisham and gets King, one may be disappointed; in addition to the shift in genres, the obvious literariness, particularly Harris's focus on Florence and its history and art, may have turned some off. O'Brien clearly illustrates this common reaction: "Epic in scope and painstakingly detailed, *Hannibal* is ultimately inferior to both *Red Dragon* and *The Silence of the Lambs*. In expanding and reworking the format that made the first two books a success, Harris has lost the focus and urgency of his earlier work" (133). However, the first two novels were just as detailed, though not as violent, as *Hannibal*. The details vary mainly in that in *Hannibal* the details often refer to Italian art, geography, and history. It does seem that these details of Florentine culture and history are the cause of many of the negative reactions, based sometimes on exaggerations or misremembered details. O'Brien, once again, is a prime example of this negative reaction to the amount of details about Florence, as well as to the amount of Dante, "often in untranslated Italian" (134). Whether he is misremembering or exaggerating, O'Brien is wrong about the large amount of untranslated

Dante in the book. Harris does include 9 lines that are untranslated, but these are paraphrased and commented on by Lecter during his lecture on them (196–97). All other lines are translated. O'Brien, however, claims that this focus on Florence and its history, art, and literature reveals "cultural elitism ... self-indulgence and lazy repetition" (134). Just as the Shiloh episode at the end of *Red Dragon* and the use of Blake were read as Harris's attempt to claim literariness and place himself above genre fiction, *Hannibal*, too, is seen as revealing Harris's desire for his work to be ranked above genre fiction, and adding literary and artistic details in order to achieve this. O'Brien suggests that Harris's gambit was successful because upon the publication of *Hannibal*, "Book reviewers who normally shunned mere thrillers acclaimed Harris as a literary genius who effortlessly blurred the line between popular fiction and 'serious' literature" (127). What these reviewers and those like O'Brien have in common is that, whether dismissing or embracing these historical and literary details, little attempt is made to understand reasons for their inclusion, including the possibility that these allusions and details emphasize particular themes or interpretations.

Many negative reviews of and reactions to *Hannibal* may be based upon having forgotten the literary qualities of both *Red Dragon* and *Silence of the Lambs*, some of which had been explored in print already (see the discussions of the works as gothic, for example). Other negative reactions may have stemmed from reading this third novel as another in a series of separate but similar works, instead of as the third part of an ongoing longer work that continues an exploration of particular themes and literary allusions. The ten-year gap between *Silence of the Lambs* and *Hannibal* may explain both of these causes of negative reviews, as the length of time between the novels makes it easier to forget the literary qualities of the earlier novels and to facilitate reading each novel as a separate work that happens to have the same characters. Those who have reacted positively to *Hannibal* often have in common the approach of reading it as a continuation of the earlier two novels. Stephen King, for example, does read the three novels as part of one work, as revealed in his positive review of *Hannibal* in the *New York Times*, in which he calls the novel "the third and most satisfying part of one long and very scary ride." One must read *Hannibal* as a continuation of an exploration begun in earlier novels, keeping in mind Harris's earlier use of Blake and what it reveals about the nature of good and evil. This attention to the Blakean allusions and connections

5. Harris's Marriage of Heaven and Hell

is quite important in reading *Hannibal* since Harris returns to explicit references to Blake here after having only implicitly alluded to Blake in *Silence*. In addition, this novel continues Harris's exploration of the coexistence of good and evil in nature and humanity, the nature of God, the importance of perspective and vision to understanding, the difficulty of easy categorization, and especially the importance of not brooding on the past but instead reconciling and forgiving — all themes and ideas connected to Blake.

Hannibal begins with Starling killing five people in a botched drug raid. One of these is the leader, a woman holding her baby. Starling must wash the woman's HIV-contaminated blood off of the child. Harris begins with the heroine, previously associated with protecting lambs, with blood on her hands. Starling's continued complexity and contradictions, as well as her growing relationship with and connection to Lecter, are a central part of the Blakean ideas Harris explores even if Blake himself is very rarely explicitly connected to either of these characters.

Only one of the Blake allusions is to one of these two central characters. When Starling receives a letter from Lecter she notices his "fine copperplate hand" (29). In *Red Dragon* Dolarhyde's copperplate handwriting is explicitly compared to Blake's (88), so here, by extension, Lecter's handwriting is similar to that of Blake as well, since it, too, is copperplate. Even here the allusion is not explicit and is only apparent to those who recognize the description as similar to that in *Red Dragon*. Lecter has an implied connection to Blake while Dolarhyde's is explicit. It is important to remember this, as well as that while Dolarhyde explicitly draws upon Blake, he misreads Blake. In *Hannibal*, as in *Red Dragon*, the character with the explicit connection to Blake is the one who misreads him.

The most explicit connection to Blake is Mason Verger's copy of *Ancient of Days*. Harris makes a point of naming and describing this painting: "A passable print of William Blake's 'The Ancient of Days' hung above the couch — God measuring with his calipers" (56). Clearly, Harris wants the reader to be aware of the image and of Blake. Interestingly, again the explicit connection to Blake is with the "villain," and again the choice of the Blake work, as well as the connection to the character's own personality, reveals a misreading of Blake. While Verger does not explicitly comment on the painting, examining his own comments regarding the nature of God, as well as his own actions, indicates this misreading. The standard interpretation of *Ancient of Days* is that it represents Urizen, Blake's Old

Testament God-like figure, who in early mythic days of formlessness, which he saw as chaos, felt the need to order, measure and impose laws upon all of creation. In the first chapter of *The [First] Book of Urizen*, in an "abominable void" (3:4), Urizen "Times on times ... divided, & measur'd/Space by space" (3:7–8). In the second chapter Urizen writes "the Book/Of eternal brass" (4:32–33), which contains "Laws of peace, of love, of unity:/Of pity, compassion, forgiveness" (4:34–35). While these laws are written with the best of intentions and sound positive, they quickly lead to the pronouncement "One command, one joy, one desire,/One curse, one weight, one measure,/One King, one God, one Law" (4:38–40). Urizen forgot that, as Blake writes in *The Marriage of Heaven and Hell*, "One Law for the Lion & the Ox is Oppression" (plate 24) and that "Prisons are built with stones of Law" (8:1). Urizen therefore represents not just the lawgiver but also the punisher, who, instead of understanding nuances of behavior, expects all laws to be obeyed at all times, and therefore inflicts punishment on transgressors. In addition, instead of creating a controlled paradise, his laws lead to the further binding of humanity and the breaking of laws. While Urizen enacts laws and codes and punishes those who disobey, Jesus rebels against laws and forgives those who transgress, understanding that all laws were made to be broken and actions must be judged in context. In the final Memorable Fancy of *The Marriage of Heaven and Hell*, Jesus is described as breaking the Ten Commandments, after which there is the statement, "I tell you, no virtue can exist without breaking these ten commandments: Jesus was all virtue and acted from impulse, not from rules" (plates 23–24). Not only does Jesus embody virtue and impulse (even breaking commandments if necessary), but also "the Spirit of Jesus is continual forgiveness of Sin" (*Jerusalem*, "To the Public" plate 3). For Blake, then, Jesus, not Urizen, is the ideal image of God, the one followers should aspire to; however, for Verger Urizen is God, representing his vengeful and hypocritical religious views.

However, like Dolarhyde's misreading of Blake and the Red Dragon, Verger's misreading is not corrected or countered by any voice in the novel. In addition, since no one in the novel explicitly comments on the painting, and Harris does not provide an authorial statement beyond its description, the role of the painting in the novel can be easily missed or dismissed. O'Brien, for example, considers the painting only a culturally elite allusion and claims, "While 'The Great Red Dragon and the Woman Clothed with

5. Harris's Marriage of Heaven and Hell

the Sun' was a central motif in *Red Dragon*, this time around the Blake reference seems an empty flourish" (134). However, it is only an empty flourish if one has not noticed the connection to Blake throughout all of Harris's novels in his portrayal of good and evil or if one does not connect the portrayal of God in that painting to Verger's vision of a patriarchal and vengeful God, one who, in Verger's words, will "will smite mine enemies and drive them before me" (59).

The painting's positioning in Verger's room is also telling, as Verger himself represents a bizarre mixture of good and evil, emphasizing the difficulty of categorization or pure binaries. He thanks God for his encounter with Lecter, in which he became horribly disfigured but survived, calling it his "salvation," and he asks Starling if she has accepted Jesus, if she has faith (58). While he outwardly is the most religious of the characters and works with the FBI to capture Lecter, he also plots Lecter's horrible torture and death and continues to torment children, making them cry so he can drink their tears in his martinis (66). It is Verger who wishes revenge on Lecter; it is he who comes closest to recapturing and punishing Lecter for his crimes. For those who wish to draw a solid line between good and evil, Verger causes difficulties. Verger suffered horribly at the hands of Lecter, and, as the lone surviving victim, we might expect that he would elicit our sympathies, that perhaps the novel would involve Starling working with Verger to capture Lecter. Yet, because Verger continues to torment children and is aligned with distasteful and mistaken characters like Krendler and Doemling as opposed to Starling, Lecter instead elicits our sympathies, as he does Starling's. This sympathy for Lecter instead of Verger, this inability to identify a pure good versus pure evil struggle in the novel, is both what led to some of the negative reviews and what aligns Harris with Blake.

Verger's association with Krendler and Doemling is central to placing the reader on Lecter's side. Operating on a surface level of style and manners, as well as indicators of intelligence, the contrast between Lecter on the one side and Krendler/Doemling on the other may seem to be reinforcing an elitism, as the contrast between Chilton and Lecter is read by some as doing in *Silence*. However, as in the previous novels, Lecter's sense of style and taste, as contrasted to that of others, may serve not just as a class marker but also as an indicator of attention to detail and the ability to read and understand the world, in part through use of imagination. As discussed in the previous chapter, Starling shares this interest in taste and detail with Lecter. This attention to and recognition of the importance of detail plays a part in this novel as well. For example, during her meeting regarding her actions at the drug bust that begins the novel, Starling sees the men's feet and identifies the specific shoes they wear, using them to help her categorize them and identify them as "country slicksters who have made it to Washington" (38). Not only does her attention to detail allow her to perform well as an FBI agent, but it also indicates her understanding of class status and categorization. This attention to detail also helps protect her; for example, she knows that Mr. Sneed is wearing a wire during the meeting and can call him on it (39). It can also help her rise above her status and break out of society's labeling of her, even if in a seemingly superficial way through outward appearance. Krendler does not share this attention to detail, or at least not to the same extent. He believes that Starling will not notice that one of the men is wearing a wire and, on a more superficial note, wears expensive suits with cheap shirts and ties, which Starling notices as well (261).

In addition, and also as discussed in the previous chapter, the vulgarity of Krendler, like that of Chilton, works to illuminate the hypocrisy and flaws of the legal system, suggesting that it is not a powerful or superior system that is always correct and must always be obeyed. The clearest example of Krendler's hypocrisy is his working with and for Verger. Like Chilton, Krendler's vision is narrow, with his goal not necessarily being bringing Lecter to justice but instead elevating his own position in Washington, D.C., while, if possible, bringing Starling down through poisoning her personnel file (38). His jealousy of Starling and his continued anger at her refusal to succumb to his sexual advances reveal his brooding on the past, leading to a desire for vengeance as well as active hindering of her career. His metaphoric murdering (hindering) of Starling, or at least her career, is emphasized through his crassness, especially when contrasted with Lecter's cultured words and taste. Krendler voices his anger toward Starling in vulgar language—for example, calling her "cornpone country pussy" (265)—creating distaste in the reader for Krendler and, by extension, the legal system that he represents.

In addition, Krendler's ego, like that of Chilton, also reveals his narrowed vision. His focus in his rise in government is not on protecting others or even upholding laws, but instead on his own ego and image. When he visits Starling in her basement office, surrounded by Lecter's information, "He could see his own photograph in association with a display like

5. Harris's Marriage of Heaven and Hell

this in the FBI museum.... He could see its enormous campaign value" (260). He works with Verger not because he wants justice or revenge against Lecter but because Verger can help further his political career. Similarly, Pazzi, too, works to capture Lecter for his own personal gain, contacting Verger instead of the FBI for financial gain instead of greater justice.

Dr. Doemling likewise reveals the faults of ego and the lack of vision and understanding of others in his narrow focus on personal success and superiority. As Krendler and Pazzi stand for the law and government, Doemling represents the flaws of the psychiatric/medical system. In his discussion of Lecter with Verger and Krendler, he not only attempts to diagnose Lecter but emphasizes his own importance as well, claiming that the illness Lecter suffers from has been named for Doemling himself, since he diagnosed it, and may be included in the next *Diagnostic and Statistical Manual* (271). Doemling also is condescending to Barney (273), clearly not seeing what both Lecter and Starling see in Barney, and his frail ego and possible motivation for revenge in helping Verger is revealed when, toward the end of their conversation, Barney reveals that Doemling was the one psychiatrist who left crying after trying to talk to Lecter and that Lecter then gave his book a bad review in the *American Journal of Psychiatry*, which may have made him cry as well (277).

Doemling and Krendler are blinded by their narrow vision and their egos, leading them to make incorrect suppositions and, ultimately, to be wrong in their analysis of Lecter and his motivations. They cannot see from his or others' perspectives and therefore cannot truly understand. Krendler's mistaken notions are, as is typical for him, more vulgar than Doemling's and are based in part on stereotypes of class and gender. The clearest example of this is when Krendler visits Starling in the basement and asks her if Lecter "hire[s] S and M whores" or "[m]ale prostitutes" (263). While Harris does not explain "Krendler's relish in the question" (263), which Starling notices because of her careful attention to detail, one can infer that Krendler wishes to be superior to Lecter, to find a detail that would debase Lecter. Krendler hopes those activities are ones that Lecter would secretly indulge in, perhaps in order to prove to himself that he is more masculine than Lecter, and therefore superior to him, because he does not need to be dominated or to pay for sexual encounters, as his statements imply Lecter does. Soon after these questions Krendler reveals, using dismissive language, that he thought Lecter was gay because of his interest in art and culture (263). Krendler misreads Lecter due to a reverse elitism in which pop culture is elevated above the arts because it is more "masculine." This is, once again, a desire to position himself above Lecter by disparaging Lecter's interests and tastes, but it is also a desire to label Lecter as different from himself, to deny any similarities between the two and box them into safe separate categories. Krendler's narrow vision prefers clear separation of people and categories.

Doemling, too, misreads and misdiagnoses Lecter. He claims that what Lecter wants is control (268), meaning that Lecter uses his understanding of Starling in order to control her and that control is in itself his final goal. Lecter's hypnotizing and drugging of Starling at the end of the novel could be seen as supporting this idea and will be further explored later. As for now, the important aspect of this diagnosis is that it is too simple. In Doemling's eyes, Lecter merely wants control. He cannot see or understand that Lecter could have a genuine interest in Starling, or in anyone else. Doemling reads Lecter's letters to Starling as only pretending to be caring and providing support and kindness (271). In Doemling's diagnosis Lecter is preying on Starling's transference while "his object is her degradation, her suffering, and her death" (276). Doemling believes that Lecter wishes simply to see her in "distress" (277). Doemling, like Krendler (and, as we will see, Verger), broods on the past, leading to his desire for revenge. He cannot forget Lecter's disrespect and dismissal of him, and therefore wants to be the one who can finally categorize and capture Lecter, blind to the fact that if it were this easy to label and catch him, it would have already been done.

Doemling and Krendler help the reader see the flaws in the legal and psychiatric systems, just as Starling comes to see them through her own corrosive experience and the guidance of Lecter. In addition, by aligning Verger with figures who wish to capture Lecter for their own gain and not some greater good, Harris works to place both Starling's and the readers' sympathies with Lecter. Doemling, Krendler, and Verger all reveal the danger of unmoving, unseeing systems and laws, emphasizing this Blakean aspect of the novel. As Starling recognizes and accepts the flaws in these systems, she gives up trying to play within the rules; she disregards the boundaries between right and wrong. Even though she had "survived most of her life in institutions, by respecting them and playing hard and well by the rules" (27), through her encounters with Lecter and her observation of those around her she learns to abandon her adherence to the rules and her desire to survive within institutions. Starling's "doors of perception" (*MHH* plate 14) are open and she can now see the corruption and hypocrisy of various systems; "she began to look at the shapes of things [and] began to credit her own visceral reactions to things, without quantifying them or restricting them to words" (225). Her vision operates now outside of labels and categories. Her acceptance of what she sees helps her "mind-forg'd manacles" slowly break so she can act on her perception and reject established rules.

It is not only Starling, though, who can see in detail the flaws of Doemling and Krendler and the complexity of Lecter, and whose senses and taste, along with imagination and understanding, have been expanded through contact with Lecter. Barney, too, undergoes this growth. In her own hunt for Lecter, Starling meets with Barney and asks him how he survived his contact with Lecter, knowing that it was due to more than just being civil. Barney's response explicitly states the Blakean idea of coexisting good and evil and echoes some of Blake's comments to Crabb Robinson (discussed earlier) regarding how all men are both good and bad: "I was working on some correspondence courses and he shared his mind with me. That didn't mean he wouldn't *kill* me any second if he got the chance — one quality in a person doesn't rule out any other quality. They can exist side by side, good and terrible" (original emphasis, 87). Barney understands that there is no simple answer or diagnosis, in part because of Lecter's helping him with his academic work and the complex ideas he encountered, and in part because Lecter did not simply categorize and dismiss him, but instead talked to him and helped him enter the world of art and thought, sparking his desire to see all the Vermeer paintings. One of the major contributions that both Barney and Starling add to an understanding of Lecter is that he will not lie. Barney tells Starling that he is not worried about Lecter coming after him because "he said he wouldn't" (88). Both Starling and Barney refuse to assume that because of his other evil acts Lecter will also automatically lie. Because Barney knows that Lecter doesn't lie, he can easily see how Doemling's simplistic reading of Lecter is flawed since that reading entails Lecter lying about not coming after Starling and lying about being concerned for her. When Doemling completes his diagnosis, it is Barney who refutes him, revealing his understanding of Lecter and his relationship with Starling, saying, "He admires and respects her courage and her discipline. He says himself he's got no plans to come around. One thing he does *not* do is lie" (original emphasis, 277).

Barney further reveals his understanding of the connection between Starling and Lecter when he tells Starling that Lecter killed Miggs because he had offended her (92). He attempts to explain this relationship to Doemling and Krendler, describing the truthful discussions the two had and how Starling was accepting of both the good and the bad that Lecter told her about herself because she knew he wouldn't lie (275). According to Barney, Lecter told him that "he could see what [Starling] was *becoming*," comparing her to a cub that will grow up to be a big, dangerous cat (original emphasis, 275). Perhaps, as implied by Lecter's suggestion in *Silence* that Starling obtain tiger's eye beads, he sees her becoming a tiger, Blake's tiger. Barney also reveals that Lecter believed that Starling "was 'cursed with taste'" (276). While Barney says he does not know what Lecter meant by this curse, it is most likely connected to not only a desire for objects and experiences beyond one's class but also Starling's ability to see and understand details, allowing her to see the truth, at times an ugly truth and one that she could then never not see.

Starling seems to be aware of this curse to some extent; at least, she is aware of her expanding tastes and attention to details. After she meets with a nurse to gather more information about Lecter and she has noticed all the small details regarding the nurse that indicate her class, and perhaps her interests, Starling comes to realize that she is "weary" of other people's indifference to detail and design and that "she was hungry for some style" (71). It is not just that she desires more elite experiences and objects, but also, and to some extent more importantly, she is bothered by those around her who do not see specifically and clearly in detail. Once again, this could be an indication of Harris's elitism, but it also could be indicative of Starling's desire for someone who sees closely, someone who pays attention to what Blake might call the Minute Particulars. This lack of sight also usually indicates a lack of insight or imagination in her world. Perhaps she has begun to recognize, even if subconsciously, Lecter's appeal. Starling longs for expansion beyond her limited senses, a greater understanding of the world. In her encounters, it is only Lecter who also sees and experiences so closely and completely. While his actions are violent, his interests are beautiful. When she stands in his now long empty cell at the closed Baltimore State Hospital for the Criminally Insane, she considers the connection of death and love, danger and beauty, thinking, "Death and danger do not have to come with trappings. They can come to you in the sweet breath of your beloved" (78–79). While she does not yet accept Lecter as her beloved or admit their relationship, she is beginning to see the intricate connection between the beautiful and the dangerous. Lecter also sees beauty and danger in Starling when he calls her "the honey in the lion" (184), the sweet out of something strong. He may be attracted most to this complexity in her and be aware that she is open to embracing it as well; as stated earlier, he did tell Barney he was interested in her "*becoming*" (275). She knows that he killed Miggs in part because Miggs offended her and realizes when she attempts to track him through his interests that she should include herself on the list. Perhaps this is part of the curse of taste as well, that those like Lecter himself (those who are interested in the mixture of danger and beauty in her) will be drawn to her. While she compiles this list to find Lecter, unlike Verger Starling does not want Lecter dead. She recognizes his importance, the necessity of his continued existence, and she tells Ardelia (her roommate) that she'd "like to see him beat the needle.... Can't waste a man that's crazy enough to tell the truth" (242).

Perhaps the truth she's heard him tell includes that of human nature, of what Lecter witnesses in himself and those around him. He does, after all, visit the exhibit of atrocious torture instruments in Florence to watch the crowd, knowing that "Elemental Ugliness is found in the faces of the crowd" (128). When he returns to the exhibit on a later visit he is seen "registering aspects of damnation from the avid faces of the voyeurs" (161). Here Lecter ponders the ugliness of the crowd, while in the earlier novels he speculates about and lectures on the cruelty and ugliness of God. Others in this novel reflect on the cruelties, or at least indifference, of God; for instance, Starling is compared to a medical missionary who knows "that God wouldn't do a goddamned thing to help" (46). It is Mason Verger who explicitly speculates about the nature of "Acts of God" and suffering, thinking, "God's choices in inflicting suffering are not satisfactory to us, nor are they understandable, unless innocence offends Him. Clearly He needs some help in directing the blind fury with which He flogs the earth" (99). This vision of God explains his ownership of *Ancient of Days*, Blake's image of the Old Testament God of laws and constraints, the God who made Job suffer. While the painting represents a controlled figure with calipers, and not one exhibiting blind fury, this is the God who in the Old Testament punished nations and unleashed fury, the one who expects blind obedience and punishes, often without explanation. This is also a God who, according to Verger, needs help inflicting and directing this fury, thereby justifying his own vengeful actions, as opposed to a Christ-like forgiveness.

While Lecter does not muse about church collapses or God's punishment in this novel, he himself had an encounter with God's infliction of suffering on the innocent. In 1944, when deserters staying at a hunting lodge had run out of meat, they ate his sister Mischa. He prayed to see her again, only to discover some of her baby teeth in a pile of the soldiers' defecation. Harris writes, "Since this partial answer to his own prayer, Hannibal Lecter had not been bothered by any considerations of deity, other than to recognize how his own modest predations paled beside those of God, who is in irony matchless, and in wanton malice beyond measure" (256). Although Simpson in *Making Murder* points to this passage as indicative of Lecter's (and Harris's) atheism (140, 216, 260), the passage may instead indicate, not that Lecter no longer believes in God, but that he now believes or recognizes that God is capable of cruelty without explanation. If God can inflict such horrors and sufferings, why can't he? He also recognizes that this God does not enact vengeance or punishment, and therefore he will not be punished by God for his crimes. Like Verger, he comes to believe in something resembling Blake's Urizen, the God of the Old Testament who punished and played with Job. The difference between his belief in this Urizenic God and Verger's belief is that Verger — as seen in the passage quoted earlier — believes that God must have reasons that we can't understand and that this God also requires help from humans in inflicting this fury. Lecter does not ask for or expect reasons and does not believe that God needs any help in being cruel. When Lecter kills the deer hunter, the one the game wardens have been hoping to catch, it is not to help God or the law mete out punishment but instead it is to protect nature itself. The deer reminds him of his childhood and his desire to help Mischa and other vulnerable creatures (283, 290). As will be seen in *Hannibal Rising*, Hannibal's connection to nature and desire to protect it is at the heart of many of his actions. The other important distinction between Verger and Lecter in regard to this God is that Verger pays attention to this God, believing him worthy of worship, while Lecter chooses to ignore him. Although Blake certainly wouldn't have condoned Lecter's murders or cannibalizing, his response to Urizen is closer to Blake's philosophy than Verger's response is: instead of worshipping Urizen, ignore him. As *Hannibal Rising* makes clear, Lecter did not come to this conclusion regarding God immediately and, in fact, was similar to Verger in his initial brooding and vengeance; here, however, he is closer to a Blakean balance and state of forgiveness.

The focus of most critics in discussing this memory of his childhood is not on Lecter's view of God, but on this event as an explanation of his evil, as his origin story. Some critics, like Robert Winder and Kristina Bross, have claimed that this memory of Mischa serves as a poor and disappointing explanation for Lecter's evil. Winder states that Lecter is now "just another crazed avenger," and Bross says, "Here his twisted ways are explained by childhood trauma." Sexton claims that "the story [is] given so surprisingly and perhaps unwisely" (80) and that "although [it] illuminatingly establish[es] that in this world God is to be seen as just the biggest predator of all ... [it] has been much reviled" (141). As Sexton and others have pointed out, it contradicts his conversation with Starling in *Silence* in which he explains that his actions and nature can't be explained by influences (19). Both in *Red Dragon* and in *Silence* Lecter tells Graham and Starling that he is evil just because it is a part of his nature, and yet here we have a starting point, an aspect of his background that made him evil. However, these two passages do not necessarily contradict each other but instead may work together, revealing that both nature and nurture created Lecter's evil. His experience as a child did not create the evil within him. As seen throughout the novels, this capacity for or understanding of evil also exists in people (like Starling and Graham, for example) who have not experienced such horrors. As with all humans, Lecter is born with the capability for evil, with evil as part of his nature; it is his choice to recognize this aspect and then decide whether to act upon it or not. Unlike most people, upon recognizing God as both the greatest predator and indifferent to humans' own acts of evil, Lecter accepts that evil portion of himself and allows himself to act on it. While this moment from his youth reveals this dual nature, he could also have accepted this part of his nature without acting upon it. His actions are driven in part by recognizing the indifference of God and the cruelty of humans and in part by his brooding on the past and wishing revenge for Mischa and those like her. He is not yet in a Blakean balance even though he has accepted his and humanity's dual nature. Not only has he accepted this duality within himself and humanity, but his acceptance of the evil within himself is so complete that others have difficulty accepting that he is not "something entirely Other ... [a] 'monster'" (137), and some even recognize Satan in him. The older gypsy, upon seeing Lecter, tries to warn Romula (149), Romula bathes her baby in holy water to protect it from Lecter, and both she and the older gypsy call him Satan (156, 166).

For those readers who believe in Lecter's pure evil, those who agree with the psychiatrists that he is a monster or with the gypsies that he is Satan, the incident from Lecter's childhood disappoints because it provides him with a reason for his actions. The experience taints his pure evil. Sexton describes this reaction well: "The angry response of so many readers shows how much they themselves had had invested in the idea of Lecter as glamourously inexplicable, thrillingly pure in his evil" (142). However, in true Blakean tradition, Harris has created a complex character who is a mix of contraries. Lecter, aware of contrary natures, embraces his own and encourages the same in others. The memory of Mischa is not the cause of Lecter's evil, but instead the moment when he became aware of these contrary natures, particularly the human face of evil and the cruel nature of God. This moment taught Lecter the lesson of Blake's "A Divine Image" from *Songs of Experience* that was used as an epigraph in *Red Dragon*: "Cruelty has a Human Heart" and "Terror, the Human Form Divine" (ll. 1 & 3). This realization in turn allowed him to express both sides of himself (the Love of the *Innocence* "Divine Image"— revealed in his relationships with Mischa and with Starling — as well as the Cruelty of the *Experience* "Divine Image"— revealed in his killings and cannibalism) instead of pretending or attempting to be wholly good.

Both those who believe that this childhood incident caused Lecter's evil and those who view him as an example of pure evil that this experience taints mirror the fault of the majority of those who attempt to capture Lecter: they look for the simple answer, the easy explanation of why he behaves as he does, and ignore any complexities. Either he is simply evil — no more need be said — or there is a specific and simple cause for his actions. For example, as discussed previously, Dr. Doemling and Krendler try to tell Verger that Lecter wants to degrade Starling and eventually watch her suffer and die and that he will exploit all he knows about her to do this while pretending to be her friend. Barney, however, knows better the complexities of the man and, as discussed earlier, explains their relationship and that Lecter does not lie. Dr. Doemling continues to insist on seeing only one side and responds that Barney's opinion is an example of "tabloid thinking" and that Lecter "does not have emotions like admiration or respect" (277). Doemling wishes to view Lecter as pure evil, refusing to see any taint of good in him.

5. Harris's Marriage of Heaven and Hell

Like Barney, Starling recognizes Lecter's sincerity and acknowledges and accepts his admiration, respect, and even vulnerability. In *Silence* Harris used the lambs as the traditional figure of innocence. Because of her desire to protect the lambs, the innocent, from slaughter, Starling joined the FBI and began her contact with Lecter, someone labeled evil. However, in *Hannibal* Lecter himself becomes like a lamb to her. When she thinks of Verger torturing Lecter to death "she shied from it as she had from the slaughter of the lambs and the horses so long ago" (397). Lecter the killer is not the tiger or the dragon, but the lamb.

Just as she once attempted to save the lambs, she attempts to save Lecter, only to be saved by him. The last section of the novel is truly a Blakean marriage of heaven and hell as Lecter literally carries Starling away with him. At first this marriage appears one-sided, as Starling is injured and Lecter uses drugs both to cure her physically and, along with hypnosis, to cure her psychologically and emotionally by helping her confront her memories of her father and correct her relationship with her past. While Lecter is controlling her, as Doemling suggested he would, it is not in order to degrade or destroy her. This is not to say that Lecter acts completely selflessly or that there may not be possible damage to Starling caused by this encounter. Just as Starling had been haunted by memories of the lambs and, to some extent, is now haunted by memories of her father and mother, Lecter is haunted by the memory of Mischa. As mentioned previously, the deer reminds him of both Starling and Mischa, and contributes to his killing of the hunter (293–321). This haunting by the past creates one of his intellectual pursuits, which is considering time and if it can be reversed. At the same time that he attempts to help Starling confront her past, he considers how he can give Mischa Starling's place in the world (436). Lecter is not in balance yet. He is not only haunted but also brooding on the past, unable to let it go. He is like one of Blake's characters, like Theotormon in *Visions of the Daughters of Albion*, who, instead of confronting the violent action that has taken place, the rape of Oothoon, stays brooding and locked up, refusing to see or listen to Oothoon, refusing to take that horrible event and try to move past it and make things better. Lecter is also like a character without his Emanation, without his female complement. While he admires Starling, he is fixated on somehow reuniting with Mischa. The Blakean marriage will occur when not only has Lecter helped Starling recover but she also has helped him put Mischa behind him in order to embrace his Emanation, Starling herself.

At first this marriage seems forced upon Starling; she is, after all, both drugged and hypnotized. However, details in the novel do point to her willingly wanting to stay, so that when at the end Harris states that Lecter uses neither hypnotism nor drugs to further their connection anymore (484), her voluntary choice is quite believable. She has never believed him to be a monster and has trusted that he will not hurt her. Her connection to him regarding taste, style, and heightened senses has already been discussed. When she reads the letter from Lecter early in the novel her thoughts are contradictory — she is both happy and sad (33). Starling is glad to hear from him and gain strength and help from him. She is also glad that the FBI can use this letter to find him, but is sad that he can now be traced. On one level she must want to protect him, keep him out there where he can provide her with help and where he can't be caught. When Crawford discusses Lecter with her and how this is her chance to redeem herself in the FBI, he does so because he believes she wants to capture Lecter, and also that she wishes to correct the future of her career, but he simplifies her relationship with Lecter and her objectives (50). The truth, even if not consciously known by Starling at this early point in the novel, is that she does not just want to chase him to catch him. There is another motive at play here, another desire. Perhaps it is to be with the one person who really knows and understands her. After Lecter is kidnapped and Starling returns home, she looks around her house, devoid of personal objects and keepsakes, and thinks of her family, asking herself who her family is, who knows and cares for her (397). An answer comes to her, a memory of what Lecter wrote in his letter to her: "*You are a warrior, Clarice. You can be as strong as you wish to be*" (original emphasis, 397). This memory not only serves to encourage her to do what she thinks is right but also indicates that the one person who knows her, tells her the truth, and wants her to act on that knowledge is Lecter.

While Starling may not have been consciously aware of her willingness to be with Lecter or her connection to him, it existed and played upon her throughout this novel (and to some extent in *Silence* as well). She had hidden part of herself from herself and was not yet ready to see it or accept it. Throughout the early part of this "marriage," while the drugs and hypnotism are still being used, Starling is both "herself and not herself" (441). She hears herself talking about her own thoughts and wonders who it is (441). She begins to be aware of her hidden self. She becomes accepting of her complexities and traumas, doing what Graham refused to do, and thereby survives.

5. Harris's Marriage of Heaven and Hell

The novel ends with Starling having been "cured" by Lecter. He makes her confront her father's memory, freely experience all of her emotions regarding her father, and reconcile herself to his memory. As she once recognized Lecter's ability to tell the truth and admired it, she now speaks the truth, allowing herself to be free with him and not try to hide any one particular facet of herself. She hears herself speaking to him and "the things she told Dr. Lecter were often surprising to her, sometimes distasteful to a normal sensibility, but what she said was always true" (447). Lecter teaches Starling to accept the truth of her father's memory and use the memory for strength instead of brooding or worrying about how he, or anyone else, would judge her (452). She accepts this and, interestingly, in return teaches Lecter to stop being haunted by the memory of Mischa, asking why, if she can carry her father's memory with her and use it without obsessing over it, he cannot do the same with Mischa's memory. The place in the world for Mischa is within Lecter's memory and imagination, not in Starling (477). Lecter realizes that he can maintain his sister's memory within him and doesn't need to fight against it. He no longer has to be afraid of that painful memory. They have cured each other. Starling has accepted the hidden aspects of herself and has moved past her father's memory and Krendler's attempt to undermine her (albeit in part through dining on him). Lecter has accepted that he can live with the memory of Mischa and with the understanding companionship of Starling. This novel's ending with the union of Starling and Lecter embodies a literal marrying of Innocence and Experience, but one that is quite complex. For it is not Starling who is innocent and Lecter who is experienced, but instead each are both. Just as in the end of Blake's prophetic poems, Emanation and Self are reunited.

However, Harris's ending left many readers and critics unsatisfied, calling it, for example, a "betrayal of a dubious feminist heroine" (Bross). O'Brien claims that when Starling embraces Lecter's world, "the finale of *Hannibal* veers sharply into a realm where our disbelief becomes difficult to suspend" (9). Many still wished to see the novel in terms of a clear struggle of binaries: pure good versus pure evil, with good triumphing in the end. Instead, the conclusion provides them with either evil triumphing through Lecter winning Starling to his side (still a simplistic reading) or instead an ambiguous ending, with good and evil mingled and no clear sense of which will lead in the future. After all, the question remains at the end of *Hannibal* as to whether Starling and Lecter murder together or have left evil behind. When Barney sees Lecter and Starling at the opera in Buenos Aires three years later, he insists on leaving for Rio right after the opera, not even seeing the Vermeer and thereby never achieving his dream of seeing them all (481). While Barney is cautious, as he always was around Lecter, there is no indication that Lecter, or Starling, would necessarily kill Barney. In fact, throughout both this novel and *Silence* Barney is certain he is safe if he is courteous and both he and Lecter follow the rules, and he trusts Lecter when Lecter says he will not harm him. While maybe Starling now also lives by her own moral code, one that would be categorized as evil, perhaps instead she can balance Lecter's tendency to act on his evil aspect. After all, as Blake said in *The Marriage of Heaven and Hell*, "Without contraries there is no progression" (plate 3), so with the joining of Starling and Lecter as contraries, Lecter may possibly, while still maintaining and acknowledging an evil side, no longer act upon it, having progressed beyond these actions. In addition, one could suggest that since Lecter has experienced forgiveness and love from Starling, and mutual sacrifice in that each was willing to risk him- or herself for the other, they have entered into the "Great Eternity," as Blake described in plate 61 of *Jerusalem*. On this plate Blake writes of how Salvation (The Great Eternity) consists of both "Continual Forgiveness of Sins" (l. 22) and "Perpetual Mutual Sacrifice" (l. 23). Now that Lecter and Starling have been reconciled to their pasts, have forgiven themselves and been forgiven by their memories, now that they are willing to accept and forgive their evil aspects, perhaps they do not need to act upon them, allowing them to live in a peaceful Eternity. Messent suggests as much, claiming that "it seems that Lecter leaves the traumatic loss of his sister—and the cannibalism that comes to be associated with it—finally behind him" (17) and that Starling "allow[s] Lecter to remember his dismembered self, curing him by making him whole" (28). Simpson reads the ending similarly, stating that Lecter "becomes wholly integrated again.... Though still a monster, he is a rehabilitated one" (*Making Murder* 219).

This peaceful and haunting coupling of Lecter and Starling at the end, while surprising for many, does flow organically from the novels, as illustrated by King's review (mentioned earlier). Ellis also comments on the rational build-up to this ending, claiming that "Starling and Lecter, as a perverse form of 'romantic' leading couple ... becomes the result of the logical developments of the narratives of the three books" (172). Szumskyj refers to the union as "an inevitable one" (208) and claims that

"Clarice's path was realistic" (209). Another insightful description of the Lecter/Starling pairing comes from Simpson, who discusses the relationship between Starling and Lecter in gothic terms, saying that in gothic

> [b]oth [the victim and the villain] are alienated from bourgeois society. Through that distant perspective they can see how fragile and illusory bourgeois values really are. Furthermore, even as they threaten one another in the dark Gothic landscape, they exhibit an odd understanding, even sympathy, for the other's lonely plight. This pairing of outsiders is demonstrated quite overtly in the fiction of Thomas Harris, through the developing Lecter/Starling alliance in *The Silence of the Lambs* and its logical sexual conclusion in *Hannibal* [*Psycho Paths* 58].

While many readers and critics do not agree with Simpson that the ending is logical and is not a betrayal of the characters, read against the Blakean allusions the novel could end no other way.

Hannibal— *Film*

As with the other Lecter novels, *Hannibal* spawned a film version, directed by Ridley Scott and released in 2001, and as with the other film adaptations, some aspects of the novel had to be changed, altering, of course, a reading of the text. For example, once again (given the nature of the medium) access to characters' thoughts without the use of potentially annoying or overwhelming voiceovers becomes difficult. Therefore, just as Graham's final Shiloh thoughts were left out of both film versions of *Red Dragon*, many of Starling's thoughts that reveal her development and acceptance of the coexistence of good and evil and her expanding taste and senses, aspects of her personality that ultimately support her joining with Lecter, are left out of the film. This necessary omission, as well as readers' reactions to the ending of the novel *Hannibal*, led to the biggest alteration — that of the ending.

In the film, while Lecter does save Starling from the rampaging pigs, after she has freed him she is suffering from a gunshot wound and not a tranquilizer. Lecter operates, removing the bullets. There is no hypnotism and no drugs (except morphine for pain). She wakes to find herself dressed in a black gown, unlike in the book, where she dresses herself and joins Lecter for dinner. Starling finds her gun and handcuffs and calls 911. While she waits for help to arrive she tries to negotiate with Lecter; when that fails, she attacks him. Starling also does not participate in the meal of Krendler's brain. In her final confrontation with Lecter, while her hair is pinned in the refrigerator door and Lecter is kissing her, she manages to handcuff him to her, causing him to cut off his own hand in order to escape. We last see him on a plane, enjoying a meal from Dean and Deluca, as well as some leftovers of Krendler's brain. A young boy asks to try the food, and Lecter, somewhat reluctantly, finally allows him to. So, while the film does not end with a marriage of heaven and hell, it does not end with a triumph of good over evil either, as Lecter is still out there, free to act on his evil impulses, and, in fact, without Starling's influence perhaps he is even more likely to continue in his evil ways, particularly given some alterations in his characterization in this film, which will be addressed below.

Ridley Scott, the film's director, claims that Harris had "been nervous about our proposed ending. The book reached for something that was in his heart, obviously ... Clarice goes off with Hannibal at the end of the book. I felt it was too much of a quantum leap that a straight arrow like Clarice would do such a thing" (qtd. in Sexton 145). Since you cannot count on viewers of *Hannibal* having read the novel (or, in fact, having seen or read *Silence*), retaining the novel's ending may in fact have been a shock. Because of this, the change to the ending is understandable, though it undercuts Harris's Blakean message regarding good and evil.

Another major change from the novel to the film is the absence of *Ancient of Days* from Verger's room. However, the filmmakers inserted a different explicit reference to Blake by using a postcard of Blake's *Ghost of a Flea*. O'Brien views the use of this postcard as something "throw[n] in" by the director that "even as an obscure *Red Dragon/Manhunter* in-joke ... seems a half-hearted gesture" (159). Given that the postcard is never identified, it could easily be categorized as an in-joke, a nod to those in the audience familiar with Blake's works. However, the inclusion of this image also maintains Harris's use of references to Blake, emphasizing the ideological connection between the two. In addition, the postcard functions to reveal a characteristic of Verger, as does *Ancient of Days* in the novel. The image is one of Blake's "visionary heads" sketched at the encouragement of John Varley, who suggested that Blake draw the figures he saw in his visions. Blake claimed that the flea told him that fleas' bodies were inhabited by the souls of bloodthirsty men. Blake's portrait is of a flea-like man, or humanoid flea, a combination of animal and human, of a dual nature. In the novel Verger's ownership of *Ancient of Days* reveals his belief in a Urizenic God and works, along with his cruel actions, to highlight his hypocrisy, his delusion that his vengeance fits well with his Christian beliefs. Here, the postcard is connected to Verger. He has chosen it as the way to set up Starling, to produce a note supposedly written from Lecter to her. Perhaps Verger chose it because he believed that Blake would be an artist whom Lecter would have an affinity with, or perhaps he hoped the gruesome image would be easily believed to be from Lecter; no matter his rationale, the image is associated with him and not Lecter, and also, though to a lesser extent, with Krendler, whose job it is to confront Starling with it. Verger is the bloodthirsty man — literally out for Lecter's blood. Krendler, while not desiring actual blood, is an accomplice in Verger's plan for Lecter and has metaphorically attempted to bleed Starling's career dry. Both Verger and Krendler are the fleas that try to hide behind a mask of humanity.

However, in the film Verger's hypocrisy and cruelty are not as clear as in the novel. He does state that he has found salvation thanks to his encounter with Lecter, a salvation that seems to be at odds with his desire for vengeance. However, in other ways, Verger's own evil is downplayed or left out of the film. His past as a child predator is mentioned, both to Starling and in a flashback of his encounter with Lecter; however, his cruelty against children appears to have ceased, for there are no children on his estate whose tears he can use in his drinks. In the film there is no Margot, so his past abuses of and continued cruelty to his sister are also not part of the film. His aide Cordell does not have a criminal past as he does in the book and is, in fact, a conflation with Doemling, being named here Cordell Doemling and having some of Doemling's lines.

It is Cordell who is with Verger at the beginning of the film talking to Barney and hearing what Barney has to say about Starling and Lecter's relationship, learning that Lecter thought Starling "was charming and amusing." As this is the main point that Barney shares, this is the first of many indications that Lecter's interest in her is mainly romantic or sexual, not intellectual or philosophical. According to Verger, speaking with Cordell, Lecter's interest is not even primarily sexual/romantic. He speaks Doemling's theory here about Lecter being interested in Starling's suffering, saying, "No matter how Barney may want to romanticize it, make it Beauty and the Beast, Lecter's object, as I know from personal experience, has always been degradation, suffering.... He comes in the guise of a mentor

... but it's distress that excites him. To draw him in she needs to be distressed. Let the damage he sees suggest the damage he could do."

Verger's willingness to use Starling as a pawn works as another indication of his character; likewise, Krendler's attitude toward and treatment of Starling reveal his own bloodthirsty character. In fact, Krendler is perhaps the least changed in characterization from the novel. In an early scene with Starling he clearly takes time to ogle her legs. Later, when he visits Starling in the basement, before he talks to her, he sees a sketch that Lecter presumably did of Starling that has a sticky note over the breasts; Krendler lifts the paper to peek at the breasts. It is in this scene that the audience learns that he made advances to Starling that were rebuffed because he was married, and he says the "town is full of cornpone country pussy" before hitting on her again. Not only has Krendler tried to derail Starling's career, but he also tries to seem superior to Lecter by, as he does in the novel, saying he always thought Lecter "was a queer" because of "all that artsy-fartsy stuff." As in the novel, in his motivations and his treatment of Starling, Krendler is set up against Lecter and is found lacking. The film therefore maintains, at least on this surface level, Harris's theme of the attractiveness of evil and the ugliness and hypocrisy of the legal system.

In the novel, Krendler and Verger misunderstand Lecter, particularly his relationship to Starling, and it is Barney who has learned from Lecter and understands him. In the film as well Barney has learned from Lecter, mentioning briefly how he would discuss his courses with him. He also emphasizes that he knew to be civil to Lecter in order to survive and that he had no fear that Lecter would come after him because Lecter "preferred to eat the rude." However, Barney does not emphasize, as he does several times in the novel, that Lecter would not lie. Also, while he says that Lecter and he discussed Starling, the only detail he gives is of how Lecter said Starling was a deep roller. Barney does not indicate, either to Starling or to Verger, that Lecter was interested in any aspect of Starling except her appearance and charm. There is no mention of her courage, or her curse of taste, or her becoming anything. Finally, on a minor but telling note, there is no mention of the Vermeers— the reason in the novel that Barney sells the Lecter memorabilia. Therefore, in the film, not only has his time with Lecter not expanded his senses, but it also is not clear what he is spending the money from the Lecter memorabilia on, leaving him to seem purely mercenary in this regard.

5. Harris's Marriage of Heaven and Hell

Starling's senses and taste in the film have also not been expanded by Lecter, at least not to the extent indicated in the novel. She does catch the scent of something on Lecter's letter to her that leads her to get the smell analyzed, and she does have a magazine open to a Gucci ad in her apartment (although Lecter may have opened the page to the ad). As said previously, there is no mention of her curse of taste and no inner reflection on her desire for taste (since these reflections in the novel occur inside her head they would have been difficult to translate to the screen). She does seem to understand Lecter well, able to explain to Krendler why Lecter ate his victims, and perhaps this understanding goes beyond a simple intellectual understanding. When Krendler enters her basement office she has been listening to a tape of Lecter talking about how it is natural to want to taste your enemies. When Krendler realizes she is there and asks what she is doing in the dark, Starling responds, "Considering cannibalism." While on the surface it means she was thinking about Lecter and the rationale for cannibalism, and the secondary meaning of considering being a cannibal herself seems like a bad joke, it is possible that for a brief time, perhaps just in the instant of seeing Krendler there, Starling truly and viscerally understood. Lecter does seem to have become a large part of her life, even while absent. When Barney asks her if she ever thinks of Lecter, she responds, "About 30 seconds every day. He's always with me, like a bad habit." However, in the novel she frequently told people that Lecter would not lie, but here, while she clearly understands Lecter better than anyone else, like Barney, she does not emphasize or even mention Lecter's truthfulness.

These lapses on the part of Barney and Starling to emphasize Lecter's telling the truth and their trust in him works with some changes in the film to indicate an altered characterization of Lecter. For example, while Starling tells Krendler that Lecter ate victims that exasperated him or whose disappearances he considered a public service, the film portrays Lecter as more capricious, killing for fun's sake alone. The key example of this is at the opera. When a young couple passes by and the woman says to her companion, "Let's get something to eat," Lecter smiles and says, "Why not?" turning to follow them, implying that he will kill and eat them, that his cannibalism is purely recreational and random now. Another change in this regard occurs at the end of the film, when Lecter includes his container of Krendler's brains as his in-flight meal and shares it with a young boy. This scene occurs earlier in the novel, as Lecter flies back to

America, and while he does have his own special meal that he has brought on board, it contains no human flesh or organs and he just wants the young boy to leave him alone. The film's ending emphasizes his cannibalism and how infectious his evil may be. Essentially, Lecter lacks depth and complexity here. While we see a sophisticated side to him, we do not see much of a human side to him. The lack of any reference to his memories or trauma over Mischa adds to this portrayal as well. In addition, the nature of his interest in Starling is not clear. At times, his interest seems merely to be motivated by physical attraction; at others, he seems to enjoy playing with her, happy that she can and will keep up; at still others, he does seem to both respect her character and want her to grow beyond her narrow worldview to see the reality of human nature and institutions like the FBI.

The letter that Lecter sends Starling after he hears about the botched drug raid begins the same way in the film as it does in the novel; however, the letter soon turns to focusing on what worries and shames her the most and then turns to Lecter himself. He talks about how he has been elevated to the 10 Most Wanted List and hopes she is on the case "because [he] need[s] to come out of retirement and return to public life." The letter does not include information that will help her grow psychologically (like thinking about her memories while looking at her reflection in the skillet) and, more importantly, does not refer to Starling as a warrior — a detail that in the novel is central in allowing her to operate outside the institutions of the law and to understand who truly knows her. On the basis of this letter alone in the film it seems that Lecter just enjoys playing with Starling. Lecter's tone of voice when on the phone with her in Italy, his playful "Nothing I would love more than to be able to chat with you.... See you around," adds to the sense that he is playing, that he sees her simply as a well-matched opponent or plaything. Missing from these two instances of contact is any indication of his admiration of, or even recognition of, her complexity. Since in the film it is no longer really Lecter who calls Starling "the honey in the lion," but instead Verger setting a trap and writing as Lecter, the audience misses this characterization of Starling and the truth it reveals about Lecter's interest in her.

The extended phone conversation between Lecter and Starling, original to the film, does, however, add a layer of complexity to their relationship and to Lecter's motivations. He begins by saying he likes to talk to her when her eyes are open (he had visited her apartment the night

5. Harris's Marriage of Heaven and Hell

before while she slept) and that she has shapely feet (he will leave her a gift of expensive shoes). These and other small moments indicate a physical attraction to her. However, he also demonstrates a concern that echoes his conversations with Barney about her being a deep roller. He says he is worried about her because she "fell in love with the Bureau" and discovered it did not love her in return, and in fact resents her. He explains that it resents her because she "serve[s] the idea of order. They don't. [She] believe[s] in the oath [she] took. They don't. [She] feel[s] it is [her] duty to protect the sheep. They don't." He tells her that those at the Bureau both hate and envy her and are weak and unruly, so she should "believe in nothing." Here it seems clear that he admires Starling for her strength of belief and difference from those around her and he wants her to recognize this strength and difference as well. However, when she says that if he turns himself in to her, she'll protect him from Verger, and he asks her if she will stay with him in his prison cell and hold his hand because they "could have some fun," Lecter seems to be focused mainly on playing with her (and perhaps his sexual attraction to her). After joking with her he turns to distressing her, asking her what she will do now, if she will work as a chambermaid like her mommy. The conversation ends, though, with an indication of the complexity of his feelings for her. He asks Starling, "What if I did it for you? ... Harmed them, the ones who harmed you? What if I made them scream apologies?" He does want to protect her, to punish those who offend her, as he did with Miggs in *Silence*. However he goes on to say that he knows she wouldn't want that because her sense of right and wrong would make her feel like an accomplice. Lecter knows he cannot make Starling compromise this strong sense of right and wrong and seems to respect it. Perhaps he respects it in part because even though Starling now knows how corrupt and hypocritical the manmade institutions are, she is still willing to protect her ideals, and in this way she does follow her own code, albeit one very different one from Lecter's.

Lecter's respect for her fidelity to her ideals, for her courage, even in the knowledge of the corruptions of institutions and their lack of respect for her, is seen again in their final confrontation in the kitchen. When Lecter tells Starling, "Given the chance you would deny me my life," Starling responds, "Not your life." She wouldn't want him dead, and Lecter knows this, responding, "My freedom." Starling, unlike Verger, does not want revenge; she wants justice. Lecter then probes further into her relationship with the FBI, saying, "Would they have you back then — the people you despise almost as much as they despise you? Will they give you a medal? Would you have it framed to look at and remind you of your courage and incorruptibility? All you would need for that is a mirror." This passage is similar to the part of the letter in the novel in which Lecter tells her to look at her reflection and later tells her she is a warrior. He does respect her strength — that, in part, is why he is attracted to her — but her strength here is why she cannot give in to him. Their final exchange is the most telling clue as to what Lecter may want from her. He asks her, "Tell me, would you ever say to me 'Stop — if you loved me you'd stop?'" When Starling replies, "Not in a thousand years," Lecter says, "That's my girl," and kisses her. The kiss and reference to love do indicate an attraction, but in addition he is happy that she would not ask him to stop in return for love. Why? He may be happy she does not love him, but it is more likely that he understands that her answer means that even if she did love him she would never make that bargain. She knows that you cannot just ask someone to stop acting on their nature because a change of nature would take more than a simple request, perhaps an exchange, a quid pro quo — of the kind in the novel regarding the healing of both of their traumas. At the end he admires her strength, courage, and insight, which is why he cuts off his own hand and not hers.

Even with the change in the ending and the lack of reciprocal healing from trauma, one striking element remains — audience interest in and attachment to Lecter. While the ending of the film differs from that of the novel, it ends with Lecter free. Two alternative endings were considered, according to Ridley Scott's commentary, of which only one was filmed. It is only in the non-filmed version that there is even a hint of Lecter's defeat. In that version, after Starling handcuffed herself to Lecter, the next scene would show both in a boat. Lecter would fling himself overboard, pulling Starling with him and forcing her, in order to survive, to produce the handcuff key. She would find the key and would free herself, leaving the viewer to watch Lecter continue to sink. The film would thus not explicitly show Lecter dying but would imply it. Scott claims in his commentary that this version was rejected and not even filmed because it seemed too much like a James Bond plot, and, more importantly, he believed audiences would want to see Lecter free. The second possible version is similar to the chosen ending; however, Starling does not handcuff herself to Lecter while he kisses her — he merely leaves after kissing her. The final scene once again is Lecter on the plane eating his meal and talking with the

5. Harris's Marriage of Heaven and Hell

young boy who is interested in the food. It is this interchange with the boy, with its subtle differences from the chosen version, that caused it not to be used, according to Scott. In this version, Lecter asks the boy if his mother ever warned him about taking food from strangers, and when the boy says yes, Lecter says it doesn't matter because the mother is asleep. Test audiences saw this as revealing how Lecter was corrupting the boy, encouraging him in cannibalism. This corruption is further emphasized in that, here, after the boy tastes the brains and says they are good, Lecter asks if he would like more and feeds him another forkful. Lecter's corruption of the boy was too much for viewers to take and so this version was not used. As both the changes themselves and Scott's commentary suggest, while we may not want Starling to go off with Lecter and would have difficulty admitting that a "straight arrow" like her could see any worth in being with Lecter, we also, like Starling in the novel, want to see Lecter free. Maybe we just like being scared, knowing that the monster walks, but maybe we agree with Starling that you "can't waste a man that's crazy enough to tell the truth" (242).

CHAPTER 6

Printing in the Infernal Method
Hannibal Rising

While critical and personal opinion of *Hannibal* is divided, the near universal reaction to Harris's fourth and final Lecter novel, *Hannibal Rising*, is negative. For example, Jason Whittaker, in discussing the use of Blake in the films adapted from the novels, states that he will be discussing the "Lecter trilogy (and, yes, I mean trilogy. Does anyone even remember *Hannibal Rising*?)." Even Peter Guttridge's review in *The Observer*, which suggests that the novel can be entertaining, emphasizes its "ludicrous" aspects. This prequel was published in 2006 after a much shorter gap between novels than usual for Harris. In addition, Harris was writing the screenplay for the film at the same time he was completing the novel, and the novel was published just a few months before the film was released. The weak quality of the novel has been suggested to be a consequence of the shorter turnaround time and writing it concurrently with the screenplay, both supposedly caused in turn by Harris's attempt to hold on to his creative property. According to Daniel Fierman, Dino DeLaurentiis wished to capitalize on the success of the previous films but there were no more Lecter novels to adapt, leading him to pressure Harris by saying that if he didn't create the prequel, DeLaurentiis would find someone else to do it.

As a prequel the novel attempts to tell the story of Lecter's youth. Regardless of how well written the novel could have been, being an origin story was bound to disappoint those who wish to think of Lecter as Satan, as someone whose evil is shrouded in mystery or has no origin. The audience disappointed by the brief mention of his childhood in *Hannibal* would certainly not enjoy an entire novel devoted to the topic. As Simpson describes it in *Making Murder*, Harris—in the eyes of those who don't like

6. Printing in the Infernal Method

Hannibal or *Hannibal Rising*—stripped "the good doctor of his mythic grandeur ... pluck[ed] him from the metaphysical realm of pure evil" (264). There is an audience that believes that Lecter is inherently different from the rest of humanity and therefore cannot have an origin. In addition, it is true, as discussed in the previous chapter, that an origin story does seem to contradict passages in the first two novels in which Lecter emphasizes that natures are given and not produced. But while it is the existence of an origin story that bothered some readers, S.T. Joshi claims that Harris did not go far enough in creating the origin story, stating that the biggest problem with the novel is that Harris was not willing "to engage in a psychological portrait of Hannibal" and so all that readers get is "a flat succession of incidents" (131). For Joshi, then, and perhaps for others as well, the problem is not that the novel is an origin story but that it is too simple to be an origin story, particular for someone as complex as Lecter.

Perhaps, however, the novel is not an origin story in the true sense of the term, nor is it meant to be. There are details in the novel that undercut its role as an origin story and imply that discovering an origin of Lecter's, or anyone's, evil or nature is difficult, if not impossible. The most explicit indication of the difficulty of pinpointing the origin for Lecter's evil in the traumatic moment from his childhood of the killing and eating of Mischa, in the memory that haunts him of seeing her teeth in stool, is that when he finds Mischa's skeleton he sees that her teeth are intact and realizes that his memory is a false one (221). In addition, the prologue indicates that Lecter's Memory Palace is fragmentary (1). Lecter, while having an impressive memory, cannot complete trust or rely on it. By extension, we, humanity in general, cannot trust memory, and if we cannot trust memory, how can we come to any conclusion regarding an event's role in the creation of one's nature? The prologue also mentions that Lecter frequently gave different dates for events in his life, including his birthdate (2); this could be a justification for the discrepancies between his age given in *Hannibal* versus that given in *Hannibal Rising* during the events at the hunting lodge, or it could be a further indication of the inability of others to truly know anyone else's past or even the difficulty for an individual to correctly and consistently recall his or her own past. A small detail, one that has been pointed out as being an error on Harris's part that reveals how rushed he was in composition and how little he cared about continuity, also may indicate how difficult it is to know anyone's past and how most people lack observational skills: Nowhere in *Hannibal*

Rising is there mention of Lecter's polydactylism. The details given in the earlier novels indicate that he should still have this extra finger in this novel, and yet, while his red eyes are mentioned, his extra finger is not. This seemingly objective, solid physical detail is not mentioned, perhaps revealing that one cannot be certain of anything, no matter how seemingly real or physical it is. Perhaps it is not mentioned because no one around young Lecter took any particular note of it, being so unobservant that they even overlooked an extra finger. Of course, it may just be a consequence of Harris rushing the novel to completion and forgetting to mention it; however, its absence, along with the other points indicating the instability of memory and the past, may be working toward a particular point. Harris may be implying the impossibility of an origin story for Lecter because, as the other novels have established, and as Blake's philosophy reveals, the beast, the evil within Lecter, exists in all of humanity, and therefore has no origin. It does, however, require an awakening or awareness in order to be acted upon. At the end of the prologue we are invited to "watch as the beast within turns from the teat" (2). It is interesting that Harris does not ask us to watch the beast within Lecter; this may have been a poetic or stylistic choice, but the simplistic description could also imply that this is the beast within all of us and we are provided with this rare chance to watch its movement. Simpson agrees with this assessment, saying that this statement in the prologue "suggests a basis in human instinct for what Hannibal becomes" and that "the beast is a metaphor for those base urges" in us all (*Making Murder* 277).

    While this Blakean theme of human nature can be found in the novel, as in *Silence* there are no direct references to Blake in this work. The closest we get is the description of Lecter's handwriting as "copperplate" (110), similar to the description in *Hannibal*, which, as explained in the previous chapter, can be linked to Blake through an explicit connection of copperplate handwriting to Blake in *Red Dragon*. The thematic connections to Blake in this novel are fewer than in the earlier ones; however, that does not mean that this book stands alone, outside of the thematic connections explored so far. If we view this not as the fourth novel in the series but as the first part of Lecter's journey, the connection to the Blakean ideas of good and evil becomes clearer. But before the novel can be read as the first in the series (the focus of the concluding chapter), the Blakean themes in the novel itself must be explored: the complex and contradictory nature of humanity and nature itself, the flaws of the institutions of law and gov-

6. Printing in the Infernal Method

ernment, the flaws of religion, and the importance of heightened senses and observation to understanding.

As in the earlier novels, we have here, too, several characters who embody contraries, beginning with Lecter's ancestor and namesake Hannibal the Grim, who made captured soldiers build Lecter Castle, then released them only to have many of them stay because of his goodness, a man who also threw enemies into the oubliette. As Hannibal the Grim is only mentioned briefly, this is all we know of him, but it establishes in Lecter's background a complex mixture of good and evil. The most prominent character, however, to reveal this complexity, this mixture of qualities, is Lecter's aunt, Lady Murasaki. Just as Lecter will later recognize in Graham and Starling this mix of good and evil natures, Lady Murasaki recognizes it in Lecter and attempts to show him proper balance. When she shows him her ancestor's armor she says that she wants him to be like his father and uncle, and like her ancestor, "but with more compassion," indicating that she wants in him, or would accept in him, a mixture of strength/violence and compassion (80). She doesn't want him to distance himself from the fierceness of the warrior who can behead his enemies, but to balance it with other qualities as well. Lady Murasaki seems to have a mixture of these qualities. Her capability for violence is revealed when Lecter attacks the butcher in her defense and she, in turn, defends him against the butcher's brother, holding "a large butcher knife against the butcher's brother's throat" (93). Her complexity is best seen, though, when, instead of turning Lecter over to the police, she protects him, not just in the moments before Popil arrives at the house, but also in her placing the severed head on the mailbox while he is interrogated (123).

Given these violent moments, it is not surprising that Lady Murasaki is often described as a hunter waiting for her prey to come to her. However, she is not a hunter in a violent sense but instead in a sexual or physical sense, and her prey is men like Popil. She also uses this seductive power to attempt to tame Lecter toward the end of the novel, but Lecter is not ready for balance yet. He is early in his journey and not quite the man he will be with Starling at the end of *Hannibal*. He is a young man of both good and evil natures, but he refuses the complete balance that he may have found with Lady Murasaki and that he doesn't achieve until he leaves behind his brooding for Mischa and comes together with Starling. Here his focus is still on Mischa, on the hole she left in his life, on the injustice of her death, and on his guilt—whether for not being able to save her or for eating her as well, as Grutas claims, or for surviving the war when so many didn't.

Even though he is not yet ready to embrace the duality of his character, it does exist. Simpson calls Lecter "the ultimate embodiment of that paradox," the paradox being that of human nature's "bestial quality hand-in-hand with its higher beauty" (*Making Murder* 281), which Harris returns to in each of the novels. This duality is seen particularly in Lecter's compassion for Mischa before the horrific events at the hunting lodge and also in his continued care for the young children at the orphanage. He protects the vulnerable and attacks bullies. As the headmaster puts it, "Hannibal can be dangerous to persons larger than himself. He's fine with the little ones" (64); he acts the same way in the village school in France (89). His reaction to the butcher later is also an attempt to protect the vulnerable, his aunt the outsider, from the bully (93). When he wants to frighten Kolnas he does so through implying that he has harmed Kolnas's children, but he has not actually done so because he would not harm the innocent and vulnerable children. Paradoxically, his complex nature, a mixture of good and evil, compassionate and violent, is revealed in the almost simplistic path of revenge he takes. His violence is directed by the desire for justice for the innocent and vulnerable (Mischa, and Grutas's other victims). This path of revenge indicates, however, how he is still out of balance, since he seems to be seeking revenge in part to guide God's hand in vengeance, aligning him with Verger in *Hannibal*.

Lecter's reaction to and interaction with nature also reveal his compassion and protection of the vulnerable against bullies, similar to his protection of the deer against the hunter in *Hannibal*. In this novel, as in the previous ones, nature is revealed to be both beautiful and dangerous, and it needs to be respected and protected. Lecter recognizes the beauty and danger of nature and how it can be either depending upon how you treat it. His relationship with nature also connects to his heightened senses in that he observes closely enough to notice and take advantage of these aspects of nature. Of all of the animals referenced in the novel, the black swans at Lecter Castle are the most connected to earlier novels and to Blakean themes. In *Silence* swans are used by Lecter to indicate the beauty that God is capable of creating, as opposed to typhoid. Here the swans are not only beautiful but also, as swans naturally are, powerful and dangerous. The alpha black swan appears early in the novel, when it comes out of the water hissing at Lecter and Mischa (5). The swan is described as knowing

6. Printing in the Infernal Method

Lecter all his life, and yet still he comes out aggressively, suggesting, perhaps, the difficulty of completely taming anything. Lecter, however, has been taught how to face down the swan: he "raised his arms to shoulder height ... his reach augmented with willow branches," giving him the "greater wingspan" (6). The swan is intimidated and returns to the water. Not only do Lecter's actions reveal a studied way of behaving in harmony with nature, not forcing the swan through violence or dominance back in the water but instead convincing it that it should go, but they also may be a subtle, perhaps even unconscious, connection to Blake. As discussed previously, Blake's images, both his paintings and his illuminated works, are full of images of birds with outstretched wings and human figures with arms outstretched as if they are wings. These images appear at moments of great pain or illumination (or both). Since they appear here and later in his adolescence when he returns to the castle/orphanage, the swans may therefore indicate that Lecter's youth is a time of painful enlightenment.

When the swans appear when Lecter Castle is attacked at the end of Chapter 3, they no longer represent just the beauty and danger of nature, but also the inhumanity and dangerous nature of humans, especially those oblivious to their surroundings and the living things around them, those who have forgotten or never learned Blake's idea, repeated in several works, that "Every Thing That Lives Is Holy." As the alpha swan attempts to lead the others away in flight, he is injured by the planes and fire and falls. His mate comes to his side and tries to move him. As a tank approaches, the swan stretches her wings out to turn it away, hissing and hitting the tank with her wings until "the tank rolled over them, oblivious, in its whirring treads a mush of flesh and feathers" (20). The humans have not seen or cared about the swans and have therefore destroyed them. As mentioned previously, Lecter re-encounters some of these swans after the war when he is back at the castle, now an orphanage. As before, the male swan comes out to confront him and Lecter spreads his arms to imitate wings, sending the swan back into the water (52). The other boys do not know how to respond to the swans or to treat them with respect; they comment on how when they tried to steal the eggs they got knocked down. When they see what Lecter does, how he controls or interacts with the swans, they respond by throwing stones at the swans (52), leading Lecter to attack them for bullying the animals. Not only does this moment indicate painful enlightenment in regard to others' natures, but it also reveals Lecter's compassionate side, and the cruelty of humans in general.

Like the swans, spiders are used to reveal both the beauty and the danger of nature. As Lecter waits for the butcher so he can kill him, he passes the time watching a spider, "a splendid yellow and black orb weaver" (101). Its work is beautiful and seems to be in time to the lute; the observation ends when a beetle flies into the web and the spider binds it. While beautiful, the spider is deadly to its prey. Not only is Lecter literally in tune with nature (here the spider as he waits), but after killing the butcher he releases both the fish on the line and the crickets that were being used for bait (104), showing compassion for living creatures. Like the crickets, the ortolans seen later in the novel are creators of song, and, like the crickets that the butcher used as bait, ortolans are eaten — however, not by fish but by humans, even though this is illegal. They are an example of not only humanity's use of nature but also its cruelty or disregard for other creatures. In addition, they exemplify humanity's cruelty and yet desire for happiness and beauty. When Lecter sees the ortolans singing in an aviary in Kolnas's café, he makes a connection between humans and birds, saying, "They're just like us.... They can smell the others cooking, and still they try to sing" (246). This is one of the few explicit statements regarding the ability of people to create beauty and live in a hostile, or at least indifferent, world; however, the entire novel is set in the context of postwar Europe, which itself reveals the duality and cruelty of humanity. The ortolans, unlike the humans, may be able to escape this dual nature of humanity, though. After Hannibal kills Kolnas, he releases the ortolans (294). They no longer have to smell the others cooking but can be free and return to their home in the Baltic, as Lecter hopes.

Many of the characters are in a similar condition to that of the ortolans: away from home, refugees, having experienced the cruelty of war — some from the victims' perspective, some from the tormentors' perspective, and some from both. If anything emphasizes humans' capacity for cruelty and blurs lines of morality and categorization, it is war. Simpson claims that "the war does suit Harris's controlling theme of the violence in the human heart, here metastasized to a global level" (*Making Murder* 313). The reactions to these experiences in war and of cruelty vary among the characters, emphasizing that one experience cannot be solely responsible for one's nature, since some react to the same or similar events with cruelty while others react with increased compassion. This, therefore, undercuts the idea that Lecter's experience at the hunting lodge created the monster he was. Many of the other characters experienced such horrors

6. Printing in the Infernal Method

and not all became what he did. Yes, Grutas and his gang became thugs after the war and were murderers and smugglers. However, judging from their descriptions early in the novel, these were already men who were willing to engage the darker side of themselves. In addition, their focus at first was an understandable one of survival; however, they took it further and used the violence and disregard for others as a way to get ahead, especially after the war. Grutas in particular narrowly focuses on his own financial and selfish gain. Like Chilton and Krendler in earlier novels, his vision is limited to only what will help further his desires; he, however, not only is blind to the needs of others but is actively cruel. This is the primary difference between Grutas and Lecter. While Grutas may share Lecter's desire for the finer things in life (a Bosendorfer piano, for instance), Grutas reveals no compassionate side, no concern for others at all. While both Grutas and Lecter were influenced by events in the war, those events are not the sole creators of their natures; if so, either both would show compassion or both would be needlessly cruel. The difference between the two lies, in part, in how well they can see from someone else's perspective, how much compassion they can show, and whether they accept the complexity and connections of the world. When young, Lecter learned from his tutor, Jakov, that "every person is worth your time.... If at first appearance a person seems dull, then look harder, look *into* him" (original emphasis, 24). Jakov, a persecuted Jew, understands, like Blake did, that every man contains both good and bad. Due in part to these lessons from Jakov, even in his quest for cruel vengeance Lecter reveals heightened awareness of the duality of the world and the interconnectedness of humans and nature, leading to moments of compassion.

This awareness is also partly due to the influence of Lady Murasaki, who herself has great reason for desiring vengeance — her family in Hiroshima. However, she is the one who emphasizes to Lecter the necessity for compassion and justice within the bounds of the legal system, even as she protects him from Popil and the law. And Popil's reaction to his experiences not only reveals further complexity but also indicates why he is portrayed in a better light than many of the other officers of the law in Harris's novels, being treated more like Graham or Starling than Krendler. Popil is not single-minded in his pursuit of Lecter, and, most importantly, he does not pursue him with only his own professional or financial gain in mind.

While Popil does try to uphold the law, unlike Chilton or Krendler, he is not using the law mainly to further his own career and he does recognize, to some extent, the flaws of the law. This is why, even though it is clear that the young Lecter does not care for him and is jealous of the attention he pays to Lady Murasaki, Popil is not portrayed as distasteful or foolish, as Chilton and Krendler are, and also does not encounter the fate of Pazzi in *Hannibal*. From Popil's experience working for the Resistance, he is able to recognize the horrors and beasts that lurk within humanity. Thus, when talking with Lecter after the butcher's death, he is able to read the young man, even through his calm veneer and in spite of the fact that his blood pressure and heartbeat never increase. Because of his "experience and knowledge of the awful," he is able to hear a slight change in Lecter's voice that he recognizes as "Other" (122). This does not scare Popil so much as thrill him because it provides him with a hunt; in this way, he is like Graham later tracking Lecter. He also, however, as Lecter discovers, was a policeman for the Vichy government who joined the Resistance when he realized that sometimes the law does not operate for justice or the good. At Louis's execution, Louis asks Popil where the police were "when the Nazis threw the children into the trucks" (195). Popil knows where the police were, as becomes clear when Lecter gives Popil the note from Louis and Popil says he "saw one of their trains" and then deserted because he finally really saw or understood what the police were allowing to happen (282). In addition, his experience in the Resistance led him to understand that sometimes uncontrolled vengeance leads to further bad consequences. Having to prove himself loyal to the Resistance, he killed a member of the Gestapo, and in retaliation eight villagers were killed, leading him to feel guilty for those deaths (282). In some ways he is closer to having his natures in balance than Lecter at this point. He works both inside and outside of the law (for example, knowing what Lecter has planned and letting him follow through, to some extent). A key indicator of Popil's being in balance is that he is not damaged as Graham is because he recognizes the cruelty of humans and accepts its existence while working for mercy at the same time. Like Lady Murasaki, he could be a guide for Lecter, could reveal a way to balance these contraries, but Lecter is not ready yet. Like others who encounter Lecter, Popil calls him a monster (282), claiming that the little boy Hannibal died at the hunting lodge; however, he, like Starling, doesn't want Lecter killed but instead locked up so "they can study him and try to find out what he is" (283). It seems that while Popil understands how good men can do evil things, and

6. Printing in the Infernal Method

how injustice and cruelty exist in the world, he does believe the monster in Lecter was created, not born, and is now a thing apart from humanity to be studied.

And yet other details point to Lecter "the monster" as not being created but instead emerging out of something that existed within him and that is now being given the freedom to act. At the end of Part I Harris writes of Lecter, "He is growing and changing, or perhaps emerging as what he has ever been" (159). Clearly, Harris does not have in mind that this novel is a simple origin explanation; it is, in fact, more complex than that, at times indicating that Lecter has chosen what he is becoming, or at least has chosen to let it out, while at others implying that it is beyond his control. For example, when Lady Murasaki tells Lecter that he is being "drawn into the dark" (252), he replies that it is not a matter of being drawn, comparing it to his years of muteness following the events at the hunting lodge: "When I couldn't speak I was not drawn into silence, silence captured me" (252). Lecter here seems to be saying that who he is or who he is becoming is not in his control, a sign that while he is already embracing his dark aspect, he may be more like Dolarhyde at this point, seeing it as separate from him and not a complete part of himself. Regardless of how well Lecter is able to recognize his coexisting natures at this point, what is established in this novel is that all people are capable of violence; the context of postwar Europe emphasizes that fact. The most explicit comment on humanity's cruelty comes as Milko prepares to kill Lecter and Harris writes that he "made the slight adjustment of the heart that we make before we kill" (258). The use of "we" here emphasizes that all humans contain this capacity for violence or evil and all it requires is a slight adjustment on our part to act on it. The important question then becomes whether all are willing to make that adjustment, and whether, once the adjustment is made, the readjustment back to good and peaceful can be made.

Lecter seems able to make this adjustment; however, he cannot yet re-adjust back at this point. He is not accepting of both of his natures, seeing them as binaries and thinking he can be one or the other but not both. His opinion of God at this point is also different than it will be later. As discussed in the earlier chapters, Lecter is not an atheist in the other books, but instead recognizes the predatory or violently indifferent nature of God. Unlike Verger he does not worship this God, but he accepts it and the fact that he is created in that God's image, both cruel and merciful.

At this early point in his development, though, he is the atheist that Simpson claims. The most explicit comment of Lecter's disbelief, his atheism, comes when he buries Mischa and he tells her "we take comfort in knowing there is no God," and that her "oblivion" is better than being in any heaven (222). Here Lecter is more like Verger or Dolarhyde than like the Lecter he will be in the other novels. This atheism does not just come from seeing Mischa's skeleton. Earlier, when he is in the orphanage, he comes to the conclusion that "the painted ceiling of his childhood" is "as thin as Heaven, and nearly as useless" (57). Because of the cruelty he has witnessed, Heaven is useless or nonexistent to him. This passage comes just before the description of the oubliette in which a dying man scratched "pourquoi" (57). At this point Lecter, like many survivors of war and trauma, asks only, *Why?* This questioning leads to a lack of faith, and his not yet believing that man, nature, and God are indifferent and that the answer may just be "because." Karim calls this passage "one of the most moving sections" of the novel and connects it to what he sees in all of Harris's other works as "a questioning of the human condition and an investigation into the nature of our own wickedness" (156). This exploration of the human condition and nature is also Harris's connection to Blake.

Karim likewise comments on how Harris continually critiques organized religion (156), another connection to Blake, as made clear in earlier chapters, and one that is revealed in the bloody connections made to organized Christianity in this novel. Lecter's reaction to the church and belief, and his disbelief in God and the church, can be seen in his reaction to his uncle's funeral, where he is "disgusted with the whining and bleating of the hymns and the droning nonsense" (97). Christianity is portrayed as a violent religion, as Blake often portrayed it, focusing on its emphasis on bloody crucifixion. When Lady Murasaki and Lecter go to see the stolen artworks, Lady Murasaki is confronted by "bloody religion pictures [that] filled one end of the hall, a meathouse of hanging Christs" (145). It is at this exhibit as well that the two look at a tapestry called "The Sacrifice of Isaac" and Lecter wonders if God was going to eat Isaac. His aunt tells him no, God wasn't, because "the angel intervenes in time" (151). Lecter's reply: "Not always" (151). Not only is God made complicit in cannibalism, but the angels, like the Vichy police, do not come to help. When Lecter lives in Paris his view of Notre Dame again emphasizes the callous nature of religion, as he sees the cathedral as a spider feeding on the city (169).

6. Printing in the Infernal Method

Interestingly, the sexton's reaction to Lecter's glowing eyes in the cathedral is similar to that of the gypsy in *Hannibal*: he at first crosses himself, before realizing that it is only a young man that he sees (170–71). What does this reaction indicate? That Lecter is already a devil? Or that he is a young man with a devil inside? Lecter's growing understanding of the devil inside all of humanity, the indifference and cruelty of life, is revealed prior to Louis's execution, when he tells Louis that since all of the pain and suffering before his birth didn't bother him, he should not be concerned about what happens after his death either (187). The implication is that suffering and pain always exist and human lives are but brief interruptions to the constant flow of pain. Most importantly, Lecter's comment indicates that humans are only concerned about the pain and suffering that affects them, not that which hurts others; humanity is a part of indifferent and uncaring nature.

Just as this novel establishes the indifferent nature of the world and the capability for both good and evil in all people, along with Lecter's allowing his evil and violent nature to emerge, it also establishes Lecter's well-known surface characteristics: his tastes and senses. While previous works set him up as an elite, here we see that he truly is descended from the elite class. This, in part, may explain his desire for and interest in high culture and art. His relationship with Lady Murasaki explains his worldliness in that it is not just Western culture and art that he is knowledgeable about but also Japanese. Her interest in drawing and painting, along with that of his uncle, helps to explain his own artistic capabilities. As in the other works, though, this elitism may not just be a class marker but may also be connected to his enhanced senses, which in turn allow him to see and accept the complexity of the world. As in other works, it is clear in this novel that Lecter's memory is excellent, though not perfect, as is his facility at acquiring new knowledge. Both of these traits are made possible through close observations. His "memory palace," after all, is based on things he has actually seen or experienced and that he can then align facts with. Once again, the sense here that seems the strongest is that of smell, connected closely, of course, with his interest in food and cooking. This sense is also connected to the women he is interested in, in that he is able to pick out their scents easily. Interestingly, Popil also shares this ability, another indication that he is closer to being like Graham or Starling than like Chilton or Krendler; he understands the intricacies and subtleties of smell. This is also a sense that many take for granted and overlook instead of cultivate, as Lecter does.

Thomas Harris and William Blake

One of the intriguing details regarding sense is young Lecter being mute for years. While, of course, it makes sense that the muteness was a psychological effect of his traumatic stress, it also allowed for several years when, since he was mute, and some — like several of the other orphans — even thought he was deaf, he could focus on observing those around him, instead of actively participating with them. This allowed him to see into their natures and into nature itself. He, perhaps, could therefore see and accept things that others could not. In other words, his muteness here may have operated like Starling's outsider status regarding gender and class: it forced close observation, which then could be used to advantage later. One of the senses that may have been honed was, of course, vision, a sense that ties in to Blake directly, as he connects vision with enlightenment and emphasizes perspective as central to imagination and understanding. Several scenes in this novel emphasize Lecter's vision. When he attacks the boy who threw stones at the swan, his face is blank except for his eyes, which are alive, and the edges of his vision are described as red (53). Later, when he confronts the butcher, we see not only this focus on Lecter's vision but also the inability of others to see from a different perspective and recognize the true nature of others. When the butcher sees Lecter, even though he was previously attacked by him, he sees a young boy who would do something like put sugar in the gas tank (102). Unfortunately for him, he does not see someone to be afraid of. Lecter, in contrast, is described as having "a sharpness of vision, with edges of refracted red" (102). Importantly, Lecter combines this intense and focused sight with his other enhanced senses. When Popil says that he would be sorry if Lady Murasaki were deported because he would miss seeing her, she asks him if he lives by his "eyes alone"; Popil in turn asks her if Lecter lives by his eyes alone (233), implying that neither relies just on vision. For both, vision is just the first of the senses that must be sharpened. It is expanded vision, along with all other enhanced senses, that leads to understanding and acknowledging the complex relationship of good and evil.

By the end of the novel, Lecter is close to what he will be in the other novels, but some aspects and characteristics are still missing. Lady Murasaki sees that "something was missing behind his eyes" (307). She believes that he is frozen inside (308). The Lecter in the other novels does not appear frozen; in fact, he seems quite lively. As he grows he will begin to thaw, begin to move beyond being just a monster out for vengeance like Dolarhyde or Verger and become more complex. While he will not achieve complete balance until the end of *Hannibal*, he does seem, in the other novels, less focused on Mischa; he broods less. He becomes more accepting of the cruelty of the world, giving up atheism for an understanding of a complex God. At the end of Part II, almost the end of the novel, he says prayers for Louis, thinking that his own will be just as good as those he could buy in a church (310). His understanding of God is already changing. He is willing to pray, even if not to the same concept of God that others have. While he may be frozen, as Lady Murasaki suggests, and he eats alone, he is "not lonely" (310). However, at the end of the novel he has "entered his heart's long winter"—a winter that may not end until he meets Starling—and we learn that he "was not visited in dreams as humans are" (310). He is still more monster than man, out of balance, and yet he is content, not driven by rage or vengeance. Simpson describes Lecter's growth as a "gradual transition from innocent child (a 'lamb' in William Blake's lexicon) to predator (the 'tyger' of Blake's poem)" (*Making Murder* 308). While on a surface level this is true, and while at the end of this novel Lecter may be in the stage of still being a predatory tiger, we must remember that, for Blake, Innocence and Experience are not so simple. It is not a simple linear path but instead a complex cyclical one, in which one can transition from Innocence to Experience and back to Innocence or be a mixture of both at the same time, since they are, as the subtitle of the work indicates, "the Two Contrary States of the Human Soul." Even more important to remember is that the tiger is not wholly predator and was in fact made by the same hand that made the lamb.

In the last chapter we see a Lecter who is no longer "torn with anger" or "tortured by dreams" (322). His killing of Grentz, the last of the men from the hunting lodge, is described as being a pleasurable holiday activity. He enacts violence now not out of hate but instead based upon his own moral code. While not commendable, he is acting in a calm manner, not attempting to be the vengeful hand of God, but instead inflicting death as he describes God doing it in the other books: indifferently, without emotion. As we last see him, we are left with the observant Lecter, the one fascinated by humanity and who attempts to see the mixture of cruelty and mercy in everyone, someone who will "look out at audiences ... and read and read and read" (323). This is the Lecter who will read into Graham and into Starling.

Hannibal Rising— *Film*

The film, written by Harris at the same time he was writing the novel, was released in early 2007, a few months after the novel's publication. Instead of reinvigorating the franchise as the filmmakers wished to do, as stated on the "Hannibal Lecter: The Origin of Evil" featurette on the DVD, the film is the forgotten or disparaged part of the franchise. While *Silence of the Lambs* swept the Oscars, *Hannibal Rising* was nominated for 2 Razzie awards: Worst Excuse for a Horror Movie and Worst Prequel or Sequel.

While all films, as discussed in previous chapters, have to simplify aspects of the novels on which they are based due to time constraints and the difficulties of sharing inner thoughts, this film is extreme in its simplification of the novel. Few of the themes remain intact because all of the characters have been simplified, thereby erasing the theme of the complexity of human nature. A few traces of these ideas exist, but not many. While there are many aspects of the film that reviewers found fault with (dialogue, length, silliness, etc.), one was the simplification. Stephen Hunter, in a review for the *Washington Post*, claims that "the movie's [one] fundamental flaw [is] — the one-dimensionality of Hannibal." In addition, there are no explicit allusions to Blake in the film; none were in the novel and, unlike in the film *Red Dragon*, none have been added here.

A few of the references to nature have been retained but the most central ones have been cut. The film opens with a close-up of a spider web in the forest and then several shots of nature and the animals at peace in the forest before the interruption of the war. Young Lecter and Mischa play by the lake at Lecter Castle, and then planes and bombs stop their play. While this sets the film up to be about, perhaps, the peacefulness of nature being disturbed by the cruelty of humanity and war, and the interplay of beauty and danger in nature (as seen in the spider and its web), this idea is not sustained. Most importantly, there are no swans at all in this film, thereby removing one of the central images that reveals both Lecter's ability to be in touch with nature and to protect it while others are harmful or indifferent to it and also the beauty and danger of nature itself. The image of the spider is repeated where it appears in the novel, prior to the killing of the butcher, perhaps emphasizing that Lecter is like the spider, capable of creating both beauty and death. Furthermore, in that scene, after Lecter kills the butcher there is an intensification of the animal and nature sounds in the background, as well as of the sunlight.

However, the meaning behind this is not clear. Is it that Lecter's senses have been heightened by the killing or that the killing is a part of nature?

In addition to the deletion of the swans, other connections to nature are gone. While Lecter does take the butcher's fish home, he does not release any crickets or fish on the line. While the ortolans are still kept at the restaurant and Lecter says of them to Lady Murasaki, "They're like us. They smell the others cooking and still they try to sing," he does not release them after he kills Kolnas. There is no discussion of crickets for Lady Murasaki, a small point but one that negates Lecter's concern for others' happiness. The only other interactions with animals in the film are a young Lecter throwing rocks at wild wolves to keep them from eating the bodies of his family, his aunt's dog growling at him and then mysteriously being nice to him when he arrives at the house, and Popil referring to him when speaking to Lady Muraski as "your pet snake." The scene with the dogs connects to the idea, referred to in a previous chapter, that Lecter is Satan because of his command over animals (for example, the wild hogs that seem to clear a path for him in *Hannibal*). Similarly, the reference to his being a snake is also an obvious connection to Satan, tempered only by the idea that he is a pet and therefore is somewhat domesticated and under control. Overall, Lecter's connections to nature or animals in the film emphasize his evil or predatory aspect, not his compassion or the complexity of both nature and Lecter himself.

Lecter's compassion is retained in that he does fight against bullies and cares for his sister. The director of the orphanage tells Lecter that he does not "honor the human pecking order" and is "always hurting the bullies." Apart from this comment, though, we see little of his gentle or artistic side. This is in part due to other changes in the plot. When he arrives in Paris, having escaped from the orphanage, his uncle is already dead and therefore cannot teach him about art and how painting can release his emotions. Lady Murasaki, in one of their first encounters, does give him a flower to arrange, but does not teach him about haiku or painting. Tellingly, she instead teaches him Kendo. She is part of his education in being a warrior, not in being a balanced human. There is an added scene where, after the insult of the butcher, she kneels in front of her altar and says, as Lecter overhears, "Forgive me, I cannot seek revenge. Hannibal needs peace," revealing that she knows that balance is necessary in life, but also giving Lecter the incentive, it is suggested, to do what she refuses to do. The relationship between Lady Murasaki and Lecter is altered as well, with the sexuality and desire between the two being made explicit, partly because the uncle is already dead in the film when Lecter arrives. In the scene where she tries to convince him to give up his revenge, she doesn't offer to be the rain to his dry ground as she does in the novel (252), but instead kisses him. Her promise here seems to be of purely a physical union and not a balance of personalities—or contraries, wet and dry—as it seems in the novel. The generalized oversimplification of the characters even alters the tone of a scene that actually is not much changed from the novel. When Lecter is about to kill Grutas, Lady Murasaki asks him to stop and instead forgive him, and Lecter says he can't. He goes on to tell her he loves her, and she asks, "What is left of you to love?" This scene comes almost directly from the novel, with a slight change in that, in the novel, Lady Murasaki does not ask Lecter to forgive Grutas but instead to turn him over to Popil in order to save himself (302). In the novel one can understand what Lady Murasaki had loved about Lecter and why she wants to save him. However, given the simplicity of the characters in the film, resulting in Lecter being a one-sided character focused on revenge, it is not clear what she could have loved about him in the first place.

In addition to Lecter and Lady Murasaki, another character who has been simplified is Popil. Importantly, there is no mention of his being Vichy. Instead of being a complex character with a conflicted past, he is a policeman out for justice. Also, in the film, Popil twice refers to Lecter as a monster, which is not a surprise, as he also does this in the novel; however, given the oversimplification of the plot and the lack of depth to both Lecter and Popil, we cannot necessarily see how Popil came to this conclusion in the film. When they are interrogating Lecter about the butcher's death, Lecter remains calm during the polygraph and Popil tells a colleague when looking at the results, "He reacts to nothing. That's monstrous." The jump from a "vanilla," as they call his polygraph, to his being monstrous seems extreme, especially given the context of postwar France, where much worse monstrosity was witnessed. Since we don't get Popil's inner thoughts of recognizing the "Otherness" in Lecter's responses, his conclusion regarding Lecter's nature does seem to be made too quickly. Now, granted, voiceover in film is distracting, but this film does use a voiceover at another point. Lacking any glimpse into his mind, we are left with no real basis for Popil's initial categorization of Lecter. The second categorization of Lecter as a monster comes after Popil speaks to him about his memories and his search for the men who ate Mischa. He tells his colleague

6. Printing in the Infernal Method

that after Lecter leads them to Grutas, they will arrest Lecter and a court will find him insane and place him in an asylum, where the doctors will study him to find out what he is. He states that the boy died in the forest in 1944 when his heart died with Mischa, and that there is no word for what Lecter is now except monster. This scene is directly taken from the novel but, as with the scene between Lecter and Lady Murasaki discussed earlier, this scene seems less believable here because of the simplification of characters, resulting in the fact that Popil does not know as much about Lecter or the evil that good men can do as he does in the novel. Because we have access to Popil's background and thoughts in the novel, his conclusions regarding Lecter do not seem hasty; here, however, they are unsupported.

The film also does not question or comment on human nature as much as the novel does, as the leaving out of Popil's Vichy past suggests. The discussion between Hannibal and Lady Murasaki about the tapestry of Isaac is retained, as is Louis asking Popil, "Where were the police?" and then having Lecter say to Popil, "He answered your questions. You didn't answer his: Where were the police?" However, there is no "prayer" over Mischa's grave about there being no God. The other small details of Notre Dame being a spider and the bloody religious images are also left out.

Finally, the novel has Lecter being arrested after the attack on Grutas and put in jail. He is released after three weeks because of protests in support of him and because prosecuting someone for the murder of war criminals and white slavers is unpopular. In addition, Lecter left little evidence behind to clearly connect him to any of his crimes. In the film, however, the canal boat explodes, leaving everyone to think Lecter is dead (this is emphasized in a deleted scene in which Lady Murasaki has his photo on the family altar). Without his arrest and subsequent release, the line between guilt and innocence and justice and law remains clear. While the film does end with him free, the legal system and humanity in general are not complicit in evils or injustice. Without his being arrested, the citizens of Paris, and by extension the audience, are not confronted with the question of whether the killing of war criminals is murder or justice. Lecter does go to Canada to collect a head, but there is no reference to his now having no nightmares or, more importantly, to his being able to read the American faces and see their true natures.

Essentially, the film creates a simplified version of Lecter. He was traumatized in the war, he enacted revenge, and he will continue to enact it. We are left with the idea that he will continue to place Grutas's face on the "bullies" he encounters throughout his life, not that he comes to a conclusion about the nature of God or nature itself. All of his acts will now be mere reenactments of his earlier revenge. He has completely given in to his darkness and has no sense of concern for others, not for Lady Murasaki or the ortolans. According to Peter Webber, the director, this in fact was the goal of the film. In the featurette "Hannibal Lecter: The Origin of Evil," he describes Lecter as being "incredibly violent, vicious, and with no mercy whatsoever." This is not the balanced, though violent and evil, Lecter we see in the novels and, to some extent, in the other films; this is not the Lecter who can join Starling and be complete. The Lecter whom Weber describes embodies only the "Divine Image" of Blake's *Songs of Experience*, revealing that "Cruelty has a Human Heart" (l. 1), while leaving out or ignoring the "Divine Image" of *Innocence* in which "Mercy has a human heart" (l. 9) as well. While the other films alter and flatten this complex Blakean view of human nature and good and evil, this film completely erases and negates it.

Conclusion
"Without contraries there is no progression"—Lecter's Blakean Progression to Balance

In *Red Dragon* Harris establishes the use of Blakean allusions and philosophies that carry through the remaining novels. While the reason for the Blake echoes can be discerned through reading the novels in their published order, by slightly reordering the novels the purpose of these connections becomes clearer. Instead of viewing the works chronologically, in the order they were published, one must instead view the four novels as a story of Lecter's progression, beginning with *Hannibal Rising* and then proceeding through *Red Dragon*, *Silence of the Lambs*, and finally *Hannibal*. However, while the purpose for the Blakean allusions and philosophies becomes clearer when the novels are interpreted and considered in the rearranged order, they should still be read in the published order, as this order allows for the establishment of the Blakean connection in *Red Dragon* that one then can hold in mind while pondering Lecter's Blakean progression. In addition, reading in the published order will ensure that readers will want to continue reading the novels. As stated in the previous chapter, *Hannibal Rising* has been universally panned and may in fact turn readers away from the other novels if read first, while *Red Dragon* will capture readers and intrigue them.

By encountering the explicit allusion to the Red Dragon painting in *Red Dragon*, the reader is also primed to notice more subtle and implicit connections to Blake. As discussed in the previous chapters, the Blakean ideas and philosophies in the novels exist even in the absence of explicit Blakean allusions. Harris's focus on the importance of perspective and vision, heightened senses, forgiveness over vengeance, the accepting the duality of nature and of humanity, the duality of God, and the intercon-

Conclusion

nectedness of good and evil are all echoes of Blake's philosophies found in his poetry. While one cannot determine intent or direct influence, it does seem as if Harris bases the progression of Lecter and the description of the relationship of good and evil not just on Blake's ideas of contraries and the relationship of good and evil but also on Blake's beliefs regarding God and Satan and how the two are intertwined. According to Tristanne Connolly, Blake's works reveal that

> only when God and Satan split completely does Satan become a force of pure evil and God a force of pure good.... The human, wanting to believe himself entirely "good" or "righteous," rejects from himself all "evil" or "sinful" elements which are externalized in the spectre. This effort to exonerate oneself from evil does not work for God or for the human, because the rejection denies the relationship between God and the devil, the human and the spectre ... the result is that the separated being can claim independence and power. God cannot make himself all good without infringing on his own omnipotence and losing control of evil; likewise, the human cannot, without falling into his spectre's power [166].

God and Satan, when interconnected, keep each other in balance. Yes, this means that evil exists but it also means that it cannot be dominant over good because good exerts an influence upon it. However, when separated from each other due to the best of intentions, the desire to eradicate all evil, the reverse happens: evil is no longer influenced or controlled or balanced by the good and actually increases. When humans view good and evil as separate, consider God and Satan as adversaries, they replicate the error of division. By externalizing one's evil impulses they, instead of being easily eradicated, can ironically gain more power and influence. This pattern of the error of division is illustrated, as discussed previously, in Dolarhyde's attempt to separate himself from the Dragon and defeat it by externalizing and ingesting it, an action that merely allows the Dragon to gain power over Dolarhyde. This is one example of how Harris's novels illustrate what happens to those who attempt to "exonerate" themselves from all evil: they are damaged. The damage may come in a subtle way (for example, Graham's drinking and obsession with work, which causes him to lose his family), or it may come in a violent and horrific way, as it does for Dolarhyde, whose attempt to "Become" at first fully Dragon and later fully separate from the Dragon leads to the Dragon's power and the deaths of many individuals, including his own. Most of the characters in Harris's novels, like most humans, attempt to separate good and evil,

Conclusion

attempt to label and therefore contain evil. Most of the characters do not succeed in identifying and eliminating evil and, in fact, are either damaged through losing jobs or reputations or are killed. However, keeping in mind the revised order in which the novels should be interpreted, three characters do not attempt to sever the tie between good and evil and therefore survive and live contented lives: Barney, Starling, and Lecter. It is their acceptance of the dual nature of humanity and nature, their understanding, their open use of their senses, and their ability to not seek vengeance that allows them their freedom at the end of *Hannibal.*

Barney, Starling, and Lecter have all at times been outsiders, and as outsiders they are able to observe without being noticed; they are able to see the structures of society, rules and expectations taken as natural by those within, as constructed and at times harmful. Barney works within the hospital as an orderly who can observe how the doctors and nurses interact with Lecter. He can see where, when, and why the doctors fail. Barney also differs from those around him in race and class. While the novels do not explicitly comment on this fact, these differences would also allow him to see things that those around him miss. Starling is a female in a masculine profession and world. She can understand the female victims, particularly the lower-class ones, in a way that her male counterparts cannot; she can also see the institutionalized sexism and patriarchy of the FBI and society as a whole. Lecter was an outsider at the orphanage, living as an orphan in his old home and having his fall in status often pointed out to him. He also was mute at this time, a further separation from the boys around him, and one that allowed him to observe silently, seeing the bullies and how the institution supported them. For all three characters, their observations reveal to them the duality of human nature and the arbitrariness of categories, leading to a greater understanding of the world and its complex nature, and the recognition that in such a complex world one must be open to different perspectives and be willing to move forward from the past.

Reading Lecter as an illustration of a Blakean philosophy, however, is not meant to justify his actions or position him as an unsullied hero; nor is it meant to vilify Blake. But keeping a Blakean context in mind does force the audience to acknowledge the complexities of good and evil and the nature of humanity, as well as emphasize that the correct response to evil should be acceptance and forgiveness instead of brooding and vengeance. Lecter is, obviously, in no way less evil than Dolarhyde or

Conclusion

Gumb; however, in Blake's terms he is more fully human because he has not attempted to separate from his spectre, but instead has recognized it as a part of himself. He has recognized that both mercy and cruelty have a human heart. Lecter has the perspective and vision to recognize and accept the complexities of the world. In addition, Lecter makes use of his vision and other senses in order to not only recognize the futility of any attempt at categorization and separation but also fully enjoy the world and all its pleasures. As discussed previously, Lecter's refined tastes, his elitism, are related to his enhanced perceptions and therefore his ability to acknowledge complexity. However, this capacity for pleasure and sensation is important for Blake for other reasons as well. In response to Lavater's aphorism 366, one of the aphorisms that emphasizes the connection between man and God and that states, "*The purest religion is the most refined Epicurism. He, who in the smallest given time can enjoy most of what he never shall repent, and what furnishes* enjoyments, still more unexhausted, still less changeable — is the most religious and the most voluptuous of men," Blake underlined the italicized portion and wrote "True Christian Philosophy" (original emphasis, 591). It is "True Christian Philosophy" for two reasons. First, enjoying all of the world's luxuries means being grateful for their existence and not letting them go to waste. In addition, Epicurism, in contrast to how most understand it now, did not just teach one to enjoy the finer things in life, but also emphasized enjoyment of all things, opening one's senses to the enjoyment of a meal of bread and water if that is all that is available. This does not mean that one should limit oneself to bread and water or not see and experience the difference between that and a gourmet meal, but instead that one should fulfill and encourage one's senses no matter the circumstances. This is related to the blurring of boundaries emphasized by Blake and the dismissal of categories. A true epicurean would not automatically dismiss the bread and water but would understand that pleasure and nourishment may be found in that as well. In addition, this Epicurism leads to the idea of being grateful for all, even the simplest and most meager things. Second, this embracing of the senses is "True Christian Philosophy" in that it also emphasizes the physical world and, by extension, Jesus' human aspects, reminding one that he was not a distant God, but an embodied one. Blake often refers to the Divine Form or Divine Human, emphasizing the connection of the spiritual and the bodily. The practitioner, then, of this "True Christian Philosophy" is more fully human, accepting of both sides, the

Conclusion

spiritual and the physical, of human nature. Lecter, even given all of his evil, is partaking of true religion, whereas others, who judge this indulgence of the senses and would deprive themselves and others of it, are countering true religion and replacing it with a false and hypocritical Christianity, with the Urizenic religion of the Tree of Knowledge of Good and Evil. And although other characters seem to share in a version of Epicurism, share Lecter's elite tastes, they are not portrayed in a positive way by Harris and would most likely not be seen by Blake as partaking in "True Christian Philosophy." The two primary examples are Verger in *Hannibal*, with his mansion and horses, and Grutas in *Hannibal Rising*, with his estate and his Bosendorfer. While both share Lecter's interest in fine-quality experiences and wish to indulge their senses, they lack compassion for others. Though their senses are enhanced in one way, they are narrow and lacking in others in that they are not able to empathize or show mercy. As indicated in previous chapters, Lecter's tastes are not merely markers of the elite or a sign of elitism, but instead, when combined with his ability to understand other humans and experience compassion for them, they are subtle indicators of the Blakean connections, particularly the importance of open senses and perception.

Reading with Blake in mind, one can trace Lecter's progression, beginning with the young Lecter revealed in *Hannibal Rising*. The young man in this novel already has more open senses and attention to detail than other characters, as his tutor Jakov has discovered. His encounters with the black swans reveal that he has learned how to interact with nature and to appreciate its beauty as well as its dangerousness. He has a desire to protect the vulnerable, beginning with Mischa but extending to others considered weak or outsiders, revealing his capacity for empathy and understanding. His experiences in the war lead him to question the nature of God, ultimately concluding that there is no God and seeing religion as a predatory spider obsessed with sacrifice and blood. After these traumatic wartime experiences, while he can still recognize and appreciate the beauty of nature, he focuses more on achieving vengeance for Mischa than on enjoying what he can or opening himself to love and balance. As he embarks on his path of revenge, he also comes to recognize the flaws in the legal system and how the system cannot help him achieve this vengeance or justice. Because his focus is unbalanced at this point, focused more on cruelty than on mercy, he leaves behind the possibility for balanced family life with Lady Murasaki and rejects Popil's overtures to help him achieve justice. At the end of this novel, Lecter is more at peace than he was earlier in the novel; however, he still has not achieved balance, is focused on his last act of vengeance, and has not yet accepted the existence of an indifferent God. He will perhaps begin to come to his balanced understanding of God by further study and observation of humanity. After all, his observation is already acute and the novel ends with his statement that in America there are so many faces to study.

The Lecter encountered in *Red Dragon*, *Silence of the Lambs*, and *Hannibal* is older and wiser, closer to a Blakean balance than the young man was. He is no longer an atheist but instead believes in a God who can be indifferent and cruel. He does not believe, though, that this God should be worshipped; however, he does seem to believe that the complex actions of humanity, its capacity for both mercy and cruelty, reflect the personality of this God. While he still acts on his evil and violent desires, his killings are no longer for vengeance. He seems to kill now for several other reasons. He does kill due to what he sees as necessity—for example, to protect himself, as seen in his murder of Dr. Fell, which provided him with an identity and access to not only shelter and income but also books and art. Some of his murders are committed in order to protect the more vulnerable—for example, his early attempt on Verger as recounted in *Hannibal*, which was meant to protect children by eliminating a pedophile, and his murder of the deer hunter, discussed in the *Hannibal* chapter, which was intended to protect nature and was connected in his imagination and memory with Mischa. Perhaps the most difficult to understand is his murdering as punishment for misuse of senses or lack of imagination, as he does to the symphony flutist. However, given Blake's insistence on the importance of imagination, if Lecter is a Blakean character, this rationale makes some sense. Remembering what Melanie Bandy suggests about Blake's beliefs, that "Blake reserves his strongest condemnation for unbelief in the Divine Humanity, the world of imagination" (51), people like the flutist are not just untalented or careless with their senses but also revealing a disregard for the divine. Since they do not recognize the Divine Humanity, in Lecter's eyes they perhaps do not deserve to partake in humanity anymore. Overall, Lecter's killing is more indifferent now, like that of God. Dr. Fell to him was like a fly to a boy, or like a worshipper at a church collapse to God.

In these three novels he also seems to be searching for someone else who can recognize the dual nature of humanity, someone who shares his

Conclusion

power of perception and understanding. He is searching in part, as becomes clear in *Hannibal*, for a replacement for Mischa, for a substance to fill that void in him. He believes he has found a similar soul in Graham, but Graham cannot fully accept his own dual nature and therefore, through his attempt to clearly separate good from evil, becomes damaged. Lecter then sees the potential in Starling, and to a lesser extent in Barney. Interestingly, and as discussed previously, both Starling and Barney are outsiders: one due to gender, one to race, and both, perhaps, to class. They both take the time not just to talk to Lecter but to speak with him, listening to what he says, and what he does not say. While both do their jobs in regard to Lecter, both are also willing to go beyond their jobs in order to discuss other interests and learn from him. They are willing to expand their relationship with Lecter beyond the strict definition or category of their encounter. Starling, after all, is willing to engage in dialogue with Lecter, although at first it is just to get information and insight from him regarding the Buffalo Bill case. Ultimately, she ends up taking his comments to heart and, for example, learns to look to her memories for strength. These dialogues move the relationship beyond that of FBI agent interviewing serial killer. Similarly, Barney discusses his classes with Lecter and learns from him, moving their relationship beyond the bounds of guard and killer. Both Starling and Barney are not locked into a narrow vision of what their exchanges or relationships with Lecter should be, indicating a willingness to ignore labels, categories, and expectations. Because of their openness and their willingness, Lecter encourages and helps both to further expand their senses and understanding. It is Starling and not Barney, though, who is sought out and engaged with more by Lecter after his escape. If he is looking for a replacement for Mischa, it makes sense that he would focus on the female and not the male; it could also indicate, as details at the end of *Hannibal* suggest, that while sexual attraction is not the driving force in his interest for Starling, it does play a role. It could also simply indicate that Starling is more open to the idea of balanced contraries and blurred boundaries than Barney is. The choice of Starling as the character who ends up balancing Lecter in the end also could indicate Harris further alluding to Blake in that the two who end up in balance are also contraries in gender and therefore reflect Blake's Self and Emanation. While Starling at first is somewhat resistant to this idea of balanced contraries, by the end of *Hannibal* she is accepting of her dual nature and the nature of life itself. She has sacrificed for Lecter and he for her. They

Conclusion

are Self and Emanation in Eternity enacting mutual sacrifice. It is the finding of a similar perspective in Starling that allows Lecter to move beyond his brooding for the past. While he had already long ago given up vengeance, he can move toward forgiveness of himself for what he sees as his role in Mischa's death and not try to bring Mischa back. He can move past brooding and into acceptance and progress. He has completed the Blakean progression and is in balance.

Because of his beliefs regarding humanity and good and evil, his reliance on senses, and his progression to balance, Lecter is the most Blakean of the characters and yet it is Dolarhyde and Verger who are explicitly connected with Blake. Why would Harris have done this? Why not associate the explicit allusions to Blake with Lecter in order to emphasize the novels' thematic connections to Blake? Harris could have created explicit Blakean connections to Lecter and used another artist for the painting and tattoo in *Red Dragon* and either described a different painting as hanging in Verger's room or left the detail of the painting out altogether. The simplest explanation is that Harris chose Blake for the explicit allusions connected to Dolarhyde and Verger due to several factors, the first being the vividness of Blake's designs. Blake's Great Red Dragon would make quite an imposing and impressive back tattoo and a large copy of *Ancient of Days* would indeed be a vivid focal point in any room. The designs thus described also clearly connect with the characters and their desires. Dolarhyde wishes to be the Dragon in control, particularly over a woman, so that he can enact metaphorical vengeance upon his grandmother. Verger wishes to be Urizen in control with his compasses, enacting laws and punishment, particularly against Lecter. A related reason for the choice of Blake is perhaps that the designs are unique and well known enough to be clearly identified by a reader who can then look them up for themselves, entering further in to the fiction. Harris merely had to describe a few of the unique aspects of the paintings to make it possible for a reader to easily find and see the painting and then be able to imagine it for the rest of the novel.

Another reason Harris may have chosen Blake is Blake's supposed connection to madness. Blake's unique approach to printing, plus some of the anecdotes told about him, not only position him as a solitary figure, a connection to both Dolarhyde and Verger, but also have led to the (mostly discredited) belief that he was mad. Instead of having a publisher print and publish his poems, Blake controlled the entire process, engraving his illuminated books on copper plates, printing them, painting the pages,

Conclusion

and then binding them. This method could be seen as the eccentric method of an eccentric man, one out of step with society. Furthering the idea of Blake as at least eccentric, if not mad, is the fact that Blake had claimed to see visions when young and visionary heads when old; in fact, he claimed he received instructions on how to execute his relief printing from his dead brother Robert. Some of Blake's poems (for example, *The Marriage of Heaven and Hell*) may lead to a further opinion of him as mad in that he clearly positions himself as a narrator/speaker who then speaks of his visions and the positive aspects of hell and devils. Robert Hunt had even called Blake an "unfortunate lunatic" in a review of his exhibition (qtd. in Adams 139). If one wanted to refer to a, maybe not well-known but certainly not obscure, artist who was associated with madness in order to emphasize the madness and isolation of the characters, one could do well by choosing Blake. While other poets and artists have reputations, deserved or not, for being mad (such as Edgar Allan Poe and Vincent Van Gogh), they are either one or the other, a poet or a painter, and not both. Since Blake was both, his visual work can be described and play a central role in the plot and his poetic and philosophical ideas as revealed in his writings can be alluded to.

However, these explanations for the choice of Blake, as stated previously, are simplistic. In addition, the danger in choosing Blake for these reasons is that any reader with a more in-depth knowledge of Blake, or one who is inspired by the novels to further learn about Blake, will be aware of not only how Blake's "madness" is now discredited but also how there are multiple copies of his works, each varying at least in coloring if not design details, leading to multiple or varied interpretations of the works. These readers with a background in Blake will be more aware of the varying contexts of the works and therefore the varying interpretations as well. Due to this knowledge of multiple contexts and interpretations, they will be less likely to agree with Dolarhyde's and Verger's interpretations of the works. These readers will know that the bearded figure is not God but Urizen and is a negative figure for Blake, and if they are even more familiar with Blake's works, they will know that while Urizen is overall a negative figure, he has the best of intentions. However, this discrepancy between what a Blake-informed reader and what a non–Blake-informed reader will take from Blake's works used out of context perhaps leads to the heart of why Harris uses Blake.

A likely reason for the use of Blake and his explicit association not

Conclusion

with Lecter but with Dolarhyde and Verger is revealed in the fact that both Dolarhyde and Verger misread Blake, as discussed in previous chapters. Both characters misread Blake in part because of their own limited perspectives. Thanks to the narrow vision that serves their own purposes, they take the works out of context. This taking out of context is connected to simplified readings of the works themselves. Dolarhyde reads the artist as being equivalent to the painting and Verger reads the work in a different, almost opposite, context than the one Blake created. For Dolarhyde, Blake is the Dragon; he approves of the Dragon and its actions. This interpretation connects with Dolarhyde's own desires in that he wishes to be the Dragon wreaking vengeance upon the woman. Because he desires this, he reads the Dragon and Blake as approving of this action. As mentioned in the *Red Dragon* chapter, Dolarhyde believed that Blake looked in his head for the image of the Dragon and therefore believes that his idea of the Dragon is the same as Blake's. While Verger does not comment on *Ancient of Days*, as discussed in the *Hannibal* chapter, he most likely identifies the bearded figure as God. He would not be likely to recognize the character as Urizen because it is unlikely that Verger even knows who that character is or has read Blake. Verger most likely sees an old white-bearded man with compasses and assumes that this is the Judeo-Christian God creating the world and its laws and constraints. Verger's vision has been narrowed by traditional institutional Christianity and he therefore reads the painting in a Christian and not Blakean context. Since Verger himself desires control and laws that would punish Lecter, it is no surprise that he reads the work this way. Because of their misreadings, Dolarhyde and Verger apply the wrong philosophies. Dolarhyde focuses on becoming and devouring, and in the process he externalizes his own bestial dragon aspect. Verger focuses on laws and vengeance, wanting to guide God's hand in wielding justice. Ultimately, these philosophies and the resulting actions lead to their own defeats and demises. Considering that not only do the two characters connected to the explicit allusions misread Blake but doing so also has negative consequences for them, Harris's use of Blake may not just be meant to indicate a particular philosophy but may be meant as well to comment on the difficulty of interpretation, the danger of quick and narrow interpretation, and the necessity of acknowledging multiple interpretations.

As discussed in previous chapters, Blake is an author/artist who is notoriously difficult to interpret and categorize, especially when aspects of his works— individual proverbs or images, for example — are taken out of context. For example, is Thel's running away from her grave positive or negative, are Blake's works misogynistic or feminist, is "Jerusalem" a patriotic hymn or a warning of England's decay? The difficulty of interpreting Blake is closely connected to the Blakean themes that Harris has borrowed and emphasizes in these novels. Since being able to categorize, label, and place in context helps or guides interpretation, the inability to clearly and simply categorize or determine the one true context hinders interpretation. Blake's works themselves not only profess the difficulty of categorization but enact this as well. They not only state the necessity of broadened perception that allows the ability to see beyond simplistic interpretations or clear binaries but also encourage or even force this broadened perspective in the attempt to interpret them, leading readers to acknowledge the existence of multiple possible interpretations. This aspect of Blake's works may ultimately be the reason for Harris's choice of him as opposed to another artist or poet. Blake's ideas of good and evil are intertwined with, and may even be secondary to, the more general idea of the difficulty or even impossibility of categorization that Lecter and Blake both embody. Blake, the uncategorizable artist, indicates the difficulty of labeling. In the novels, as discussed previously, the characters who attempt to clearly label and define are damaged, while those who are more open to complexity and recognize the difficulty inherent in categorization, even of good and evil, survive. Dolarhyde and Verger not only attempt to categorize but also have narrowed and limited perspectives of the Blake art they each are connected with, leading to narrow and incomplete interpretations. While Harris's possible reasons for choosing Blake and using the explicit allusions that he did may now seem obvious, Dolarhyde's and Verger's misreadings of Blake go unnoticed or commented upon within the text, with even Dolarhyde's mistake of Butts's name uncorrected, as discussed previously. This lack of commentary, lack of any indication of a misreading, de-emphasizes the connection between interpretation, perspective, and the central thematic idea of the interconnectedness of good and evil and the necessity of acknowledging complexity and multiple perspectives. This lack of commentary also, sadly, cements the connections between Blake and Dolarhyde and Verger instead of more clearly aligning Blake and Lecter, thereby obscuring Harris's thematic use of Blake. One possibility, far-fetched though it may be, could be that Harris hoped to broaden his readers' perception by making them work and look more deeply than they expected to. Perhaps the few explicit references to Blake in the novels are meant to entice the reader, leading to investigation into who Blake is and not only how Dolarhyde and Verger have misread him but also how Lecter is the most Blakean of the characters and that the Blakean themes are central to the novels. In this case, Harris's references to Blake would operate as Lecter's quoting of "Augeries of Innocence" does in the film *Red Dragon*, leading Graham — the reader — to insight and enlightenment, broadening experience, knowledge, and a new way of considering the world.

Lecter's quoting of Blake leads Graham to useful knowledge, at least for discovering Dolarhyde — as discussed previously, Graham is not yet ready to fully accept the knowledge Lecter has of the complexity of human nature. Harris's quoting of Blake may likewise lead the reader to the discovery that Lecter is the figure of Blakean balance. Lecter also embodies the difficulty of categorization and labeling, not just in that he attacks those who attempt to label him and not just in that readers are drawn to him while he enacts vicious revenge, but also in that it is difficult to acquire a true and reliable knowledge of his background. The contradictions (usually considered mistakes made by Harris) that some have identified in Lecter's background may be purposeful indications of the impossibility of correct categorization and complete knowledge. One cannot accurately label without complete and reliable truth. As discussed in the *Hannibal Rising* chapter, Harris himself has indicated how unreliable the record of Lecter is. Readers have not only the seemingly contradictory suggestions of his evil being part of his nature and its being caused by his wartime experiences but also his different birthdates and ages, as well as a reference in *Red Dragon* to his early sadism to animals that is countered by his kindness to animals in *Hannibal Rising*. Most surprisingly, and most difficult to explain or smooth over, is the very physical objective detail of Lecter's extra finger, which is never mentioned in the last novel but, because it was not removed until the events of *Hannibal*, should be present. However, maybe these aren't mistakes or indications that Harris was making it up as he went along and couldn't keep track of inconsistencies. As discussed previously, the preface to *Hannibal Rising* indicates that Harris is well aware of these inconsistencies. These may be further clues to the Blakean idea of the difficulty of labeling and categorization. These contradictions may suggest that humans by nature have limited knowledge of others and even of themselves at times. While one can attempt to see and understand

Conclusion

from another's perspective, one can never fully do so, leading inevitably to moments of misunderstanding; one must accept the possibility of mistakes and not be wedded to a limited or incorrect perception, as Dolarhyde and Verger are. Additionally, one may believe society's labeling and may create "mind-forg'd manacles," which not only block external truth or alternate perspectives but also may limit one's own understanding of oneself. Like Starling in *Hannibal*, one under the influence of this narrowed perception may even lie to themselves regarding their pasts, and may need a radical change of vision in order to see the truth — in Starling's case, the truth of her father, which was in turn intimately connected to her view of herself.

At the end of *Hannibal*, while readers may not have all the correct details of his life, and while they may lack the full truth regarding Lecter, Harris has provided enough detail about Lecter and enough allusions to Blake to enable the recognition of Lecter as embodying Blakean philosophy. It is perhaps this embodiment of supposed contradictions and contraries that allows Lecter to continue to intrigue audiences. Blake could have been speaking of Lecter when he wrote in an annotation to Boyd's *Historical Notes* on Dante, "the Grandest characters wicked. Very Satan. Capanius Othello a murderer. Prometheus. Jupiter. Jehovah, Jesus a wine bibber" (634). Lecter, too, is a grand and wicked character; as discussed previously, he is often compared to — or even identified as — Satan. Interestingly, though, Blake includes Jehovah and Jesus in his list of grand and wicked characters, revealing once again the complexity of good and evil and how they cannot be separated, which is perhaps the central theme of the Lecter novels.

While some, like Simpson, would suggest that "the fiction of Thomas Harris offers a bleak assessment of the human plight" because "he proposes that human beings suffer from a radical dualism in their natures" and that "all people are born with the potential to kill" (*Making Murder* 315), Harris is not, in fact, pessimistic or bleak. The knowledge of our duality does not lead to a more predatory or vicious world, for while Harris shows that evil and good coexist, he does not claim or suggest that evil must be acted upon. It is the acknowledgment of the complexity of good and evil that Harris emphasizes. While he does, as Simpson suggests, propose that all humans are capable of killing, he does not suggest that humans are incapable of recognizing this potential and never acting upon it. Harris proposes instead that acknowledging and understanding this capability

Conclusion

inherent in all of humanity can actually lead to balance and perhaps fewer killings, a quite positive assessment. Simpson errs as well when he claims that "once they [Harris's characters] become dedicated murderers, they are finally at peace with themselves" (*Making Murder* 316). Verger and Dolarhyde are certainly not at peace. While they are clearly not morally conflicted about their violent or predatory actions, both are also searching for something else that will give them peace. Dolarhyde believes, at first, that completing his "Becoming" will bring peace, and perhaps quiet the memories of his grandmother; he later, after falling in love with Reba, believes that devouring the Red Dragon painting will bring him peace. Verger is obsessed with Lecter and believes he will find his peace when Lecter is fed to the pigs. Barney also reveals Simpson's error in that he recognizes the duality of human nature and never gives in, never becomes a "dedicated murderer," and yet is at peace. Lecter does seem quite at peace with himself throughout the novels; however, as becomes clear in *Hannibal*, he is still haunted by memories of Mischa and believes that when he has found a space for her in this world he will be at peace. If one believes that when Starling and Lecter are united at the end of *Hannibal* they kill together, then Simpson is correct in that it would seem that only when Starling embraces her evil aspect and killing potential and acts upon them is she free from her past and at peace. However, as discussed in the *Hannibal* chapter, while Barney is cautious upon seeing the couple, there is no indication that the two kill. Instead, it is quite possible that now, with both of them having sacrificed for the other and placed their haunting memories to rest, with Starling no longer concerned with her father and Lecter letting Mischa's memory and his guilt go, they have joined together in balance, at peace with themselves and therefore not acting upon evil natures, not killing. Harris does not paint a picture of a universe of predatory duality in which one must act on evil urges in order to be at peace. He also does not suggest that one must suppress and deny these urges; in fact, he indicates that if one attempts to defeat or deny these urges, one is damaged. Instead, in Blakean fashion, Harris reveals that in order to achieve peace and balance, one must accept that these urges exist and then decide how to react appropriately to them.

If, as Blake writes in an annotation to Lavater, "human nature is the image of God" (597), then both humanity and God have a dual nature. Mercy and cruelty both have a human heart, which should come as no surprise since God made both typhoid and swans. To reject one's nature is to reject God, so what can one do but accept one's nature, which, as Lecter told Graham in *Red Dragon*, was "issued to us along with our lungs and pancreas"? (259). Harris uses Blake to emphasize that evil urges are natural, that they exist alongside good, and that all of nature and humanity is a mix of these contraries. If readers do not see this theme or this connection to Blake at first, it merely reveals that they need to return to the novels with enhanced vision and be open to new perspectives. Examining the novels through a Blakean lens reveals that Lecter's progression has been one of accepting contraries and has led him to achieve balance, completion, and peace. While there are other possible explanations, of course, for why Harris alludes to Blake, and one cannot dismiss them because dismissing them indicates adhering to a narrow vision that does not accept other perspectives, this thematic connection seems the most probable and compelling. Blake stated in *The Marriage of Heaven and Hell*, "Without contraries there is no progression" (plate 3), and showed readers "the Two Contrary States of the Human Soul" in his *Songs of Innocence and Experience*. Through Lecter and his relationship with Starling, Harris embodies these ideas and draws his readers into a world of blurred boundaries and shifting labels, in which our desire for Lecter's survival and delight in his charm reveal our own contrary natures.

Bibliography

Adams, Hazard. *Blake's Margins: An Interpretive Study of the Annotations*. Jefferson, NC: McFarland, 2009. Kindle edition.
AFI 100 Years 100 Heroes and Villains. CBS, 3 June 2003. Television.
Amis, Martin. "Hannibal, the Camus of Carnage." Review of *Hannibal*, by Thomas Harris. *Talk* (September 1999): 222+.
Bandy, Melanie. *Mind Forg'd Manacles: Evil in the Poetry of Blake and Shelley*. Tuscaloosa: University of Alabama Press, 1981.
Blake, William. *The Complete Poetry and Prose of William Blake*. Edited by David V. Erdman. Commentary by Harold Bloom. 1965. Rev. ed., Berkeley: University of California Press, 1988.
Bross, Kristina. Review of *Hannibal*, by Thomas Harris. *Commonplace* 1, no. 3 (April 2001).
Connolly, Tristanne. *William Blake and the Body*. New York: Palgrave, 2002.
Crabb Robinson, Henry. *Blake, Coleridge, Wordsworth, Lamb etc: Being Selections from the Remains of Henry Crabb Robinson*. Edited by Edith J. Morley. Manchester, UK: Manchester University Press, 1922. The Internet Archive. Kindle edition (no pagination).
Damon, S. Foster. *A Blake Dictionary: The Ideas of Symbols of William Blake*. Rev. ed. Hanover, NH: University Press of New England, 1988.
Demme, Jonathan, dir. *The Silence of the Lambs* (1991). Los Angeles, CA: The Criterion Collection, Orion HomeVideo, 1998. DVD.
Dent, Shirley, and Jason Whittaker. *Radical Blake: Afterlife and Influence from 1827*. New York: Palgrave, 2003.
Dortort, Fred. *The Dialectic of Vision: A Contrary Reading of Blake's Jerusalem*. Barrytown, NY: Station Hill Arts/Barrytown Ltd., 1998.
Ellis, Phillip A. "Before Her Lambs Were Silent: Reading Gender and the Feminine in *Red Dragon*." In Szumskyj, *Dissecting Hannibal Lecter*, 160–75.
Fierman, Daniel. "Lecter Loses His Bite." *Entertainment Weekly* (online), 16 February 2007.
Goode, Mike. "Blakespotting." *PMLA* 121, no. 3 (May 2006): 769–86.
Guttridge, Peter. Review of *Hannibal Rising*, by Thomas Harris. *The Observer*, 9 December 2006.
Harris, Thomas. "Foreword to a Fatal Interview." In *The Hannibal Lecter Omnibus*, vii–x. London: William Heinemann, 2000.
_____. *Hannibal*. New York: Delacorte Press, 1999.

Bibliography

_____. *Hannibal Rising*. New York: Delacorte Press, 2006.
_____. *Red Dragon*. New York: G. P. Putnam's Sons, 1981.
_____. *The Silence of the Lambs*. New York: St. Martin's Press, 1988.
Hunter, Stephen. "'Hannibal Rising': Broken 'Silence.'" *Washington Post* (online), 9 February 2007.
Joshi, S. T. "Suspense vs. Horror: The Case of Thomas Harris." In Szumskyj, *Dissecting Hannibal Lecter*, 118–32.
Karim, Ali S. "*Hannibal Rising*: Look Back in Anger." In Szumskyj, *Dissecting Hannibal Lecter*, 147–59.
King, Stephen. "Hannibal the Cannibal." Review of *Hannibal*, by Thomas Harris. *New York Times* (online), 13 June 1999.
Magistrale, Tony. "Transmogrified Gothic: The Novels of Thomas Harris." In Magistrale and Morrison, *A Dark Night's Dreaming*, 27–41.
Magistrale, Tony, and Michael A. Morrison, eds. *A Dark Night's Dreaming: Contemporary American Horror Fiction*. Columbia: University of South Carolina Press, 1996.
Mann, Michael, dir. *Manhunter* (1986). Los Angeles, CA: Starz/Anchor Bay, 2001. DVD.
Messent, Peter. "American Gothic: Liminality and the Gothic in Thomas Harris's Hannibal Lecter Novels." In Szumskyj, *Dissecting Hannibal Lecter*, 13–36.
Morgan, Jack. *The Biology of Horror: Gothic Literature and Film*. Carbondale and Edwardsville: Southern Illinois University Press, 2002.
Morrison, Michael A. "After the Danse: Horror at the End of the Century." In Magistrale and Morrison, *A Dark Night's Dreaming*, 9–26.
O'Brien, Daniel. *The Hannibal Files: The Unauthorised Guide to the Hannibal Lecter Trilogy*. London: Reynolds & Hearn, 2001.
Ratner, Brett, dir. *Red Dragon* (2002). Los Angeles, CA: Universal Studios, 2003. DVD.
Schorer, Mark. *William Blake: The Politics of Vision*. New York: Henry Holt, 1946.
Scott, Ridley, dir. *Hannibal*. Los Angeles, CA: MGM Home Entertainment, 2001. DVD.
Sexton, David. *The Strange World of Thomas Harris: Inside the Mind of the Creator of Hannibal Lecter*. London: Short Books, 2001.
Skal, David J. *The Monster Show: A Cultural History of Horror*. New York: W. W. Norton, 1993.
Simpson, Philip L. *Making Murder: The Fiction of Thomas Harris*. Santa Barbara, CA: Praeger, 2010.
_____. *Psycho Paths: Tracking the Serial Killer through Contemporary American Film and Fiction*. Carbondale and Edwardsville: Southern Illinois University Press, 2000.
Spector, Sheila. "Blake's Graphic Use of Hebrew." *Blake/An Illustrated Quarterly* 37 (2003): 63–79.
Szumskyj, Benjamin, ed. *Dissecting Hannibal Lecter: Essays on the Novels of Thomas Harris*. Jefferson, NC: McFarland, 2008.
_____. "Morbidity of the Soul: An Appreciation of *Hannibal*." In Szumskyj, *Dissecting Hannibal Lecter*, 200–211.

Bibliography

Tasker, Yvonne. *The Silence of the Lambs.* BFI Modern Classics. London: British Film Institute, 2002.

Taylor, Dena Bain. Review of *"Wonders Divine": The Development of Blake's Kabbalistic Myth*, by Sheila A. Spector. *Blake/An Illustrated Quarterly* 38 (2004): 79–85.

Webber, Peter, dir. *Hannibal Rising.* Los Angeles, CA: Weinstein Company, 2007. DVD.

Wells, Paul. *The Horror Genre: From Beelzebub to Blair Witch.* London: Wallflower, 2000.

Whittaker, Jason. "Cannibalising Blake." *Zoamorphosis: The Blake 2.0 Blog.* 25 February 2010.

Whittaker, Jason, and Steve Clark, eds. *Blake, Modernity and Popular Culture.* New York: Palgrave, 2007.

Williams, Nicholas. "Eating Blake, or an Essay on Taste: The Case of Thomas Harris's *Red Dragon*." *Cultural Critique* 42 (Spring 1999): 137–62.

_____. *Ideology and Utopia in the Poetry of William Blake.* Cambridge Studies in Romanticism. Cambridge: Cambridge University Press, 1998. Kindle edition (no pagination).

Winder, Robert. Review of *Hannibal*, by Thomas Harris. *New Statesman* (online), 21 June 1999.

Index

Adams, Hazard 171
America 31, 43, 44, 45
Amis, Martin 117
Ancient of Days 14, 17, 18, 24, 41, 50, 65, 93, 119–121, 127, 136–137, 170, 172
androgyne 29–30, 36, 65, 69
Annotations to Boyd 175
Annotations to Lavater 21, 36–37, 166, 176
Annotations to Swedenborg 35, 47
Annotations to Watson 42–43
atheism 56–57, 76, 128, 153–154, 157, 168
"Augeries of Innocence" 40, 93–94, 174

Bandy, Melanie 26, 34, 37, 47, 48, 70, 168
Beulah 27
Blake and the Popular Conference 9, 11
A Blake Dictionary 24, 55
Blake, Modernity and Popular Culture 9, 11, 15
Blake Society 9, 11
Blakespotting 13–15, 17
The Body of Abel found by Adam and Eve 93
The Book of Los 41, 42
The Book of Thel 39
Bromion 43, 45, 48
Bross, Kristina 129, 133
Butts, Thomas 40, 46–47, 63, 72, 88, 173

Connolly, Tristanne 46, 164
contraries 12, 21, 22, 28–30, 32–33, 35, 36, 41, 49, 58–59, 62, 66, 68–69, 71, 84, 97, 98, 99, 101, 106, 108, 130, 134, 147, 152, 157, 160, 164, 169, 175, 177
Cox, Brian 84, 88
Crabb Robinson, Henry 30, 33, 36, 125

Damon, S. Foster 24–25, 55
DeLaurentiis, Dino 12, 144
Demme, Jonathan 108, 109
"A Divine Image" 39, 48, 62, 68, 130, 162
"The Divine Image" 39, 48, 61, 68, 130, 162
doppelganger 20
Dortort, Fred 32n1

Ellis, Phillip 134
Emanation 20, 42, 98–99, 106, 131, 133, 169–170
Enitharmon 31, 42, 49
Erdman, David 33
Eternity 23, 26–27, 29, 30, 41, 47, 65, 106, 134
Europe: A Prophecy 14
"The Everlasting Gospel" 35, 41

Fierman, Daniel 144
The [First] Book of Urizen 41–42, 120
forgiveness 12, 19, 24, 26, 31, 37–38, 41, 43, 47, 48, 119, 120, 128, 129, 134, 163, 165, 170
Foster, Jodie 59–60
Fuller, Bryan 12

Generation 27, 29, 47, 65, 106
Ghost of a Flea 136–137
Gnosticism 24, 62
God Blessing the 7th Day 93
Goode, Mike 14
gothic 12, 57, 58, 64–66, 118
The Great Red Dragon and the Woman Clothed in the Sun 18, 24, 50, 64, 68, 69–73, 81–83, 88, 89, 90, 93, 114, 120–121, 163, 170, 172, 176
Guttridge, Peter 144

Hannibal (tv show) 12
Hannibal Lecter Studiolo 17, 61
hermaphrodite 29–30, 65–66, 69
"Holy Thursday" 20, 39
Hopkins, Anthony 17, 55, 88, 91, 110, 115
horror 12, 19–20, 63, 64, 108
"The Human Abstract" 43, 68, 79
Hunt, Robert 171
Hunter, Stephen 158

imagination 19, 25, 26, 34–35, 37, 47, 53, 67, 86, 92–93, 95, 97, 99, 100, 104, 121, 125, 126, 133, 156, 168

183

Index

Jerusalem (illuminated book) 25, 27, 32n1, 37, 65, 120, 134
"Jerusalem" (lyric) 13, 71, 173
Jesus 13, 32, 37, 120, 121, 166, 175
Joshi, S.T. 145

Kabbalism 24, 38
Karim, Ali 56, 154
King, Stephen 51, 58, 117, 118, 134

"The Lamb" 32, 74
Laocoön 38
"London" 44
Los 23, 27–28, 31, 41–42

Magistrale, Tony 19, 58, 64–66, 71, 106
Mann, Michael 81, 82–83, 86, 87
The Marriage of Heaven and Hell 14, 25, 27, 30, 32, 33, 35, 40, 42, 46, 48, 55, 60, 64–65, 75, 79, 120, 124, 134, 171, 177
Messent, Peter 134
Milton 13, 32n1, 42, 45, 71
Morgan, Jack 59
Morrison, Michael 19, 58, 59

negation 28–29, 48, 58, 70–71
Noonan, Tom 81, 83

O'Brien, Daniel 54, 55, 61–62, 74, 81–82, 83, 84, 87, 112, 117–118, 120–121, 133, 136
Oothoon 43–44, 45, 46, 48, 131
Orc 44, 45

perspective 12, 18, 20, 22, 30–31, 35, 37, 38–44, 49, 52, 55, 59–61, 76, 85, 92, 93, 97, 106, 119, 123, 150, 151, 156, 163, 165, 166, 172, 173, 175, 177
Pity 45
Prometheus 45, 64, 175

Ratner, Brett 88, 94

Satan 34, 35, 42, 49, 54–56, 64–65, 107, 129–130, 144, 159, 164, 175

Satan Exulting Over Eve 45
Schorer, Mark 24
Scofield, John 46–47
Scott, Ridley 135, 136, 142–143
Sexton, David 52, 53, 61, 74, 79–80, 116, 117, 129, 130, 136
Shadowy Female 44–46
Simpson, Philip 11, 18, 56, 57–58, 61, 74, 75, 79, 82, 86, 102, 128, 134, 135, 144, 146, 148, 150, 154, 157, 175–176
Skal, David 108
The Songs of Innocence and Experience 20, 32, 39, 55, 61–62, 68–69, 71, 80, 157, 177
Spector, Sheila 24n1, 38
Spectre 27–30, 42, 58, 164, 166
Szumskyj, Benjamin 56, 134–135

Tasker, Yvonne 59, 60, 99, 101, 106, 109, 112, 114, 115
Taylor, Dena Bain 32
Thel 39, 106, 173
Theotormon 43, 45, 48, 131
"There Is No Natural Religion" 85
"The Tyger" 32–33, 68, 73–74

Ulro 27
Urizen 23, 24, 29, 31, 41–43, 49, 65, 70, 119–120, 128, 137, 167, 170, 171, 172

"A Vision of the Last Judgment" 33–35, 40, 41
Visions of the Daughters of Albion 20, 31, 43–45, 131

Webber, Peter 162
Wells, Paul 108
Whittaker, Jason 9, 144
Williams, Nicholas 12, 15–16, 18, 46, 61, 62–63, 64, 72
Winder, Robert 129

Zoamorphosis 13, 15

www.ingramcontent.com/pod-product-compliance
Lightning Source LLC
Chambersburg PA
CBHW020935230426
43666CB00008B/1685